SHENANDOAH NATIONAL PARK
Luray, Virginia 22835

TELEPHONE NUMBERS
(Area Code 703)

999-2266.   Recorded message about what's open, road and weather conditions, etc.

999-2243.   For additional information and Park business, during regular working hours.

999-2227.   Emergency number for use when there is no answer at 999-2243.

GUIDE TO
SKYLINE
DRIVE

AND
SHENANDOAH
NATIONAL PARK

By HENRY HEATWOLE
Maps and drawings by the author

Published by
SHENANDOAH NATURAL HISTORY ASSOCIATION
Luray, Virginia 22835
Bulletin No. 9

Copyright 1978, 1981, and 1985
HENRY HEATWOLE
All rights reserved

First Edition, 1978
Reprinted with Corrections, 1979
Second Edition, 1981
Reprinted with Corrections, 1983
Third Edition, 1985
Reprinted with Corrections, 1986

Library of Congress Catalog Card No. 85-61538
ISBN 0-931606-13-6

Printed in United States of America by
GOOD PRINTERS, Harrisonburg, Virginia 22801

CONTENTS

HOW TO USE THIS BOOK

By means of this guidebook I hope to lead you down Skyline Drive and into the surrounding woodlands, just as if I were with you in person; to point out things that have given me pleasure, and to tell you what I've learned about them. As we go along I'll anticipate some of your questions and answer them.

Q: How can you do that on a printed page?

A: Like this.

We'll start with some background material, for orientation in time and space. I believe you'll enjoy your park experience more if you know where to go and what to look for, and if you have some idea of what happened here a hundred years ago, and a billion years ago. For a well-exercised mind, the knowledge I want you to carry is not a heavy burden.

After the introductory pages, the rest of the book is keyed to Skyline Drive, mile by mile. The first thing you'll see on each page is the mile number, so you'll know exactly what point on the Drive I'm talking about. Thus, if you know the mile number of where you are, you can turn at once to my discussion of that area.

Q: And how do I know the mile number of where I am?

A: There are mileposts—concrete with black numbers—beside the Drive. If you're going "south" on the Drive, that is, away from Front Royal and toward the Blue Ridge Parkway, the mileposts are on your right, and the mile numbers increase as you go. Of course if you're going "north" they're on the left, and the mile numbers decrease.

Q: Why do you put "north" and "south" in quotes?

A: Because they're not compass directions, but a useful convention. The drive twists and turns and doubles back, so that compass directions are useless for describing it. Therefore we'll agree that if the mileposts are on the right, you're driving "south". It follows that if you're driving "south", things on the right side of the Drive are on the "west" side, regardless of what your compass says. And now that you know what the quotation marks mean, I won't use them any more.

Q: I haven't noticed any mileposts. Where am I now?

A: Here are a few of the places you might be:

Mile   0.6. Front Royal entrance station.
Mile   4.6. Dickey Ridge Visitor Center.
Mile 22.2. Mathews Arm Campground.
Mile 24.0. Elkwallow Wayside.
Mile 31.5. Thornton Gap (U.S. 211 interchange).
Mile 31.6. Panorama Development.
Mile 36.7. Pinnacles picnic area.
Mile 41.7. Skyland (north entrance).
Mile 51.0. Big Meadows.
Mile 57.5. Lewis Mountain Campground.
Mile 65.5. Swift Run Gap (U.S. 33 interchange).
Mile 79.5. Loft Mountain Wayside.
Mile 104.6. Rockfish Gap entrance station.

Mile 105.4. Rockfish Gap (interchange with Blue Ridge Parkway, U.S. 250, and I-64).

If you can, take a few minutes to thumb through the book and find out what you have here. Study the table of contents, so you'll know how to find the information you need *now*. If time is short, turn directly to the part of the log that deals with where you are. If you want to start hiking *now* (and, I hope, read the introductory material later) turn to page 59 for a list of recommended hikes. The list tells the milepoint at the trail head, length, amount of climbing, difficulty, and approximate time required.

Q: Actually, my problem is this. I plan to visit 24 National Parks in two weeks, and I have only three hours for this one. What do you suggest?

A: Get in your car and drive. If you go at exactly the speed limit you can do the whole of Skyline Drive, from one end to the other, in exactly three hours.

Q: But I've heard about viewpoints, overlooks, magnificent scenery.

A: Yes. As you pass each overlook take a glance at the scenery, but don't slow down. Skyline Drive is a thin gray line that passes through three hundred square miles of woodland. If you follow the line and keep moving, you can have a fine, brief, one-dimensional experience.

Q: How could I add a dimension?

A: Slow down. Have lunch at a picnic ground, or a wayside, or a lodge. Stop at the overlooks—all of them. Read what I say about them. Study the sketch, if there is one, that identifies the mountains you see. Don't just glance at the view, but invest a little time in it. Your investment will pay interest.

Q: And three dimensions?

A: Follow a trail into one of the hollows, down where the streams and waterfalls are; then climb back. Or climb a peak, and sit on the edge of a cliff, and look down between your feet at the scenery. You'll be sharply aware of a third dimension.

Q: About those sketches that identify the mountains. I'm just passing through, and I don't plan to come this way again. Why should I learn the names of your mountains?

A: After you've seen the same mountain from several different overlooks and several different angles, identifying it each time because it's named on the sketch, that mountain will begin to be, for you, a real and individual thing—not just another hump in the scenery. If you follow a trail to the top of that mountain, and get very tired doing so, then, wherever you may go, it will be not just my mountain but yours, forever.

Q: I was kidding about having three hours to spend. There's plenty of time.

A: Then if you'll bear with me and work a little; if you'll learn to know this place and cover a significant part of it on your own two feet; if you learn something of its trees and flowers, bears and deer, chipmunks and salamanders; if you become conscious of the people who once lived in these mountains, and know how to find and interpret the evidence of their life here; if you learn to read the stories written in the rocks; if you can see this National Park not as a thing but as a process; if you become more aware of your surroundings, and aware of yourself as an organism in this environment and the most recent event in its history; if you can become a friend of weather—all kinds of weather—and a connoisseur of solitude; then I promise you a polyfaceted, multidimensional, quality experience. Intellectually, as well as monetarily, the rich get richer.

Q: I'm not buying a package like that, but I'll take an option.

A: Read on.

SHENANDOAH NATIONAL *WHAT?*

Shenandoah National *Park.* That's where we are, and that's what this book is about. On the cover I've mentioned the Skyline Drive first and the Park second. That's because a strictly accurate title might have been misleading. Skyline Drive is famous and the Park is not. As you approached the Park you saw signs directing you to Skyline Drive. Not until you reached the Park boundary did you see a sign about the Park.

It's true that Skyline Drive is a magnificent scenic parkway. But more than that, it's a quick and easy way to reach the other features of the Park.

Shenandoah National Park is long and narrow, straddling the crest of Virginia's Blue Ridge Mountains for nearly 75 miles. It varies in width from less than one mile to about 13, so that the views from peaks and overlooks include not only the Blue Ridge itself, but also the patchwork of woods, farmlands and orchards on either side. Here and there the Park touches the Shenandoah Valley on the west side, or the Piedmont on the east; but throughout most of its length the Park boundary is partway up the mountain slope.

Shenandoah National Park is so long and narrow that I need two maps (pages 4 and 5) to show it. The shaded area on the maps is the Park; the wiggly solid line that runs the length of it is Skyline Drive. The dotted line that parallels the Drive is the Appalachian Trail, which extends some 2,000 miles from Maine to Georgia; about 95 miles of it are within the Park. You can get within a very few miles of any part of the Park either by car on the Drive, or by foot on the Appalachian Trail. The dozens of side trails begin either at the edge of the Drive, or a short distance from the Drive via the A.T.

Take another look at those two maps. Try to fuse them in your mind so that you visualize the Park as a whole. Note that two main highways cross the park, dividing it into three parts:

The *North Section,* from Front Royal to U.S. 211.

The *Central Section,* from U.S. 211 to U.S. 33.

The *South Section,* from U.S. 33 to U.S. 250 and I-64.

For convenience I've divided the log of Skyline Drive into these three parts. Please note one more thing on the map of the southern half: the Park appears to end at Jarman Gap. Originally it did, and the Blue Ridge Parkway began there. Now the Park and the Skyline Drive continue to Rockfish Gap, although for most of this distance the Park is no more than a narrow

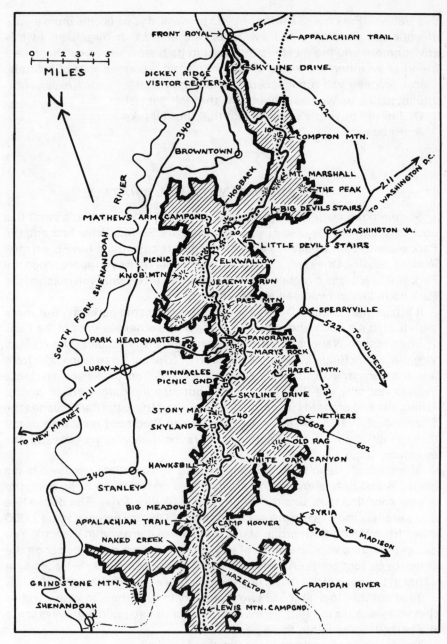

Shenandoah National Park — North Half

right-of-way on either side of the Drive. At many points between Mile 97 and Mile 105 you could throw a rock from the edge of the Drive onto private property (although I'm not advocating that you do so.)

Between Mile 97 and Mile 105 the Park has bought a scenic easement on private land beside the Drive, where landowners have agreed to build no

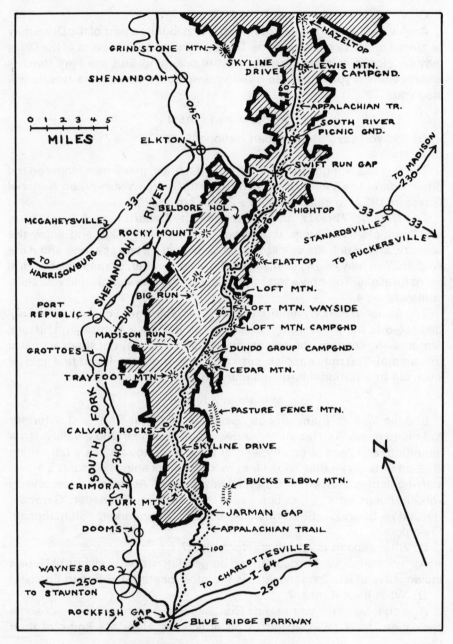

GRINDSTONE MTN.

HAZELTOP

SKYLINE
DRIVE

LEWIS MTN.
CAMPGND.

SHENANDOAH

60

340

APPALACHIAN TR.

SOUTH RIVER
PICNIC GND.

0 1 2 3 4 5
MILES

ELKTON

SWIFT RUN GAP

TO MADISON

230

BELDORE HOL.

HIGHTOP

33

MCGAHEYSVILLE

ROCKY MOUNT

70

STANARDSVILLE

33

33

TO
HARRISONBURG

FLATTOP

TO RUCKERSVILLE

SHENANDOAH RIVER

BIG RUN

LOFT MTN.

80

LOFT MTN. WAYSIDE

PORT
REPUBLIC

340

LOFT MTN. CAMPGND

MADISON RUN

DUNDO GROUP CAMPGND.

GROTTOES

CEDAR MTN.

TRAYFOOT MTN.

PASTURE FENCE MTN.

CALVARY ROCKS

90

SKYLINE DRIVE

SOUTH FORK

340

BUCKS ELBOW MTN.

CRIMORA

TURK MTN.

N

JARMAN GAP

DOOMS

APPALACHIAN TRAIL

100

TO CHARLOTTESVILLE

WAYNESBORO

I-64

250

TO STAUNTON

250

ROCKFISH GAP

6

BLUE RIDGE PARKWAY

Shenandoah National Park — South Half

roads, put up no buildings, and cut no trees except in accordance with agreed-on rules.

Note that from Jarman Gap to Rockfish Gap the Appalachian Trail continues more or less parallel to the Drive. Here it's on a right-of-way easement on private land, or on land bought by the Park or by the Appalachian Trail Conference.

Q: When is the Park open?

A: Always, every day, for 24 hours. Occasionally a part of the Drive may be closed because of snow or ice. During hunting season parts of the Drive may be closed at night, to help control poaching. But the Park itself is always open. If you choose to hike in when the Drive is closed, no one will stop you.

Of Parks and Forests

Q: Did you say "Shenandoah National Forest?"

A: No.

There *was* a Shenandoah National Forest once, in the mountains on the other side of the Valley. It was changed to George Washington National Forest in 1932, to celebrate GW's 200th birthday.

The *National Forests,* administered by the Department of Agriculture, are "multiple-use" areas where you can not only hike, and enjoy the scenery, and watch the wildlife; you may also, in certain seasons, shoot the wildlife. You may, with permission, "harvest" timber, or mine coal, or drill for natural gas. You may even rent a piece of the forest and build yourself a summer home.

The *National Parks,* administered by the Department of the Interior, are dedicated to the *preservation* of certain areas—their natural and historic features and scenery, their plants and wildlife. You may not shoot or molest any animal. You may not pick, cut, chop, dig, or collect. If you find gold (or even *oil*) in a National Park, it's going to stay there.

What's in a Name?

Shenandoah is many things besides a National Park and a former National Forest. As you surely know, it's also a river and a valley. It's a mountain, a college, a county, and at least three towns. It's a tall sailing ship, an ill-fated airship, and a sleek modern motor ship. It's a song, a movie starring James Stewart, and a Broadway musical. At various times and on various documents it has been spelled Cenantua, Chanador, Gerando, Gerundo, Shendo, Sherando, Senantoa, Shanandoe, Shanandoah, Shanidore.

Q: Shenandoah is an Indian word, right?

A: It *must* be. My Mexican friend Jorge Alatriste, who claims to be part Indian, says that "Shenandoah" is the most beautiful sound in English.

Q: What does it mean?

A: You'll be sorry you asked. The "experts", each writing with some conviction, have galloped off in all directions. Here are some of their theories:

1. It means "Daughter of the Stars".
2. It means "Silver Water".
3. It's from *Schinhandowi,* meaning "River through the Spruces".
4. It's from *Onandagoa,* meaning "River of High Mountains".
5. It's from the Iroquois *Skahentowane,* meaning "Great Meadow" or "Big Flat Place".
6. It's named for the fallen chief Sherando.

7. It's named for a tribe of losers called the Senedoes, who lived in the Valley until about 1730, when they were exterminated by another tribe that wandered up from the south.

Of these possible meanings I find "Big Flat Place" (referring to the Valley) most plausible, and "Daughter of the Stars" most pleasing. I choose pleasing over plausible. If you'll agree, then "Shenandoah" shall henceforth mean "Daughter of the Stars"; for the river has its sources in high mountains, and on a clear night in those high mountains the stars seem very close indeed.

A Recycled Park

Q: In glancing back at the maps to get re-oriented, I note that the Park is shaped like a ruptured gerrymander. What happened to it?

A: The Park follows the Blue Ridge, which is long, narrow, and wandering. The torn and tattered boundary (which I have somewhat simplified and straightened for the purpose of these maps) is a result of how the Park came to be. Because the boundary rarely follows any natural or man-made feature, such as a road, a stream, or a ridge crest, it's an administrative nightmare. The Park has a continuing policy of land acquisition by donation and land swapping, both aimed at straightening the boundary.

Most of our National Parks have been created simply by reclassifying what was already government land. In only a few was private land involved. In Acadia and Grand Tetons, the Rockefellers bought large areas of land and donated them to the government.

In 1930, what is now Shenandoah National Park was entirely private property. There were some large tracts of second-rate pasture and cut-over timberland. There were hundreds of small subsistence farms—many of them as small as five acres. Some two thousand mountain people lived here in 1930—most of them on land that was stripped of timber, badly eroded, and increasingly unproductive.

The act of Congress that authorized this Park specified that no federal money could be spent to acquire land for it. The Virginia State Legislature appropriated over a million dollars, and small contributions from the people of Virginia made up the rest. There were a few donations of sizable tracts. Thousands of people contributed the price of an acre of land, and school children contributed pennies. This Park is a gift to the nation from the people of Virginia, who bought it for us—one small parcel at a time.

And that accounts for the ragged boundary, which shows where the money ran out, where land was more productive and therefore more expensive, or where reluctant owners successfully resisted condemnation proceedings.

This has been called a recycled Park because it started with ruined land which, under the protection of the National Park Service, has begun its long recovery toward primitive forest, and has reached the intermediate stage that we see now.

The Theme is Change

The recovery of this land from man's abuse, and the succession of plant and animal life that goes with such recovery, will continue. Some roads will become trails, and some trails will vanish. Access to the Park from the bottom of the hollows may get easier, or it may become impossible. The number of visitors will increase, and Park personnel must cope with the resulting pressures. The Park has recently spent large sums to build new sewage treatment plants. Eventually it may be necessary to ration access to the Park in order to protect those things the Park was created to preserve.

This book will be a little out of date before it gets into print, and worse before you see it. I'll point out, as we go along, subjects on which you should check with the rangers for the latest information. But that's all I can do. There is no facet of this Park that's immune to change.

Speaking of Rangers . . .

The people you see with dark green uniforms and flat-brimmed hats are Park Rangers—*not* Forest Rangers. Rangers may belong to the Protective Division or the Interpretive Division, and you can't tell which by looking. All wear the same uniform.

Rangers of the Interpretive (or Naturalist) Division are those who answer questions at the Visitor Centers, lead conducted walks, and put on campfire programs.

Rangers of the Protective Division work entrance stations and campgrounds, and patrol the Drive and the backcountry. It's their job to "protect the Park from the visitor, and protect the visitor from the Park", to enforce Park regulations and state and federal laws, and to preserve order.

Park employees in green or gray work uniforms belong to the Maintenance Division. They keep the Park clean, the Drive open, and the facilities working.

Rangers of both divisions, and maintenance personnel as well, will answer your questions if they can, and help you if you need help. All may be called on to fight fires, or participate in search or rescue missions.

If you have a complaint about the Park, take it up with any ranger. If you feel that you can't get satisfaction from the ranger, phone the superintendent at (703) 999-2243. Better still, write him a letter. That will give him time to investigate your complaint before he answers. Write:

Superintendent
Shenandoah National Park
Rt. 4, Box 292
Luray, Virginia 22835

(If you compain to your congressman about something that happened in the Park, he will forward your letter to the Superintendent for reply.)

Some Numbers

Here are some approximate statistics, all of them subject to change:
Total area of the Park, about 195,000 acres.
Number of visitors per year: about two million.
Park employees. Permanent: about 90. Peak seasonal: about 120.

Concession employees. Permanent: about 50. Peak seasonal: about 250.

Total roads: about 300 miles, including 105 miles of Skyline Drive.

Total trails: about 500 miles. (Note: some of the roads have been reclassified as trails, and are no longer used by vehicles.)

There are 57 separate water systems in the Park; five campgrounds with a total of 708 sites; eight picnic areas with a total of 299 sites; six restaurants with a total of 826 seats. The lodges at Skyland and Big Meadows, plus the cabins at Lewis Mountain, can accommodate a total of 911 people.

The Park has more than 60 peaks with elevations of more than 2,000 feet. Some of the highest are:

```
Hawksbill . . . . . . . . . . . . . . . . . 4049
Stony Man . . . . . . . . . . . . . . . . 4010
Hazeltop . . . . . . . . . . . . . . . . . 3815
Blackrock . . . . . . . . . . . . . . . . 3721
The Pinnacle . . . . . . . . . . . . . 3720
Bearfence. . . . . . . . . . . . . . . . 3640
Hightop . . . . . . . . . . . . . . . . . . 3585
Marys Rock . . . . . . . . . . . . . . 3514
Hogback . . . . . . . . . . . . . . . . . 3474
Trayfoot . . . . . . . . . . . . . . . . . 3380
```

Hogback is in the North Section, Hightop and Trayfoot in the South. All the rest are in the Central Section. The summit of Fork Mountain, elevation 3852, is just outside the Park boundary in the Central Section.

Waterfalls

During most of the year our waterfalls display a rather modest volume of water. Because they're fairly close to the top of the mountain, the streams that form them drain relatively small areas. Even so, our falls are often spectacular in springtime, when warm rains melt the accumulated snow.

Here is a list of our highest falls. At several of these the water drops in two or more steps; the listed height is the total for all the steps. Where there are two or more falls on the same stream, I've numbered them from the top down.

The only waterfall visible from Skyline Drive is at Mile 1.4. It has no name, and it's dry for part of the year. The next closest is Dark Hollow Falls, 0.7 mile from the Drive. You can walk to any falls on the list. Some of the trails are difficult, others fairly easy. All of them are among the recommended hikes in the list that begins on page 59.

Falls	Height, ft.	Section	Trail Head
Overall Run No. 2	93	North	Mile 22.2
Whiteoak No. 1	86	Central	Mile 42.6
South River	83	Central	Mile 62.8
Lewis	81	Central	Mile 51.2

Falls	Height, ft.	Section	Trail Head
Dark Hollow	70	Central	Mile 50.7
Rose River	67	Central	Mile 49.4
Doyles River No. 2	63	South	Mile 81.1
Whiteoak No. 2	62	Central	Mile 42.6
Whiteoak No. 6	60	Central	Mile 42.6
Whiteoak No. 5	49	Central	Mile 42.6
Jones Run	42	South	Mile 84.1
Whiteoak No. 4	41	Central	Mile 42.6
Whiteoak No. 3	35	Central	Mile 42.6
Cedar Run	34	Central	Mile 45.6
Overall Run No. 1	29	North	Mile 22.2
Doyles River No. 1	28	South	Mile 81.1

The Names of Places

Names tend to evolve, and you'll find minor variations in spelling as you read various books, maps, and signs. Don't let it bother you. Doyle's River, Doyles River, and Doyle River are the same small body of water. Whiteoak may be one word or two. And so on, endlessly. (But there are two *different* Fork Mountains, and two *different* Blackrocks.)

How places got their names is a subject that fascinates me, although not everyone shares my enthusiasm. I'll deal with some of the names at appropriate points in the log.

The truth is that many of the place names are so old that no one knows how they came about. Here are six names that you'll find on the latest maps: Shenandoah River, Conway River, Hawksbill Creek, Swift Run Gap, Devils Ditch, Naked Creek. But you'll also find them in the journal of Thomas Lewis, who passed this way in 1746.

Some names describe physical features; those are the easy ones, such as Stony Man, Hightop, Big Run. Some things are named for wealthy absentee landowners; for example Mt. Marshall, Browns Gap, Patterson Ridge. Others, such as Nicholson Hollow, Cubbage Hollow, and Dean Mountain, were named for the people who lived there.

Some names, such as Marys Rock, give rise to legends. The origin of still others, like Fort Windham Rocks and Dog Slaughter Ridge, remains obscure, mysterious, tantalizing.

WHAT'S IN IT FOR ME?

What can you do here? You already know about the Drive, and the views from its overlooks. The appeal of these vistas grows stronger, not weaker, as they grow more familiar. I still stop to absorb the scenery at overlooks beside the Drive, though I've been doing so for many years.

Perhaps the most rewarding thing you can do, to start with, is nothing at all. You'll find that difficult at first. You're accustomed to the demands of your work and your home, and the thousand pressures applied by fellow members of an exploding population. Try, for a while, to get out from under.

Convince yourself that, for now, you don't have to do *anything*. Try to believe that the most profitable way to spend your minutes is to throw some of them away. If the weather is right for it lie down in the grass, in the sunlight. Close your eyes. Shift your mind into neutral. Stay there till the tension seeps away.

The Green Museum

Shenandoah, like our other National Parks, is a museum. Its exhibits are scenery, wildlife and flowers, clean air and clear water—samples of America as it used to be. In this museum you can find instruction as well as rest.

But Park visitation, like population in general, is exploding. Some parts of the Park, at certain times, are intolerably crowded. At the height of fall color the Park has more than fifty thousand visitors a day. The summit of Old Rag can be thrilling if you're alone there, or with a close friend. But on a Saturday afternoon in summer you may find a hundred people on Old Rag summit, and it's elbows in the ribs for everyone.

Nevertheless the Park offers solitude, if you know where and when to look for it. Crowds love summer, good weather, weekends, holidays. Crowds love those few overpopular spots where crowds already are. But even if a sunny summer weekend is all you have, you can still escape from crowds and elbows. Instead of mingling with the multitude at the bottom of 70-foot Dark Hollow Falls, move on down the ravine another tenth of a mile. Pick out your own three- or four-foot waterfall. You can get very close to it, and you can probably have it all to yourself.

In the worst case—a holiday weekend—keep walking down the hollow until the trail leaves the stream; then follow the stream. You'll find yourself alone.

Small and Subtle Pleasures

I suggest that you spend some time alone, staring into running water, letting the sound of it fill you. Let your mind run as fast as the water if it wishes; let your mind have its way. Then you may find *yourself;* you may begin to know yourself better, and find out if you're good company. If you come on a shrew or a snake or a bear or a beetle, stand still and watch till it moves out of sight. If you find an anthill bustling with ten thousand ants, take a minute to watch just *one* of them. You may be surprised to learn that the principal activities of ants are shirking, dithering, featherbedding, and coffee breaks. Or, in a different season, catch a single flake of fine dry snow on the sleeve of your jacket; look at it closely (through your magnifying glass if you have one) while holding your breath so as not to melt it. You'll see, maybe for the first time, that it's a six-sided crystal just as the books say it is, except that one of the six sides broke when it struck your sleeve. Keep trying until you find a perfect crystal.

And now, if you're thinking impatiently that these are not suitable activities for an adult, go back to lesson one. Lie down in the grass and close your eyes.

You're in luck if it's berry season. Picking berries is a quick and thorough cure for being too adult. In spite of the general "no picking" rule you're free to collect berries, fruits, and nuts, as long as they're for your personal use here in the Park. Strawberries grow in open places, and ripen in June; scarce in some years and plentiful in others, depending on the weather. They're small but tasty. Later come the blueberries, also small, also tasty. Blackberries and raspberries are uncommon but good. Dewberries, which look like blackberries, are common; they're edible, but hardly delicious.

Wineberries, which you're most likely to find in the South Section of the Park, are shining red translucent raspberries that look like jewels. When they're fully ripe, so that they almost drop into your hand at a touch, they taste as good as they look. Thimbleberries look like big flat raspberries, which they are. Some are dry and seedy, others quite good.

Cherries are common and we have several species, most of them rather sour. We have a few peach trees, but bears eat all the peaches before they're ripe. Grapes grow around old homesites but I find them too sour to eat. There are hundreds of apple trees in the Park. The apples are about what you'd expect from trees that haven't been pruned or sprayed for fifty years. You may find a persimmon tree here and there; the fruit is good when it's fully ripe, and very bad when it isn't.

The American chestnut trees were killed by the blight; but some of their roots are still alive, sending up shoots that live for several years before the blight kills them. Some may live long enough to produce nuts. If you're lucky enough to find the right tree at just the right time, you may be able to collect half a handful of chestnuts.

There are five species of hickory in the Park; two of them produce bitter, inedible nuts. The sweetest are those of the shagbark, which is easy to identify. When you find hickory nuts on the ground, look at the trunk of the nearest tree. The bark of shagbark hickory is conspicuously shaggy.

Hazel nuts (called filberts in the supermarket) are common throughout the Park, and in midsummer you'll find bushes loaded with them. But you may never see a hazelnut ripe enough to eat. The deer, bears, squirrels, and chipmunks are less particular than we are.

Walking, Seeing, Learning, Knowing

Walking is fun. After a day on mountain trails your thighs will ache and your feet will complain; and you'll feel great. But I think of walking mainly as a way to promote seeing—a means of transportation from one small and subtle pleasure to another. That's why, in my list of recommended hikes, the "Time Required" is longer than you'd expect. It includes time for seeing.

(There are Walkers who deserve a capital "W". They love to spend the whole day Walking, and the whole night talking about how far they Walked. I'm not one of them. Neither are you. If you were you'd be out there Walking, not reading a book.)

Seeing and learning—each strengthens and sharpens the other. And learning can be fun, once you're safely out of school and no longer *have* to do it. That pink-magenta flower in the grass—the one with the tiny white spots on its petals—that's a Deptford Pink. Unlike many of our wildflowers, that bloom for only a couple of weeks, this one stays all summer. It's named for the town of Deptford, near London, England. Because it was brought to America by the colonists it's considered an "exotic," a foreigner, a recent immigrant in this land, just like you and me. (If you're an American Indian don't feel smug; your people too came from somewhere else.) The Deptford Pink belongs to a group of plants called the Pink Family, *Caryophyllaceae.* Maybe you know other members of this family, such as garden dianthus, and carnation, and chickweed. Not all pinks are pink; the name refers not to the color, but to the teeth on the ends of the petals, which look as if they'd been snipped with pinking shears. The Deptford Pink, like all our wildflowers, has a scientific name in Latin. If you like words, and the sound of words, you'll enjoy the feel of *Dianthus armeria* on your tongue. (Even more fun is the Latin name of flannel mullein: *Verbascum thapsus.* Say it over and over; it makes a dandy mantra.)

As you can see, my knowledge of the Deptford Pink is trivial, rather than profound. You'll never earn a cent with such information, not even on a quiz show. Nevertheless, a flower means more to me if I know a couple of things about it. I'd like to try an analogy, even though it may not work. Let's say that you have a good close friend. You know a lot about him: his age, his education, his work, his family, his tastes, his strengths and weaknesses. Each time you meet him there's a flash of recognition and perhaps a brief warm emotion, because you know him. It's possible to have a similar emotion, on a smaller scale, each time you see a Deptford Pink. (Or a skink. Or a skunk. Or a water strider.)

Textbooks and Teachers

Books on many subjects—trails, trees, flowers, ferns, mushrooms, mammals, birds, insects, geology, the mountain people—are for sale at points throughout the Park. You have a limited choice of books at lodges and waysides. There's a wider selection at the two Visitor Centers (Dickey Ridge at Mile 4.6; Big Meadows at Mile 51.0).

Our naturalists and interpreters are primarily teachers. They will answer your questions if they can; if they don't know the answer they'll try to find it. Their campfire programs are informal talks often illustrated with color slides, and provide a learning experience as well as entertainment. During the summer season there are campfire talks every night at Big Meadows and Loft Mountain; and less often at Mathews Arm, Skyland, and Lewis Mountain. You can learn even more from a conducted walk, because you can talk directly to the naturalist and ask questions about the things you see.

The schedule of campfire talks and conducted walks may change somewhat from year to year. For current information get a visitor activities sheet, or a Park newspaper called "Shenandoah Overlook." Both are free at Visitor Centers, lodges, and entrance stations. Or look for an outdoor bulletin board: the activities schedule is posted there. There are about 50 bulletin boards in the Park: at picnic grounds, campgrounds, waysides, lodges, and some of the overlooks.

The Park offers more than vistas and walking, seeing and learning. Camping is a major pastime, not just a way to sleep and eat. Setting up your tent or trailer, building your fire, preparing your food and cleaning up, can occupy your time. Here are other ways:

Fishing

Fishing is limited because our streams are small: they start near the top of the mountain, and quickly reach the Park boundary. Nevertheless, we have a number of trout streams that you may find worth while. There are rules, of course. You may take only trout, and you may use only artificial lures. You'll need a Virginia fishing license, which you can get at a lodge or wayside. Two streams (Rapidan River and Staunton River, both on the east side in the Central Section) are "fish for fun" streams. That means you must use a barbless hook, and gently return the fish to the water after you catch it. (Darwin Lambert calls this "cruelty for fun"—a point of view worth considering.)

The Park has a mimeographed list of trout streams, available free at Headquarters and at the two Visitor Centers. The ranger there will show you, on the topographic map, how to get to the best places. Designated trout streams, rules, and regulations are subject to change from year to year. So check with a ranger for the latest information.

Skiing

We have no ski lift here, no downhill run. The rangers tell me that cross-country skiing is encouraged, but few places are suitable for it. The trails are narrow, and go up and down a lot. But the upper part of the Rapidan Road, Mile 51.3, is smooth and nearly flat. You may ski on the Drive itself when conditions permit.

Bicycling

Bicycling is discouraged within the Park. Bikes are forbidden on all the trails. They are confined to specially designated parts of fire roads, the campground roads, and Skyline Drive. The ups and downs on the Drive look a lot steeper from a bicycle than they do from your car. Bicycling on the Drive is strenuous exercise, and it's dangerous.

Swimming

There are no swimming pools near the lodges or campgrounds, in spite of public demand. For one thing we're on top of a mountain, where there's very little water; it takes nearly all we can get just for drinking and flushing the toilets.

But you can swim. All the major streams have small pools where you can get thoroughly wet and *very* cool. There's a restriction: if you swim within sight of a trail, you're required to wear something. For skinnydipping, find a stream that has no trail beside it. Naked Creek (Mile 53.2) might be appropriate.

Horseback Riding

We have more than 150 miles of yellow-blazed horse trails and fire roads where horses may be ridden. You can bring your own horse if you have one or, from May to October, you can rent one in the Park.

Your own horse: ride in on one of the designated horse trails, or bring your horse in a trailer. Park the trailer in the stables parking lot at Big Meadows. Backcountry camping trips on horseback are permitted, but there are strict rules—not for your annoyance, but to protect the Park and the other visitors. Ask at one of the Visitor Centers, or write to Park Headquarters (Luray, Va., 22835) for a free map of horse trails and a mimeographed sheet of regulations.

Renting a horse is less complicated. There are stables at Skyland (turn in at the south entrance, Mile 42.5, then stop at the first parking area on the left). All horseback trips are guided; you can't rent a horse and take off on your own. For children, there are pony rides at Skyland and wagon rides at Big Meadows (Mile 51.2). Ask at the stables, between 8 and 5 o'clock, for information, schedules, and reservations.

What Else Have You Got?

The two lodges have recreation rooms where you can find such things as card tables, checker boards, pingpong, and TV. There's a dining hall at each lodge, with good (if not gourmet) food at a reasonable price. The tap rooms offer a wide choice of drinks, from champagne cocktails to "white lightning" in a fruit jar.

Q: Why couldn't they fill a swimming pool during the winter? Why no swimming pool, golf course, tennis court, ski lift, drive-in movie?

A: All those things are available nearby, outside the Park. If we had them here we would attract people who want only to swim, or only to play golf. The result: more pressures on limited facilities. And, for those who come to enjoy things that are unique to the Park, more elbows in the ribs.

WHERE CAN I STAY?

This article is a summary of park facilities, including food and lodging. The Park Service itself doesn't provide lodging and doesn't sell food (or anything else, for that matter.) Lodging and sales items are private enterprise, provided under contract by concessioners. There are three concessioners in Shenandoah:

ARA Virginia Sky-line Co., Inc., which operates the Lodges, Waysides, and gas stations.

Shenandoah Natural History Association, a non-profit organization that sells books, postcards, color slides, maps, and related items at the two Visitor Centers. SNHA also publishes books—this one, for example.

Potomac Appalachian Trail Club. This is primarily an association of Walkers. It maintains six locked cabins in the Park, which are rented to PATC members and to the general public at reasonable rates. I'll tell you where they are and how to reserve them in the article on hiking.

Lodging

Motel-type units and rustic cabins are available at the two lodges (Skyland, Mile 41.7, and Big Meadows, Mile 51.2.) There are a few housekeeping cabins for rent at Lewis Mountain, Mile 57.5. You'll find one or both lodges open from early April through November. Lewis Mountain facilities are usually open from early May to late October. Limited facilities are sometimes available before or after the main season, but this tends to vary from year to year. Vacancies are rare during the summer, especially on weekends, so make your reservation as far in advance as you can. Contact ARA Virginia Sky-line Co., Inc., P.O. Box 727, Luray, Virginia 22835. Telephone (703) 743-5108.

Food

You can buy meals in the Park, as well as groceries to prepare your own meals if you're camping.

Dining halls: Two of them: Skyland (Mile 41.7) and Big Meadows (51.2). Both are closed between meals and after 9:00 p.m. For dinner during the summer season allow plenty of time; you can expect to wait a while for seating.

Restaurant: Panorama Restaurant (31.6). Open 10 to 6, or later.

Cafeterias: at Elkwallow Wayside (24.0), and Loft Mountain Wayside (79.5). Usually open from 9 to 6, but this is subject to change.

Grill Room: at Big Meadows Wayside (51.2). Breakfast, lunch, snacks. Closes at 5:30 p.m. during the summer, so as not to compete with dinner at the lodge.

Groceries (plus other camper supplies and equipment, soft drinks, and beer): at Elkwallow Wayside (24.0), Big Meadows Wayside (51.2), Lewis Mountain Campstore (57.5) and Loft Mountain Campstore (near Loft Mountain Campground, a mile or so from the drive at Mile 79.5).

Gasoline

There are gas stations just outside the Park, at each end of the Drive. Also (mid-May to early November, 9 a.m. to 6 p.m.) at Elkwallow Wayside (Mile 24.0), Big Meadows Wayside (51.2), and Loft Mountain Wayside (79.5). In mid-season the station at Big Meadows may be open as late as 8 p.m. Note that gas stations within the Park have nothing but gasoline and oil, air and water. They don't make repairs, change tires, or lend tools.

You can find a gas station within 6 to 8 miles of the Drive, in either direction, at both of the main highway crossings: U.S. 211 (Mile 31.5), and U.S. 33 (Mile 65.5); but these are small-town stations, not likely to be open after dark.

Campgrounds

Campgrounds are crowded in the summer. To give more people a chance at them, you're limited to a *total* of 14 days camping each year between June 1 and October 31. (During the rest of the year nobody's counting.) A fee is charged for camping.

There are four campgrounds, all with sites for both tents and trailers (but no trailer hookups):

Mile 22.2 Mathews Arm,   186 sites.
     51.2 Big Meadows,   255 sites.
     57.5 Lewis Mountain,   32 sites.
     79.5 Loft Mountain,   231 sites.

The Big Meadows campground, or at least a part of it, is open all year except in January and February. The rest are open during the summer season, May through October. All but Lewis Mountain have a trailer sewage disposal site. All but Mathews Arm have showers and laundry facilities.

Dundo Campground (Mile 83.7) is only for organized youth groups. (Boy Scouts, for example). Its facilities are rather primitive, and you need a reservation. Write to Shenandoah National Park, Rt. 4, Box 292, Luray, Va. 22835.

Picnic Areas

Seven of them, all with picnic tables, fireplaces, drinking fountains, and comfort stations:

Mile 4.7 Dickey Ridge	57.5 Lewis Mountain
24.1 Elkwallow	62.8 South River
36.7 Pinnacles	79.5 Loft Mountain
51.2 Big Meadows	

There are picnic tables on the lower level at Skyland, and at a number of places beside the Drive.

Comfort Stations

(During the summer season). Downstairs at the dining halls at both lodges, from about 7 a.m. to 11 p.m. At Waysides and Visitor Centers during the day. Comfort stations in campgrounds and picnic areas are open day and night. There's a comfort station in the woods at the south end of Stony Man Mountain Overlook, Mile 38.6. That one, like those in some of the picnic areas, has no electricity. Carry a flashlight if you go there after dark. The comfort stations at the Dickey Ridge Visitor Center (Mile 4.6) and at Panorama (Mile 31.6) are open day and night, all year 'round.

Drinking Water

During the summer season, water is no problem. There are dozens of outdoor drinking fountains. They are in picnic areas, campgrounds, at Panorama Restaurant, at both Visitor Centers, and at several of the overlooks. During the rest of the year, usually mid-October to mid-May, when the pipes are in danger of freezing, the fountains are turned off and drained.

Don't drink from streams or springs unless you boil the water. In the coldest part of winter you may find the springs and streams completely frozen.

Facilities in Winter

All of the following information is vulnerable to change.

Food and Lodging. Except in January and February, Big Meadows Lodge

(Mile 51. 2) keeps 30 to 40 rooms open, plus a recreation room and a tap room. The dining hall is closed, but meals are served at the Wayside. Ask at the Wayside about reservations, or write to ARA Virginia Sky-line Co., Inc., P. O. Box 727, Luray, Virginia 22835. The winter telephone is (703) 743-5108 (from 8 to 5 only.)

Except in January and February, the Big Meadows Wayside keeps its campstore, gift shop, and gas station open, and sells firewood and ice.

Campground. Parts of the Big Meadows campground, and the comfort stations that serve these parts, are open except in January and February.

Visitor Center. Big Meadows only. Open 9 to 5 except Christmas Day and certain days in January and February.

Picnic areas. All of them are open except Loft Mountain and Lewis Mountain. But their comfort stations are closed, and their drinking fountains are dry. All picnic areas have pit toilets for winter use. Some, but not all, have a frost-free water faucet.

The *Trailer Sewage Disposal* facility at Big Meadows is open, and there is a frost-free faucet beside it.

There is a pit toilet behind the comfort station at Stony Man Overlook, Mile 38.6.

Backcountry Camping

The "backcountry" takes in most of the Park—everything that's more than half a mile from any developed area. (Developed areas are Visitor Centers, Waysides, Lodges, Campgrounds, backcountry Huts and Shelters, and Picnic Areas.) Winter or summer, camping in the backcountry can be a delightful experience. You carry your food and lodging, and everything else you need, on your back. You're self-sufficient, on your own. No pavement, no neighbors, no noise. You'll spend your days walking and seeing, and your nights under the stars, listening to the sound of running water, and sometimes the call of a whip-poor-will or the hoot of an owl. This the authentic flavor of wilderness.

In theory, that is. Sometimes things don't work out the way they ought to. As I write this, Shenandoah has (maybe I should say "suffers from") more than twice as many backcountry campers per square mile as any other National Park. To preserve the woodlands, the Park must make rules for their use. No glass containers allowed. Hang your food high, between trees, where the bears can't reach it. No fires, except in the fireplaces at the huts and cabins. No camping within sight of a trail or road, or another camping party, or a sign that says "No Camping." You must get a backcountry camping permit during daylight hours only from Headquarters, or a Visitor Center, or an entrance station. Before issuing the permit, the ranger may interview you to see if you know the rules, and to make sure you have the necessary knowledge and equipment to camp safely.

All of which is reasonable. But there's a hitch. Most of the Park consists of steep, waterless, rocky slopes, entirely unsuitable for camping. (I remember walking mile after mile, looking for a flat place big enough to pitch a five- by seven-foot tent.) Many of our most scenic areas are off limits to camping because they're small, or because they're narrow, steep-sided gorges. Because of the rules (camp out of sight of shelters, trails, other camping parties), popular backcountry areas usually have only a handful of legal campsites. Naturally, these sites get constant use. The much-trampled soil becomes compacted, and in rainy weather it turns to mud. Nothing grows there, and erosion begins. These sites must be put off limits for overnight camping until they recover, which may take years.

When a camper walks for hours with a heavy pack, and reaches his destination at dusk but finds no legal campsite, he has two choices: carry that heavy pack back up the trail in the dark, or camp illegally. The second choice seems to be more popular. Because the Park Service is required by law to protect its wild areas, it must take countermeasures.

Rangers must enforce the rules, and they will have to restrict access to the backcountry. For any given area, only a limited number of camping permits can be issued for any given night. Some places, as I said, have been put off limits. Several of the backcountry shelters seemed to invite illegal camping, and it was necessary to remove them.

I'm truly sorry about that. The wilderness experience is something of great value. But it's clear that we can't all find solitude in the same place at the same time.

Any Questions?

Q: What's a "shelter"?

A: An open-front structure, usually of stone and logs, provided with a table, fireplace, pit toilet, and spring. I'll say more about the shelters in the article on hiking.

Q: Do rangers patrol the backcountry at night?

A: You bet. They can't visit every possible campsite every night, but they check as many as possible.

Q: What's a "frost-free faucet"?

A: A vertical pipe with a handle on top; operating the handle opens a valve that's a couple of feet underground, below the frost level, and water flows. When you shut it off, the pipe drains itself automatically. (If you find a frost-free faucet with a curved handle that makes it look like a miniature pump, don't be fooled. You don't have to pump to get water.)

Q: Who owns the lodges and waysides?

A: The Government owns the land. The concessioner owns the buildings and fixtures.

Q: Who sets the rates for food and lodging?

A: The concessioner sets the rates, subject to approval by the Superintendent. Prices must be comparable to those charged for similar food and lodging outside the Park.

Q: When the campgrounds are full may I camp beside the Drive, or in a picnic area, or at an overlook?

A: No. There are a number of private campgrounds nearby, outside the

Park. To be sure of a campsite in the Park in summer, avoid weekends and holidays. Beware of good weather. And get here early in the day.

Q: Can I reserve a campsite?

A: Maybe. At present you can reserve a campsite at Big Meadows Campground only, between late May and late October. At other times and other places it's still First Come, etc. There's a reservation fee in addition to the usual camping fee. There are three ways to make a reservation:

1. Go to the Big Meadows Campground Ranger Station between 8 a.m. and 10 p.m.

2. Get a mail order form at a Visiter Center, an Entrance Station, or at Park Headquarters. Fill it out and mail it to Ticketron Reservation Office, P. O. Box 2715, San Francisco, CA 94126.

3. Look for a Ticketron sales outlet. They are said to be located in department stores, sporting goods stores, and automobile clubs in most major cities. Lots of luck.

Q: Will the campgrounds be expanded, or new ones built?

A: Probably not. We can't have more camping space without giving up something else of value. The 14-day camping limit is, of course, a form of rationing. If necessary the annual camping ration may be cut to ten days, or seven. Actually, at present, the number of people turned away because the campgrounds are full is small compared to the number who find campsites.

Q: May I park beside the Drive and eat a picnic lunch?

A: Sure. Clean up afterwards.

IN CASE OF EMERGENCY

I can summarize this article in a single sentence: If there's an emergency that you can't handle without help, tell a ranger or phone Park Headquarters. Call 999-2243. If no answer, call 999-2227.

Personal Injury

Give first aid. Stop the bleeding and restore breathing, if necessary. Then, if the injury is severe, get help.

Most Park Rangers are qualified to give first aid, and many are Emergency Medical Technicians or Park Medics. Rangers routinely administer advanced life support to seriously ill or injured visitors, and then take them to the nearest hospital. If *you* take an injured visitor to a hospital please report the incident to a ranger as soon as possible, so that the safety hazard, if any, can be eliminated.

Lost Person

If some member of your party went hiking and is now overdue, be patient. Give him a little extra time, because most hikes take longer than the hiker thinks they will. But if the missing person is hours overdue; if you have good reason to think he may have overestimated his strength and endurance; or if the weather turns bad and you know your missing hiker is not equipped to cope with it—then get help. If necessary, rangers will get out of bed to organize a search party, although they don't enjoy that sort of thing any more than you would.

When a child is lost your problem is more serious. Make a quick search of the area, but don't wait too long before you ask for help—especially if it's getting late in the day, or if the weather is turning bad. A small child lost in winter is an instant, full-blown emergency.

The behavior of a lost child who's too young to reason—say five years or younger—or of a retarded child, will often though not always follow a predictable pattern. He may choose the direction in which he thinks safety lies and then take off, going as fast and as far as his strength permits. He may quickly become frightened, and hide when a hiker or searcher comes near; and he may not answer when called by name. He is more likely to travel uphill than down, and he may climb a slope that's both steep and rough. He will probably go farther and faster than you think. For all of these reasons, get help promptly.

Snakebite

Snakebite is unlikely, but it could happen. (*Prevention* of snakebite is discussed on page 24.) If you plan to spend some time in the backcountry, I suggest that you buy a snakebite kit. They're usually available at the campstores and waysides. Read the instructions before you need them. If someone in your party is bitten, try to keep him calm. See that he avoids unnecessary exertion. And get him to a doctor or hospital as soon as possible.

Car Trouble

In spite of careful and prudent driving, an occasional Park visitor will strike a deer (or, very rarely, a bear) with his car. If that should happen to you, remember that a large wounded animal—either bear or deer—can be dangerous. Stay away from it; there's nothing you can do to help it. (Do *not* try to load a wounded deer into your car with the idea of taking it to a vet.) Just notice where you are (note the nearest overlook or milepost) and then report the incident to a ranger as promptly as you can. You will not be arrested, or even lectured.

Your car may break down somewhere along the Drive, or it may not start because of a weak battery, or you may run out of gas. A ranger can help you get started, and he can sometimes provide enough gas to get you to the nearest gas station. For more serious problems he will call a tow truck from a nearby town.

If you have a CB radio in your car you may be tempted to call the tow truck yourself. Don't. In the past it has happened that several different CB users, passing a parked car with its hood up, have each called for a tow truck. And then two or more tow trucks appeared, only to find the trouble fixed and the "broken down" car long gone.

Now, no one will send a tow truck into the Park unless the call comes from Headquarters. If you're broken down and want to use your CB, try to contact Park Headquarters on the emergency channel. If you can't reach them, try to reach someone who will phone Headquarters for you.

How Can I Find a Ranger?

In the daytime, during the summer season, it's fairly easy. You can find a ranger at either Visitor Center. Concession personnel at the lodges or waysides will call a ranger for you. During the summer season campground entrance stations are manned all day, and fairly late in the evening. Park entrance stations are usually manned until 11 p.m. in summer; some of them, when the budget permits, are open all night.

Rangers patrol the Drive, but not on a fixed schedule. Patrol frequency depends on traffic, season, weather, and time of day—or in other words on how many visitors are likely to need help. A ranger might pass a given point twice an hour on a Saturday afternoon in summer, or not at all on a winter night.

If you can stop another driver, ask him to report your trouble to a ranger. If you're in trouble on a trail, ask another hiker to report it. (There's no harm in asking two different hikers to report your trouble. Rangers are in touch with each other, and with Headquarters, by radio. They aren't going to send two different rescue parties for you.)

The rangers maintain four offices in the Park, in addition to those at Headquarters and the Visitor Centers. They are usually open during "working hours."

Mile 22.1, Piney River. Turn into the road on the east side of the Drive (not the Mathews Arm Campground road on the west.) Go about a tenth of a mile, and look for the office trailer diagonally ahead on the right.

Mile 41.7, Skyland. The Ranger Station is located in Boulder Cabin, at the north end of the lower level of Skyland. It's manned infrequently, from late May through October.

Mile 51.2, Big Meadows. From late May through October, the Big Meadows Ranger Station is located at the campground. During the rest of the year it's just inside the Maintenance Area near the stables.

Mile 73.2, Simmons Gap. Turn into the road on the east side of the Drive. Take the first left turn, into the maintenance area; then the first right turn, into the residence area. The office is on the left. It's open intermittently.

Outdoor Telephones

If you can reach a telephone, calling Headquarters is the fastest way to get help. They can contact a ranger by radio, and send him to where you are. The Headquarters telephone is manned 24 hours a day. The number is 999-2243. If no answer, call 999-2227. From an outdoor telephone you can reach the operator without a coin. There are outdoor phones at the following locations:

Mile 4.6, Dickey Ridge Visitor Center. On the patio near the south end of the building.

Mile 22.2, Mathews Arm Campground. At the entrance station (0.7 mile from the Drive via the campground road, which is closed to automobiles in winter.)

Mile 24.0, Elkwallow Wayside. The phone is in sight from the Drive.

Mile 31.6, Panorama. The phone is out of sight from the Drive, on the far side of the information station.

Mile 41.7, Skyland. The phone is outside the Recreation Hall (see map, page 143.)

Mile 51.2, Big Meadows. Three phones: at the Visitor Center parking lot, the gas station, and the campground entrance station.

Mile 57.5, Lewis Mountain. The phone is outside the Campstore, about 0.2 mile from the Drive. (The campground road is closed in winter, but you can walk in.)

Mile 65.5, Swift Run Gap. There's a phone on the side of the entrance station.

Mile 79.5, Loft Mountain. Three phones: in front of the Wayside; at the Campstore; and at the campground entrance.

You Say You're Locked In?

Each of the three sections of Skyline Drive—north, central, and south—has a sturdy gate at each end that can be closed and locked. The gates are closed when snow or ice begins to accumulate dangerously. Rangers try to make sure that no cars will be locked in, but they may overlook one that's parked away from the Drive. In hunting season one or more sections of the drive may be closed "During Hours of Darkness" to help control poaching. There's a sign at each end of the section to be closed, but you might overlook it. Or your hike may take longer than you expected. Or your defini-tion of "Darkness" may be darker than that of the ranger who closes the gates. (Mine is.)

From late October to late April there's always a possibility, however remote, that you'll find yourself locked in and wanting out. What to do depends on where you are.

North Section, north end (Mile 0.1). Turn around. Take the road on your left at Mile 0.3; drive through the residence area and out into the World.

North Section, south end (Thornton Gap, Mile 31.5). Walk a few steps beyond the gate and look to your left to see if the entrance station is open. If it is, ask the ranger to open the gate. If it isn't, walk across the overpass to the information station on the right. Phone Headquarters (999-2243 or 999-2227) from the outdoor phone at the far side of the information station.

Central Section, north end (Panorama, Mile 31.6). Call Headquarters from the phone at the far side of the information station.

Central Section, south end (Swift Run Gap, Mile 65.5). Walk down the entrance road to the entrance station, which is just around the bend. There's a phone on the side of the building.

South Section, north end (Swift Run Gap, Mile 65.5). Cross the overpass, turn left, and walk down to the entrance station. Use the phone on the side of the building.

South Section, south end (Rockfish Gap, Mile 105.4). Walk across both overpasses and phone Headquarters (999-2243 or 999-2227) from one of the motels or restaurants on the right.

And now that you know how to cope with emergencies, I have a few suggestions for avoiding them.

WHAT'S GOING TO GET ME?
(Notes on personal safety)

What comes now is a medium-sized solid block of advice. It's intended for safety-conscious readers who want to know the causes of accidents in the Park so they can take precautions to avoid them. I suppose this is a matter of personal taste. If you're one of those people who absolutely refuse to fasten their seat belt, you may as well skip ahead to the next topic.

I'll start with a couple of questions that Park visitors often ask at the Visitor Centers.

Q: Are the bears dangerous?

A: Yes and no—mostly no. Visitor interest in bears is so strong that I'll give them a separate article in just a little while.

Q: Are there poisonous snakes in the Park?

A: Yes, two species: rattlesnake and copperhead. They're fairly common in the Park, although you're unlikely to see one—especially near the Drive or in a developed area such as a campground. Snakebite is rather rare in the Park, but it sometimes happens.

Poisonous Snakebite

I have the results of a study of 190 cases of poisonous snakebite in Virginia (outside the Park) during a ten-year period ending in 1953. That was a long time ago, but the habits of snakes haven't changed very much since then. There are several points of interest:

July is the most dangerous month. A breakdown of the 190 cases by month: 3 in April; 18 in May; 31 in June; 60 in July; 36 in August; 37 in September; 5 in October; none from November through March.

The bite of a copperhead is rarely fatal to an adult, even if untreated. Rattlesnake bites are more dangerous. Any poisonous snakebite is especially dangerous to children. In this study 52% of the victims were under age 16.

On cool days in spring or fall you may see a snake in the trail, soaking up the sunlight. During most of the summer snakes stay under cover in the daytime. Daytime snakebites result from turning over stones or logs, or gathering firewood, or thrusting ones hands into bushes (as, for example, when picking blueberries).

Snakes come out of concealment at night, and bite when they get stepped on.

Anti-snake precautions are simple: Watch where you put your hands and feet. Don't sit down without looking. Carry a flashlight at night. And keep an eye on the kids.

Q: Is it OK to kill poisonous snakes?

A: Absolutely not. The Park is a sanctuary for all wildlife. If you see a poisonous snake in the backcountry, walk around it. If you see one in a campground or picnic area call a ranger, who will remove it to the back-country.

The Cause of Accidents

I've studied the rangers' accident reports for a number of years. Except for freakish one-of-a-kind things, accident statistics are fairly consistent from year to year—so much so that I can predict next year's accidents and be surprisingly close. Here's more or less what will happen next year— whatever year that may be.

Seventy people—most of them children—will be injured by falling; this is by far the biggest single cause of accidents. Children run on trails or in the campground, then slip or trip and fall. Children take shortcuts where trails double back, and they slip and fall. Children climb trees and then fall out of them. But a dozen people—mostly young adults, will fall over cliffs or waterfalls. Some of them will be cut and bruised; some will break bones, one or two may die.

Four people—all of them young adults—will take a "bad trip" on drugs.

A dozen people will be injured in auto accidents, including four collisions, four cases of fingers smashed in doors, and four miscellaneous incidents such as a car falling off a jack.

Four people will be hit by rocks falling or rolling from above.

Ten people will be injured in bicycle accidents, and five in motorcycle accidents. Horses will bite, step on, or otherwise abuse ten people. There will be ten accidents related to firewood: people will cut or chop themselves, or be struck by flying wood. There will be half a dozen painful burns—some of them caused by pouring gasoline or other fuel on a fire or on hot coals.

Five people will be bitten by dogs. There will be one case of poisonous snakebite. Four people will be affected by carbon monoxide because of riding in a station wagon with the rear window down. Ten visitors will be severely stung by bees or wasps, including three who will step on, or blunder into, a hornets nest. But no one will be injured by a bear.

Many children will feed the squirrels; two squirrels will bite the hand that feeds them. Three children and seven dogs will be sprayed (but lightly) while chasing skunks, and one child will be bitten when he actually catches a skunk.

There will be a few severe reactions to sunburn and poison ivy. Five people will slip and fall on the ice next winter, but no one will die of exposure. And that's about it. With two million visitors, the Park is statistically a rather safe place, even though things may be unpleasant for the handful of visitors who make the statistics.

Now that you know the causes of accidents I have no reason to write a long list of safety precautions. The precautions suggest themselves. Even so, I'd like to touch on a couple of points that deserve special emphasis.

Special Precautions

If you have small children, keep an eye on them. (I remember suggesting that you lie down in the grass and close your eyes. Parents of small children should close only one eye.) It's very hard, and maybe unwise, to keep kids from running. So carry a first-aid kit, or at least a couple of band-aids.

Children seem to have a natural urge to throw rocks from high places.

But trails often pass below high places, and rocks thrown from above can be lethal.

Cliffs and ledges are exposed to sudden gusts of wind that can throw you off balance. The rocks are often slicker than you might expect, especially if you're wearing smooth-soled shoes. Cleated soles of rubber (or of composition such as Vibram) give secure footing when both shoes and rocks are dry. But cleats can pick up a load of slippery mud and carry it to the rocks. All rocks, however small, are dangerously slippery when wet, or when covered with ice or snow.

There is no reason for going to the top of a waterfall. You can't see the falls from there. The rocks at the top of the falls are always slippery because of spray, moss, and algae. In Shenandoah even deer sometimes fall over waterfalls.

People are no more honest in a National Park than they are back where they came from. Protect your property. Lock your car. Don't leave valuables such as wallets, purses, cameras, binoculars, on the seat of a car, even if it's locked. Put them in the trunk.

Photographers: Please don't put the viewfinder to your eye and then step back for a better view. I feel strongly about this because two photographers of my personal acquaintance died this way. One stepped off a construction scaffold and the other off a mountain cliff, both while looking through the viewfinder of a camera.

Walking beside the Drive is unsafe; but in a couple of cases it's the only way to get from a parking place to a trail head or other attraction. I'll call your attention, in the log, to several viewpoints beside the Drive where there's only a narrow strip of grass between the wall and the road. If you choose to go there on foot, give only part of your attention to scenery and camera; save most of it for the cars that are passing just behind your heels.

Park Regulations

The Park has a rather long list of regulations, which have the force of law. Willful and knowing violations are punished. Copies of the list are posted on bulletin boards, and are available on request at Headquarters and the two Visitor Centers. Their purpose is to protect the Park—its physical features; its buildings, roads, trails, and other facilities; its plant and animal life—all of it; and its visitors.

With that purpose firmly in mind you could sit down and write a useful list of regulations yourself, without ever seeing the Park's list. Therefore I'll keep this discussion short, and summarize only a few of the more important rules.

Don't collect anything: rocks, plants, animals (including insects), or souvenirs. Leave *everything* where you find it (except nuts, fruits, berries.) Unauthorized possession of any wild animal, dead or alive, or any part of one, or any flower or other plant material, is evidence of violation. To remember your stay in Shenandoah take pictures, or take notes.

Vehicles. Watch for posted speed limits. No wheeled or motorized vehicle may be taken off the pavement (except that you can park your car in the grass or unpaved parking areas at the edge of the Drive.) Snowmobiles are not permitted anywhere in the Park.

Wildlife. It's illegal to kill, wound, frighten, capture, attempt to capture, pursue, feed, or annoy any bird or animal, including snakes and fish. When you see a deer or bear, observe it from where you are; don't try to get closer.

Fires. Permitted in fireplaces in campgrounds and picnic areas, at cabins, and at most shelters. Nowhere else. Be sure your fire is out before you leave it.

Campers. Don't dig or level the ground. Keep your campsite clean. Don't clean fish or wash clothes at the campground hydrants, or in the comfort stations. Don't drain or dump water or sewage from your trailer except at designated places. If you have a radio keep the volume down, and turn it off by 10 p.m.

Don't fish without a license, or camp in the backcountry without a permit.

Pets. Must be under restraint at all times: crated, in your car or trailer, tied up or on leash. Dogs are prohibited on conducted walks and on a few very popular trails (with a sign to that effect at the trail head.) No animals (except Seeing Eye dogs) are allowed in public buildings within the Park.

Firearms and other weapons must be unloaded, disassembled if possible, and packed away. "Other weapons" include air rifles, air pistols, bows and arrows, crossbows, and slingshots. The use of fireworks in the Park is forbidden.

There. So much for advice. (For a while, at least).

IS HISTORY IRRELEVANT?

History deals with the past, which is dead and gone. The future does not exist. We spend our lives on a razor-thin edge of time that separates the dead from the non-existent. The present is a precarious perch to live on without a thought for the past, wherein lie our perspective, our roots, our identity.

The historian's job is to collect quantities of source materials: to evaluate, sift, winnow, and cull; to assign different degrees of credibility to different witnesses; and to distill a product which, if it can't be called "Objective Truth", is at least plausible.

Source materials are, in order of decreasing credibility: documents (courthouse vital statistics and land records); family bibles, diaries, journals, letters and photographs of people who lived the history we hope to learn; physical evidence (in our case the mountaineers' cemeteries, those possessions and tools that still exist, and the ruins of their homesites); eyewitness accounts by outside observers, written at the time of the event reported; oral history—people telling what they remember of events, or of what their parents told them; last and least, writers who have made use of these primary sources with various degrees of skill.

Courthouse records give names and dates, and tell who owned what piece of land. The mountain people wrote few diaries or letters. History passed down by word of mouth is a story told by storytellers, who know that their first responsibility is to tell a good story. If the teller fails to hold the listener's attention, then the story is at fault and must be improved. Eye-witness accounts by outside observers tend to contradict one another; an observer sees more or less what he expects to see, and filters his account through his personal preconceptions. And as for other writers, I find many of them more credulous than credible.

Therefore, when I tell you of Shenandoah's past, please remember that each sentence begins with an unwritten "maybe".

In The Beginning

The story begins eleven thousand years ago, give or take a handful of centuries. The form of the Blue Ridge was very much as we see it now. With a present-day topographic map we would have been able to identify all the familiar peaks and hollows. Hawksbill, then as now, was the highest point. There were cliffs on Mt. Marshall, waterfalls in Whiteoak Canyon, and talus slopes on Blackrock and Trayfoot.

But we would have found the climate uncomfortably cold. The most recent ice age was nearing its end, but there still were glaciers 200 miles to the north. The mammoth, the mastadon, and the long-horned bison were still the dominant animals, though all three were now endangered species. Hemlocks, balsam fir, and gray birch grew in the Valley and the Piedmont. And on the mountain—who knows? Perhaps no trees at all; only an alpine flora of very small and hardy plants.

That was the setting when man first appeared here: very primitive Indians (we think) who must have come from somewhere in the West. These people were wanderers who lived by hunting. At places suitable for camping—more or less flat areas beside the streams—the hunting parties left physical evidence of their passing: spear points, knives, and scrapers chipped from quartzite, and the chips that were their byproduct. (As you might expect, these same sites were later used by more recent Indians, and then by the white settlers who became our Mountain People, and now by backcountry campers.)

Over a period of perhaps fifteen hundred years, say 9,500 B. C. to 8,000 B. C., the ice age ended and the glaciers retreated far to the north. The great mammals of the ice age became extinct. The climate slowly grew warmer. The gray birches and firs and hemlocks, which do better where it's cold, retreated to the colder mountaintops. And they moved northward as well as upward; so that those we now find on the mountain are isolated, stranded, with no place to go. The Indians remained primitive, few in number, nomads and hunters still.

Q: How can a glacier, or a tree, "retreat"?

A: Figure of speech. The glaciers melted, from south to north. A tree produces a great many seeds, which are spread in all directions by wind and water, birds and mammals. Seeds that sprout where conditions are suitable will prosper; those that sprout elsewhere will die. By this means, over a period of many tree-generations, hemlocks moved from the valley to the mountain. It took a long time, but Nature has all the time in the world.

Then Came the Woods

Over a span of many years, say from 8,000 B. C. to 1,000 B. C., the Blue Ridge changed slowly. The deciduous forest of oak, hickory, and chestnut gradually developed, and the animals that thrive in such a forest—deer, bear, turkey, elk, and woods bison—appeared and slowly increased in numbers. (I don't mean to imply that the trees or the animals developed as species; they merely returned from farther south, where they had earlier "retreated" before the advancing glaciers.) The hemlocks moved to the coolest places—the north-facing slopes of high ridges.

During this time the Indians became foragers for wild foods as well as hunters, collecting nuts, fruits, berries, and edible bulbs and roots.

And "Modern" Indians

Between 1,000 B. C. and the appearance of European settlers in Virginia, change accelerated. Agriculture began; the Indians raised corn, and probably squash, and possibly beans. Because farmers can't be nomads, a more or less settled village life developed. Pottery, which was unknown to the more primitive Indians, came into use. Hunting (to say nothing of warfare) was easier after the invention of bow and arrow. Broken pottery and burial mounds show us where the villages were. Both are common in the Shenandoah Valley. On the mountain we find arrowheads, spear points, some broken pottery, and various stone tools. Clearly, hunting parties roamed the mountains, and may have camped here for extended periods during the summer. But there were few if any permanent villages within what is now the Park.

Even in the valley, the villages were only semi-permanent. They were moved or abandoned when game or firewood got scarce, or pollution became unpleasant, or the occupants fled from hostile raiders. The Indians, in spite of what we may have read or imagined, were not conservationists. Hunting parties sometimes burned hundreds of acres of forest, to drive game animals to a point where they could be easily killed. The first white man to climb the Blue Ridge and look down into the Shenandoah Valley did not look down on unbroken forest, but on forest spotted with clearings. Indians sometimes drove herds of bison over a cliff, but used relatively few of the dead animals. It was because of their primitive technology, and because by various means they contrived to limit their population, that they did relatively little damage to the environment.

The Tribes

Here's how things were when Jamestown was settled in 1607. The Powhatans occupied most of tidewater Virginia, and their villages surrounded Jamestown. Farther west, in the Piedmont, were tribes of the Manahoac and Monacan confederacies. The Shenandoah Valley was sparsely populated. There were a few Shawnee villages (one report says Moneton and Saponi also.) The Valley was unpopular because it was a dangerous place to live. Raiding parties of Catawbas from the south and Delawares from the north swept through the Valley from time to time, killing, looting, and burning (as did the Yankee troops of Phil Sheridan in a later, more civilized age.)

The Powhatans, so I've heard, were friendly and hospitable toward the white settlers. Until, that is, they found out that the white men were not just visiting, but intended to stay forever. The Powhatans might then have wiped out the colony, except for their perennial enemies, the Monacans. Because the Powhatans feared a two-front war they dallied too long—until the white man's numbers became, as Indians tend to say in western movies, like the sands of the desert. They yielded at last to the white man's pressure and moved westward, forcing the Monacans northward and westward before them. Pressure and movement continued for a century and a half, until the Indians were gone from Virginia.

The First Explorer

The Colony of Virginia, by virtue of its Royal Charter, claimed lands that extended to the Mississippi River and the Great Lakes. In the mid-1600's settlement was almost confined to tidewater; the western lands were wilderness over which the colony had neither economic nor political control. Virginia therefore encouraged exploration. In 1669 Sir William Berkeley, Governor of the Colony, sent John Lederer, a "German scholar", to explore the Blue Ridge.

Lederer, with the help of his Indian guides, reached the crest of the mountain on March 18, 1669. He later made two more trips to the Blue Ridge, reaching the crest at two other points, and then went home to write his journal. Lederer reported wolves, beavers, "great herds of red and fallow deer feeding, and on the hill-sides bear crashing mast like swine." (The "deer" were probably Virginia white-tail and wapiti; "mast", in case you don't have a dictionary handy, refers to acorns and chestnuts.)

Because Lederer had no maps of the Blue Ridge and the peaks had no names, we can only guess, from his rather hazy descriptions, the points at which he reached the mountain crest. Various guesses include Manassas Gap (a little way outside the Park, to the north), Big Meadows (Mile 51.2), Milam Gap (52.8), Bootens Gap (55.1), and Hightop (66.7).

Lederer gets credit for being the first white man to climb the Blue Ridge. Which is somewhat irrelevant, and probably false. I strongly suspect that a few white trappers and traders had crossed the mountain before Lederer climbed it. The true accomplishment of John Lederer should be more accurately defined. He was, so far as we know, the first person of either sex and of any color to climb the Blue Ridge and leave a written account of his trip.

Golden Horseshoes

Lederer's trip did nothing to promote settlement of the western lands. Virginians began to worry that the French, moving down from Canada, might get there first. To publicize the land beyond the Blue Ridge, Governor Alexander Spotswood in 1716 led a party of men across the mountain to the Shenandoah River and back again. Those are the bare facts. Filling in the details gives this expedition a quality of legend.

The principal source of information is the diary of John Fontaine, a member of the party. There have been several other accounts, some of which must be classified as "historical fiction".

The Governor's party consisted of 63 men: the Governor himself, 16 "rangers", a number of "gentlemen", and their servants and guides. They took 74 horses and several hunting dogs. The party moved slowly because of minor accidents, rough country, steep slopes and thick underbrush. There was a long time-out when they decided the horses would need shoes because of the rough going ahead. (Legend: during such delays they passed the time by toasting the King. Fontaine says, "We had several sorts of liquors, viz., Virginia red wine and white wine, Irish usquebaugh, brandy, shrub, two sorts of rum, champagne, canary, cherry, punch, water, cider, etc.")

The explorers ate venison, bear meat, and other wild game, roasted on "wooden forks." (Legend: at each meal they drank to the health of the King, and to each of his children, and to anyone else who came to mind.) But the "gentlemen" were unaccustomed to sleeping on the ground; they suffered from aching bones, chills and fever (and, I should imagine, an occasional hangover.)

Fontaine saw the tracks of elk and bison, vines with a sort of "wild cucumber", shrubs with fruit like currents, and good wild grapes. The party crossed the mountain and descended into the valley, where they found a northward-flowing river which they called the Euphrates; it was "very deep", and "fourscore yards wide in the narrowest part." They drank some healths, and took possession in the name of George I. At dinner they drank the King's health in champagne and fired a volley; they drank the Princess's health in Burgundy and fired a volley; they drank to other members of the royal family in claret, and fired a volley; they drank the Governor's health, and fired a volley. (After which, I presume, they got down to serious drinking.)

Governor Spotswood later presented each member of the expedition with a small golden horseshoe bearing the inscription *Sic jurat transcendere montes.* Some of these golden horseshoes became prized family heirlooms, although not one of them can be located now.

It has been assumed that the Spotswood party crossed the mountain at Swift Run Gap (Mile 65.5). Monuments beside the highway there commemorate the crossing, and that part of U.S. 33 is called the Spotswood Trail. But a more recent theory favors Milam Gap (Mile 52.8) as the crossing point. Fontaine says they climbed to a spring near the ridge crest. A "musket shot" from there, on the far side of the ridge, they found another spring. They tried to descend westward from the second spring, turned back when they came to a precipice, and then made a "good, safe descent" from another point. From the foot of the mountain they travelled seven miles before they reached the river. None of that fits very well at Swift Run Gap. But if we assume that they went to Milam Gap, then Lewis Spring, then Lewis Falls, then Tanners Ridge, it fits like a glove.

Q: Were these men really such heroic drinkers? Was the Shenandoah

River deeper and wider then than it is now?

A: Everybody wants to make a good story better.

Settlers

The Spotswood expedition brought quick results. Settlers of English and German ancestry began moving into the Piedmont and toward the mountains. James Taylor II, an ancestor of presidents Madison and Taylor, built an estate in 1722 near the present town of Orange. Spotswood had, some time before his expedition, established a colony of Swiss and German artisans at Germanna (between the present cities of Fredericksburg and Culpeper.) Some of the Germans from this colony moved in 1725 to the foot of the Blue Ridge, at the mouth of Whiteoak Run. Some of their descendants are still there.

The Governor had made grants of large areas of land, including much of what is now the Park, in 1712. James Barbour bought a large part of this area in 1730, and began selling small tracts on the Blue Ridge to prospective settlers. He later bought back many of these tracts, and regained possession of others when the buyers abandoned them.

The Blue Ridge, with no roads across it, was still a barrier to settlement of the Shenandoah Valley from the east. But not to settlement from the north. In 1727 Germans from Pennsylvania crossed the Potomac and moved up the Shenandoah Valley, where they started a settlement called Massanutten, west of the present town of Luray. During the next ten years German Quakers and Mennonites from Pennsylvania established several other settlements in the Valley.

The first settler in this part of the Blue Ridge was probably Michael Woods, who built a home near Jarman Gap in 1734. Records show that Francis Thornton owned the land east of Thornton Gap in 1733, although he lived on the Piedmont, south of the present town of Sperryville. It was not until 1740 or 1750 that settlement of the Blue Ridge hollows began. At that time there was plenty of land available in the Piedmont and the Valley. But some people chose to live in the mountains, probably because they or their parents had come from the mountainous parts of Europe.

The Northern Neck

The Northern Neck includes more than half of Shenandoah National Park, or almost none of it, depending on how you look at things. The Northern Neck is bounded by the Chesapeake Bay, the Potomac River, the Rappahannock River, and a line connecting the sources of the two rivers.

In 1649 King Charles II of England granted this tremendous area to seven English noblemen. One of the seven was Thomas, Lord Culpeper, who later bought the shares of the other six. The Northern Neck was owned, successively, by:

Margaret, widow of Lord Culpeper

Catherine (the widowed Lady Fairfax), daughter of Margaret.

Thomas (sixth Lord Fairfax), son of Catherine.

Lord Fairfax was living in England when he inherited the Northern Neck. He visited his Virginia property in 1736, and was profoundly impressed by it. He instructed his agents to do two things: begin a survey to locate the sources of the rivers, and start selling land. He then returned to England to dispose of his Scottish and English properties. He came back to Virginia in 1747 and spent the rest of his life here, an eccentric but apparently contented bachelor.

The Fairfax agents followed orders. They immediately began selling tracts of land, many of which lay within other grants, especially Barbour's. And they surveyed all branches of both rivers, finally choosing the Conway River as the principal source of the Rappahannock. Colonel William Byrd, an ancestor of a distinguished Virginia family, protested vigorously. He got nowhere.

The agents of Lord Fairfax made two possible errors. First, they chose the Rapidan, rather than the Rappahannock, as the source of the Rappahannock. Second, they chose the Conway, rather than the Rapidan, as the source of the Rapidan. These two choices brought the size of the Northern Neck to about five million acres—nearly double what it should have been. Whether these mistakes were honest and therefore pardonable errors, I can't say. But I can grumble "The rich get richer."

The Fairfax Line

Ten years later, in 1746, the agents of Lord Fairfax undertook to survey a line that would connect the sources of the two rivers, and thus determine the missing boundary of the Northern Neck. They led a surveying party to Bootens Gap (Mile 55.1 on the Drive), where they spent several days trying to decide which of the three small branches at the head of the Conway River was the true source of the Rappahannock. They finally decided that none of the three was the source, and led the party four miles back down the river to the mouth of Devils Ditch. The Fairfax agents then suggested that the trickle of water that issues from Devils Ditch was in fact the true source of the Rappahannock. The surveyors rejected this suggestion as preposterous, and the party returned to Bootens Gap.

If the Fairfax Line had been run from the head of Devils Ditch, at about Mile 57 on the Drive, Lord Fairfax would have acquired an additional 50,000 acres. But I can't condemn these men. They were simply exercising a very human trait that all of us possess in one degree or another, namely greed.

A Century of Litigation

During the last half of the eighteenth century, agents of Fairfax and Barbour continued to sell land in what is now the Park: Fairfax as far south as the Fairfax Line at Bootens Gap (and occasionally much farther south); Barbour as far north as the Hazel Country (and sometimes farther north.) Much of what is now the Central District of the Park was claimed by two different owners. The resulting disputes and court actions continued almost until the Civil War.

This concerns us only in that it gives some insight into the character of the Mountain People. It has been reported that they were surly and hostile and suspicious of strangers, whom they called "furriners". In some cases this was true, and for various good reasons. The disputed land was one. When a stranger comes to tell you that you're only a squatter on land your grandfather bought and paid for, you're entitled to feel hostile, and your children will remember.

In 1795 James Barbour (who was probably a grandson of the original James Barbour) had a survey made of the Barbour property. His surveyors reported that it consisted of 42,700 acres, and extended as far north as Thornton Gap. On display in the Byrd Visitor Center (Big Meadows, Mile 51.0) is a photostat of a map drawn by the surveyors. Noted on it are the names of 33 people who were apparently "squatters" on the Barbour land. More likely they had bought the land they were living on, but not from Barbour. Incidentally, several of the "squatters" have the same surnames as families who were displaced by the Park 135 years later.

The Golden Age

The Golden Age of the Mountain People, during which a reasonable amount of labor could ensure them a reasonable standard of living, lasted until the Civil War. The first settlers moved into a magnificent forest, where one tree in five (or possibly one in three) was a chestnut; and each chestnut tree might produce a bushel of food each year. Wild game was abundant, and fish swam in every stream. The soil, though thin and rocky, was rich enough to produce good crops.

One by one, roads were built across the mountain: first at Jarman Gap (Mile 96.8); then, in 1785, at Thornton Gap (31.5). Roads at Browns Gap (83.0), Swift Run Gap (65.5), and Fishers Gap (49.4) were completed long before the Civil War. These roads ensured Virginia's political control of the Valley, and provided a means for transporting its produce to eastern markets.

After the Revolution, settlement accelerated. Virginians of English descent farmed the Piedmont, all the way to the foot of the mountain. More Germans, my great great great grandfather among them, moved from Pennsylvania to the Shenandoah Valley. And as the population increased, industry expanded. Cider presses and tanneries, grist mills, carding mills, and up-and-down sawmills—all operated by water power—sprang up at the foot of the mountain hollows. The mills used the products of the mountains, and encouraged more and more people to settle in the hollows.

Valley farmers bought large tracts of land near the top of the Blue Ridge, and used them for grazing. They allowed poorer families to live on the land, to build homes and raise gardens, and to graze sheep and cattle of their own—in exchange for labor: protecting the owner's cattle, and keeping the fields free of locust trees and brambles.

Thus some of the mountain people were employees of absentee owners. Some were squatters, who simply moved in and built homes. But most of them owned the land they farmed, or at least thought they did.

Between 1800 and the Civil War, the isolated people of the mountain hollows were probably as well off as small farmers in the Valley and the Piedmont. Some time around 1810, prosperity in the hollows must have reached its maximum. But by 1840 the mountains had passed their carrying capacity; and after that, as the population continued to increase, things could only get worse.

To Make a Living

The mountain people were farmers. They cleared the land for homes and fields by cutting trees, pulling stumps, and laboriously moving rocks. During many years of work the clearings grew larger, as did the piles of rocks stacked here and there throughout the fields. Rock walls served as fences and boundary markers, sometimes with the help of split-rail fences and, much later, barbed wire. A few trees were left in the meadows to make shade for cattle. (Which is why, as you hike through young second-growth forest, you'll occasionally see a tree much bigger than the rest.) Each family had chickens and a hunting dog or two. Most had one or more cows; many had sheep or goats, sometimes horses or mules. All had hogs, which they ear-marked and then allowed to forage for themselves, to be rounded up at slaughter time.

The people lived in log cabins, usually with a single room and a loft; the adults slept downstairs, the children in the loft. A wood-burning fireplace gave radiant heat downstairs, and warmed the loft by convection. Access to industries at the foot of the hollow was, at first, by trail. Later the people built roads, using hand tools and a little help from horses or mules. On sloping ground, which is to say nearly everywhere, they built up the lower side of the road with stones, to level it and keep it from washing away. The roads were rough, and barely wide enough for a team and wagon. Traces of the old roads are still there, and you'll see them when you hike in the hollows.

Wealth came from the forest. Black walnut trees provided food and dye, as well as wood. From the chestnut trees they cut logs for cabins and rails for fences. They used the wood of oaks and hickories to make roof shingles, furniture, farm tools, and webbings for chairs and baskets. The nuts and acorns were food for domestic animals and wild game. Black birch was one of many trees and herbs that they used for medicine; its inner bark was thought to cure rheumatism. And the crushed end of a black birch twig became a toothbrush with a built-in wintergreen flavor.

They hunted the large game animals while they lasted, and when these were gone they trapped or hunted coons, bobcats, foxes, possums, squirrels, rabbits, beaver, mink, and muskrat. There was a ready market for furs and hides.

The mountain people gathered chestnuts, walnuts, and berries, for their own use and to sell. They cut trees and dragged the logs to the up-and-down sawmills, where they exchanged them for cash or lumber. They took hides to be tanned, and paid the tanner with hides. They took wool to the carding mills (which made it suitable for spinning) and paid with wool. They took corn to be ground at the grist mills, and paid with corn.

Every mountain home had a few apple trees, and sometimes an

orchard of an acre or more. They ate the apples raw; they peeled and sliced them, and dried them on the cabin roof for winter use or for sale; they made cider, and vinegar, and apple butter, and applejack.

The mountain people preserved vegetables and fruits, and smoked or salted meats for winter use. They stripped tanbark from the chestnut oak trees and sold it to the tanneries. They collected wild honey. They made moonshine whiskey, and sold a part of it.

They wove woolen cloth and made their own clothes; they made their own shoes, household furnishings, and sometimes farm implements. But no one farmily tried to do everything. There were farmers especially skilled at butchering, and they performed that service for their neighbors. Others had special skill as stone masons, or shoemakers, or blacksmiths, or carpenters. The people used the skill of their specialists, and paid them with goods or with their own special services.

The Mountain Culture

The mountain people had a rich traditional culture. They were isolated, it's true; the next-door neighbor might be a mile away. And they spent most of their time working to make a living. But those things were true also of small farmers in the Valley and the Piedmont. The only schools were at the mouth of the hollows, which might be several miles from home. Nevertheless the mountain children attended school when they were not needed for work on the farm. Most had dropped out completely before the fifth grade. And those things too were true in the Valley and the Piedmont. Before the Civil War, the illiteracy rate in the hollows was probably about the same as that of the general population.

Many parents taught their own children to read, write, and do simple arithmetic. Some families owned books. Most had a Bible, and read from it, though not easily. A typical mountain man might have said (though I'm sure none ever did), "Well, yes, I kin read. But I don't take no pleasure in it." Oral tradition was strong; folklore and folk wisdom, legends, ballads, and tall stories—all were passed down by word of mouth.

Medicine was mostly home-made, from garden herbs and plants of the forest. Few of the mountain people ever saw a hospital. And they rarely sent for a doctor although, oddly enough, the doctor usually came when sent for.

The mountain people were mostly Baptists, and many attended church, even though that might involve a walk of several miles. After the Civil War, as families became poorer, church attendance declined. Many felt that their clothes weren't good enough for church. Some were "excluded" by the church in an attempt to regulate their morality. But the people continued to observe Christmas as a religious holiday; some exchanged presents; some decorated Christmas trees. Many families hid eggs at Easter. There were religious revivals in the mountains from time to time. Crescent Rock (Mile 44.4) was the site of frequent meetings and revivals. (They continued for a while after the Park was established, which accounts for the extra parking space there.) Most of the mountain people were superstitious; they believed in ghosts and signs and omens, as did country people in the Valley and the Piedmont.

Because of the distance between homes, "hollering" was a useful means of communication, and different hollers conveyed different messages. When a mountaineer went to visit a neighbor he stopped at the edge of the dooryard, gave the appropriate holler, and waited for an answer. To walk up to the door without hollering was a breach of courtesy, and sometimes dangerous.

They made their own music, mostly with fiddle, banjo, and guitar. Here again they depended on specialists; each major hollow had its own musicians. They had square dances in their houses, and sometimes on wooden platforms they built in the woods. Raising a new house or barn was often a cooperative effort and a social occasion. So, too, was apple-butter boiling in the fall, with music and dancing, courting, drinking moonshine and homemade beer, games, and fighting.

In the musical play "Shenandoah", a chorus of young men sings "Next to lovin' I like fightin' best." Fighting was a frequent pastime. The mountain people admired feats of strength. Such feats became legends, to be passed down by word of mouth, and the legends grew larger with the passage of time.

War Between the States

When war came, some of the mountain men went off to join the Confederate Army. Others chose not to. A squad of soldiers might come into the mountains from time to time to search for draft evaders; but there were plenty of hiding places, and hollering gave ample warning.

There was little military action in what is now the Park. Stonewall Jackson, during his Valley campaign, marched his army across the mountain twice at Browns Gap (Mile 83.0), and once at Fishers Gap (49.4). Early's army retreated through Browns Gap in 1864, and there was a minor skirmish there. A few cavalry engagements took place near the foot of the mountain, on both sides. And that's all.

But there were major battles in the Shenandoah Valley, which was of strategic importance as the back door to Washington. It was also important as the bread basket of the Confederacy. Phil Sheridan's scorched-earth policy was designed to empty the basket, and it did. After Sheridan passed through, some people actually starved to death in the Valley.

My great grandfather, who was a Mennonite and therefore a conscientious objector, spent a large part of the Civil War in the mountains, safe from Federal troops as well as conscription squads. When Sheridan came my great grandfather looked down at night, and the light of burning barns flickered like fireflies in the Valley. This is oral history, passed down in my family.

Decline and Fall

One by one, sources of wealth in the mountains withered away. The woods bison disappeared in colonial times, and the elk soon after. Deer and bear followed, and then the smaller animals, until at last there was nothing to hunt but squirrels and rabbits.

After the war Virginia was an impoverished land. Barns, livestock, and farm implements were gone. Slaves, once a major asset of the big landowners, had been freed. Confederate money was worthless. Taxes were high, and had to be paid with Yankee dollars. The landowners did what they could to regain their lost fortunes. Those with mountain land sent in logging crews who stripped the forests; within a generation nearly every tree worth taking was gone.

When the Shenandoah Valley railroad was completed in 1882, steam-powered mills were built beside it. The primitive water-powered industries at the foot of the mountains could not compete, and were quickly abandoned. The mountain people could no longer cut trees and drag them to the sawmills. They could no longer barter corn for meal, or hides for leather. The people now had to pay cash for meal, flour, and shoes, while means for earning cash were dwindling.

As I've said, the mountains had passed their carrying capacity. At first a man grew corn until the soil was exhausted, then cleared another patch and let the old one grow up in brambles. Finally no suitable land was left to clear. The people used up the mineral wealth of the soil, and had no way to replace it. Bad farming practices, clear-cutting of the forests, and repeated burning, all caused rapid erosion. When a mountain man died, his land was usually divided among his children. Thus farms became smaller and smaller, while each acre produced less and less.

The mountain people too had to pay taxes, and when they couldn't pay they lost their land. Others, when times were hard, borrowed from banks; and if they could not repay the loan they lost their land. Population in what is now the Park may have been more than 10,000 in 1900. In the next 25 years it dropped by half. When the Park was established, half the remaining families were squatters, tenants, or sharecroppers on land they no longer owned.

Public schools came to this area in 1870; then the railroad, and finally the automobile. Country people in the Valley and Piedmont had increasing contact with the outside world; they acquired new ideas, new technology, and to a small extent new patterns of speech. And the mountain people, by remaining unchanged, became different.

Child labor was urgently needed on the mountain farms. And children were reluctant to go to school, where their poor clothes and strange ways might be laughed at. Illiteracy increased.

Some of the mountain people now worked as hired hands for farmers outside the mountains. Some made axe handles, or baskets, or other handicraft items that brought in a little cash. A few found work at the Skyland resort. The mountains still produced blueberries each summer, and they could be sold for 25 cents a gallon. The sale of tanbark from the mountains reached its peak about 1900, and tanbark brought as much as nine dollars a cord. Each September a man could gather a bushel of chestnuts in a day, and sell them for up to twelve dollars.

Then came a one-two punch. The tanneries developed a new process, and the market for tanbark disappeared. The chestnut blight reached the Blue Ridge about 1915, and within a few years the chestnut trees were dead.

As other sources of income dwindled or vanished, the moonshine industry became more important. Lookouts and hollering warned of approaching revenuers, who rarely caught anyone making moonshine, but who destroyed many stills. Disputed lands, tax sales, foreclosures, and broken stills—all the work of strangers. As I've said, some of the mountain people had reason to be suspicious and hostile.

Exodus

When the Park was established there were still 432 families, with about 2,250 people, living within its boundaries. Some of them had been unable to leave their worn-out farms; they had no savings, no marketable skills, nothing to help them get started in a strange and frightening outside world. Others stayed because they wanted to, hard times or not; because the mountains were home.

But all of them had to leave. A few did so without help. The Resettlement Administration of the Department of Agriculture set up resettlement communities at seven points near the Park, where a displaced family could buy a house and land with no down payment, and a 30-year mortgage at very low interest. Many families moved to these communities. The rest were resettled by the Virginia state welfare department.

Seventeen older people were allowed to live out their lives here. The last of them left the Park in 1975.

The displaced families were moved to more comfortable houses on more productive land. They were closer to schools, jobs, and stores. In the mountains they had spent all their time trying to scratch out a living. Now the living was easier, and people had leisure time. Just the same, they tell us, life in the mountains was better.

Reminders

Many employees of the Park and the concessioner are from families that were displaced when the Park was established, and some of them were born here.

You can't take a hike of any distance without seeing evidence of the mountain people. Traces of the roads they built will be visible for decades more. Many of their rail fences are still standing, though most have fallen and decayed. Some cabin foundations are intact, and around many home-sites you can find battered tubs and buckets, broken tiles, bottles, and crockery. Most of the cabins were torn down, but a few dozen were not; these are now in ruins. Many of the cabin chimneys are standing, some of them as good as new.

There are dozens of cemeteries in the Park. Families or private organizations can maintain them if they wish; the Park does not. The Dean Cemetery

(Mile 63.2) and the Tanners Ridge Cemetery (51.6) are large and well maintained. (Burials may still take place there, as in other family burial areas, until the remaining space within these surveyed sites is filled.) Most of the rest are inactive, with no recent burials, and get little or no maintenance. Many are badly overgrown, and the headstones are leaning or falling.

Graves marked with inscribed headstones belong to families that had enough money to pay the stonecutter. Many graves are marked only by a small slab of fieldstone with no inscription. Who is buried beneath these slabs was a part of the oral tradition, a chain of information that was broken when the culture was disturbed in 1935. Now no one knows who is buried there, and hardly anybody cares.

The cemeteries, like the roads and cabins, will slowly melt into the land. The most durable reminders left by the mountain people are the great piles of stones that they heaped up while clearing their fields. Those will last a thousand years. (Want to bet?)

I've heard that many families tore their cabins down and took the logs to the new homesite, to rebuild their old homes on the new land. I've heard that some cabins were demolished when the family threatened to return to them. The Park Service made a study of the remaining cabins to see which should be preserved as historic structures. But preservation and maintenance of scattered cabins would have been costly, and no money was available. Matters drifted, and the cabins decayed.

What Were They *Really* Like?

The people who lived for generations in these mountains—what were they really like? Was the mountain man like Davy Crockett? Daniel Boone? Snuffy Smith? You can decide for yourself. And whatever you decide, there's plenty of expert testimony to back you up.

Mozelle R. Cowden studied the mountain people in the early 1930's, and paints this picture of the "median" family. There are five people, farming five acres, with a total cash income of from $100 to $150 a year. The family head is between 36 and 40 years old; his wife between 31 and 35. The adults have from one to four years of schooling; the children have none. The children are of normal height and weight. Their general health is good; their teeth are bad. The log house is reasonably clean, and flowers are planted around the door. The people are not hungry. They have chickens and a cow; and a hog to kill for winter meat. They have stored food to take them through the winter: canned fruit and vegetables, dried apples and beans, potatoes, pumpkins, cabbage, and at least ten gallons of kraut. Their cash income is enough to buy a year's supply of flour, meal, salt, sugar, and coffee.

It has been reported that the mountain people suffered a chronic malaise, a gnawing discontent. Darwin Lambert, who lived with a mountain family for nearly three years, tells me that, despite hardships, they enjoyed life as much as anyone he has ever known.

It is reported that intermarriage caused stupidity and wretched health. It is also reported that only poverty—not heredity or inbreeding—caused the degradation of the mountain people, for after leaving the Park they did as well as anyone else.

Dr. Roy Lyman Sexton, an eyewitness, wrote that the mountain people were moronic, improvident, lazy, stupid, and mean. Cowden, also an eye-witness, wrote that they were kind, helpful, generous, thrifty, accurate in speech, truthful and honest, with a keen sense of justice.

Several writers have mentioned family feuds among the mountain people. Sexton wrote that there were no family feuds because the people didn't have enough energy to keep them going.

Surely there were "good" and "bad" people in the mountains, as there are everywhere. There were good and bad hollows, just as there are good and bad neighborhoods in a city. And in most cases, it seems, "badness" and poverty go together. Most of the mountain people were reasonably well behaved, clear thinking, and industrious.

The Park: An Outline of History

In 1923, the only National Park east of the Mississippi is Acadia, in Maine. But various people have recommended creation of another eastern Park. This year Stephen T. Mather, Director of the Park Service, submits a report recommending that a Park be established in the Appalachian Mountains.

1924. Hubert A. Work, Secretary of the Interior, appoints the Southern Appalachian National Park Commission. Its assignment is to study possible sites for National Parks in the East, and to make recommendations. Various groups are vigorously promoting their favorite sites, including the Great Smoky Mountains of North Carolina and Tennessee, and the Massanutten and Blue Ridge Mountains of northern Virginia. The Commission recommends that *two* Parks be created, one in the Smokies and one in the Blue Ridge. (It's likely that George Freeman Pollock, founder and owner of the resort at Skyland, was instrumental in persuading the Commission to recommend the Blue Ridge.) The Commission, in its report, suggests that a Skyline Drive in the Blue Ridge park would be its outstanding feature, and writes "Few scenic drives in the world could surpass it."

1925. An Act of Congress authorizes and directs the Secretary of the Interior to determine possible boundaries for the proposed Shenandoah National Park.

1926. An Act of Congress authorizes establishment of the two parks, Smokies and Shenandoah. It specifies that land for the Shenandoah park be acquired at no expense to the Federal Government, and that the Park have a minimum area of 521,000 acres.

1928. An Act of Congress reduces the minimum area of Shenandoah National park to 327,000 acres. An Act of the Virginia Legislature authorizes the state to acquire land for the Park and donate it to the Federal Government. The Legislature appropriates $1.2 million to buy land, and this sum is to be matched by private donations. On the recommendation of Governor Harry F. Byrd, the Legislature creates the Virginia State Conservation and Development Commission to supervise land acquisition for the Park. (Acquisition will take years. Eventually 3,870 separate tracts will be bought, many of them with unclear titles and uncertain boundaries.)

1931. Construction of the Skyline Drive is begun, with money from the Federal Drought Relief Administration, as an emergency relief measure to provide work. Land acquisition is still under way, and there is no Park as yet. A 100-foot right-of-way for the Drive is acquired by gifts and special purchase.

It's now clear that money appropriated by the Virginia Legislature, plus private contributions, can't buy the amount of land specified by Congress as a minimum area for the Park. So Congress passes a new act, reducing the minimum to 160,000 acres.

1933. Young men of the newly created CCC (Civilian Conservation Corps) move into the future Park. They fight fires, work to reduce fire hazards, control erosion, and grade and plant the areas beside the Drive.

1934. The CCC force increases, and eventually numbers about 1,000 men, in six separate camps. They begin to build trails and shelters; this, and work on the Drive, will continue until the Corps leaves the Park at the outbreak of World War II. On September 15 of this year the central section of Skyline Drive is opened to the public, although the guard walls and many of the overlooks are still incomplete. During the first few days, long lines of cars wait bumper-to-bumper to get onto the Drive.

1935. Picnic grounds are opened at Pinnacles and South River. (Those at Elkwallow, Dickey Ridge, and Big Meadows, will come later.) On December 26, Secretary of the Interior Harold Ickes accepts deeds from the Commonwealth of Virginia conveying 176,429 acres to the Federal Government, and Shenandoah National Park is officially established.

1936. On July 3, President Franklin D. Roosevelt dedicates the Park in a ceremony at Big Meadows. On October 1, the north section of the Drive is opened to the public.

1937. The Park Service signs a contract with the Virginia Skyline Company of Richmond to provide food and lodging in the Park. The company takes over the existing dining room, cabins, and stables at Skyland, and the restaurants and gas stations at Thornton Gap and Swift Run Gap. They enlarge and modernize all three, and begin construction of a dining hall at Dickey Ridge. The Big Meadows Campground is opened to the public, and the first camper appears within five minutes.

1938. The Dickey Ridge development is opened, with a dining room, coffee shop, outdoor dancing terrace, and gas station. Waysides are opened at Big Meadows and Elkwallow.

1939. The Big Meadows Lodge, built of stone and chestnut, is completed and opened to the public; it has a dining hall for 150 people, and 26 guest rooms. At Dickey Ridge twelve cabins of native chestnut are completed; they have from two to four rooms each, and can accomodate a total of 60 guests. On August 29 the southern section of the Drive is opened. The Skyline Drive is now complete (at a total cost of about $5,000,000, or $50,000 per mile.)

1940. Lewis Mountain campground and picnic ground are opened "for Negroes." During this year the last of the mountain people are resettled outside the Park.

1958. The former dining hall at Dickey Ridge is converted to a Visitor Center, and the cabins to ranger quarters. (The cabins will later be demolished or removed because of maintenance problems.)

1961. The new highway interchange in Thornton Gap is completed. During construction the old restaurant and gas station have been demolished, and the present facilities built.

1964. Loft Mountain campground opens.

1966. Big Meadows Visitor Center opens.

1967. Mathews Arm campground opens.

1983. A very ambitious project begins: resurfacing Skyline Drive and rebuilding the stone walls beside it. This will take many years to finish.

The Land Recovers

The Park was created on eroded clearings and cut-over forest. Cutting, plowing, and grazing were stopped abruptly, and the scarred earth began to heal. The mountain people had built an extensive network of roads and trails. The Park continued to maintain a few of them, but abandoned most. Men of the CCC graded and cleared the best of the trails, and chose a few mountaineer trails and roads to make "truck trails". The roads of the mountain people had been rough and narrow. The truck trails were rough and a little wider. When World War II ended, and the Park could resume its development, it improved some of the truck trails to make fire roads and administrative roads, to facilitate backcountry patrol and firefighting. Other truck trails were abandoned.

Some environments are fragile. In meadows of the high Sierras, for example, an abandoned road or trail might last for centuries. But the Blue Ridge ecosystem is tough and resilient. An abandoned trail will disappear within a few years. The old roads last longer, especially where the sides were built up with rocks. But these too will disappear.

Thistles and brambles moved quickly into the abandoned meadows; black locust, hazel and pine soon followed. In the cut-over forests young oaks and hickories grew unhindered, and began slowly to replace the pioneer species in the meadows. With the return of food and cover the birds came back, then small mammals, and finally the deer and bear. The change goes on. If the wilderness remains undisturbed it will begin, within a century or two, to approach the climax forest that the first settlers found here. But it can never return entirely to its primitive state because the area is too small, too closely hemmed-in by civilization.

Ah, Wilderness!

In November of 1976 the Congress passed, and the President signed, a Wilderness Act that set aside a number of natural areas for preservation, including a large part of Shenandoah National Park. If the law remains in effect it will ensure the return of our mini-wilderness to climax forest. As I've said, we're running a museum here, and a climax forest would make a magnificent exhibit.

The law provides that there shall be no man-made development in the wilderness areas. To comply with this law, the Park has "put the wilderness to bed." Shelters and bridges in the designated areas have been removed. All fire roads and administrative roads in the wilderness have been redesignated as trails. Culverts have been removed and the natural drainage of the area restored. The former roads are permanently closed to vehicles by large boulders at each end.

The future of trails in the wilderness is uncertain. The Park plans to keep them open, but just "one person wide." If you meet someone, you'll have to edge by sideways. Horse trails will be kept "one horse wide", so that when two horses meet the results should be interesting. At the height of the growing season, trails "one person wide" can grow completely shut in a few weeks. Unless, that is, we keep them buzzing with maintenance crews, which would conflict with the basic idea: to create a refuge where you can get away from, and put out of mind, your fellow man and all his works. It's possible that some of the trails will be abandoned.

The more extreme advocates of wilderness would like to go further. They would like to demolish the lodges, close the campgrounds, and tear up the Skyline Drive. I've head some of them say that no one should have access to any part of this Park except on foot. I don't agree with this view, but I think we need it to counterbalance the opposite fringe. For there are people who want swimming pools, golf courses, self-guiding motor "nature" trails, more lodges, more campgrounds, and a four-lane Skyline Drive.

Whether we who walk the middle ground will continue to have a Park here, I don't know.

ABOUT THE BEARS

Hundreds of times in a summer season, a visitor will buttonhole a ranger and ask, "Are there any bears?"

Ranger: Well, yes, we have bears here.

Visitor: How many?

Whatever the answer, the visitor will be vaguely discontented with it. Trouble is, he didn't ask the right questions. He doesn't really care how many bears there are; he wants to know whether he's likely to see a bear, and is it going to be dangerous, and if so what should he do about it, and if not where can he go to see one. This is a complicated subject. To sort it out, why don't you (Q) interview me (A) on the subject of bears.

Q: So, how many bears are in the Park?

A: Who knows? The Park boundary is hundreds of miles long. Bears come and go, and mostly stay out of sight.

Q: An estimate, then.

A: In summer, about 300. In winter maybe half as many.

Q: What's your estimate based on?

A: A wild guess, supported by a bear census.

Q: Tell about the census. Who made it?

A: Park rangers, working with people from the Virginia state wildlife commission. Bears were trapped, tranquilized, marked with a metal tag in the ear and a tattoo inside the lower lip, measured, weighed, relieved of one small and relatively unused tooth, detranquilized, and released.

Q: Why the tooth?

A: They can tell the bear's age from a cross section of it.

Q: And they kept on trapping until all the bears were tagged?

A: No, that would be impossible. But after fifty or sixty had been tagged the number of "repeats" increased, until most of the bears that entered the traps had already been tagged. From that, an expert can estimate how many bears would have to be tagged before the number of "repeats" rose to a hundred percent.

Q: Isn't there a more accurate way to count bears?

A: Maybe. One suggestion was to put out bait, and spray the bears with yellow paint when they come to it. When you can find no unpainted bears, you have a fairly accurate count.

Q: What's wrong with that?

A: It would take more time than it's worth. And as soon as a painted bear stepped outside the boundary, the superintendent would get an angry phone call: "One of your bears is digging up my garden."

Q: Tell me about the bear trap.

A: It's a piece of corrugated iron pipe, maybe three feet in diameter and eight feet long, mounted on wheels to make it a trailer, and painted Park Service green. The bear enters, takes the bait, and a steel door clangs shut behind him.

Q: That sounds dangerous.

A: It would be a dangerous thing for children to play with. The trap has the word DANGER, in red letters a foot high, on each side. In developed areas the rangers don't set the trap until late at night, and they take it away early in the morning.

Q: And they made these traps just for the census?

A: No. When bears get too numerous in the campgrounds, they are trapped and released in other parts of the Park. If a bear shows signs of becoming dangerous, or if it has a history of damaging tents or cars, it is trapped and released in the George Washington National Forest.

Q: What kind of bears do we have in Shenandoah?

A: Only one kind: the black phase of the Eastern Black Bear, *Ursus americanus*. (It's *Euarctos americanus* in some books, but all experts agree on the common name "Black Bear".)

Q: No grizzlies?

A: None.

Q: And the bears that killed two young women in one of the western parks a few year ago were . . .

A: Grizzlies.

Q: You said something about bears becoming dangerous.

A: Bears are incredibly strong, and fairly stupid. That's a bad combination. Park bears are not tame; they are wild animals that have, in various degrees, lost their fear of man. That makes them potentially dangerous.

Q: But they don't actually attack people. Do they?

A: I've never heard of an unprovoked attack. But it's the bear, not you, who decides when he's provoked. Let's say, for example, that you want to be nice to a bear, so you start feeding him hotdogs. And some time later you decide to stop feeding him hotdogs and save a few for yourself. The bear might consider that a serious provocation. He might insist on eating the rest, and he would use whatever force he thought necessary to get them.

Q: You suggested that some bears are more dangerous than others?

A: An occasional bear may grow so fearless as to drive people away from a picnic table and eat their food.

Q: If that happens to me, what should I do?

A: Leave the table, and let the bear have your food. Find a ranger, and ask him to set the trap.

Q: There's nothing I can do to save my supper?

A: You can yell at the bear, or bang on metal pans; that might scare him away. But a bear that bold has heard enough yelling and banging to know they're harmless.

Q: Has anyone been injured by a bear in the Park?

A: I've heard of several incidents. If a bear smells food inside a tent, he's likely to rip a hole in the side of it and walk in. Anyone inside the tent is in danger of getting stepped on. So never keep food in the tent, not even a candy bar. Don't eat in the tent, even if it's raining. Never let the smell of food get into your tent. Keep your food in the trunk of your car.

Q: How about a strong metal ice chest?

A: A bear can probably open your ice chest. If not he can give it a severe beating, or carry it off. Bears sometimes break up or carry off empty ice chests, because they associate their shape with food.

Q: Any injuries other than getting stepped on?

A: I heard of a man who found a bear eating his food off the picnic table. The man picked up a stick and hit the bear with it. The bear countered with a left hook to the chest. The man went down, scratched and bruised, and the bear continued eating.

Q: And the man's mistake was . . .

A: He violated one of the cardinal principles of Machiavelli, which I can paraphrase like this: Don't take a swing at a powerful enemy unless you're sure you can knock him out with your first punch.

Q: Any more incidents?

A: A seasonal ranger stepped outside his trailer and started off on some errand in total darkness. He either walked into a bear or realized he was about to do so. He spun around and ran as fast as he could, right into a tree. Bruises, cuts, and contusions.

Q: And his error was . . .

A: He should have carried a flashlight.

Q: What should I do if I meet a bear on the trail?

A: Talk, or sing, or make some other noise to let him know you're there, and that you're human. Bears are nearsighted. The danger is that a bear might get close before he's aware of your presence, and then be startled.

Q: If he keeps coming toward me on the trail, what then?

A: I suggest that you step well off the trail, and yield the right of way.

Q: Would you care to summarize your bear wisdom concisely?

A: I'd love to. Don't feed the bears. Never take food into your tent; keep food locked in the trunk of your car. Never get between a mother bear and her cubs. Don't take a bear by surprise; let him know you're there. If you're having trouble with a bear make noise, but DON'T ATTACK OR THREATEN IT. If a bear just won't leave you alone, you can be sure it's interested in your food, not you. The quickest way out of trouble is to abandon the food; walk away from it, and let the bear have it. Do not seek the company of bears; avoid them when you can.

Q: But let's say that I like bears, and want to watch them. Where can I go to see bears?

A: In all seriousness, I recommend the Zoological Park of any large city. Bears sometimes come to campgrounds, especially at Mathews Arm and Loft Mountain, but the Park is doing what it can to discourage them. The trash cans are bearproof, and regulations require that you keep food where the bears can't get it. If you camp in the backcountry, string up your food between two trees, high off the ground.

Q: A bear in the backcountry—what does he find to eat?

A: Ants, grubs, beetles, and sometimes honey. Some roots, some bulbs, and the stems and leaves of some plants. Fruits, nuts, and berries. In the fall in Shenandoah they eat large quantities of apples. In the winter, acorns provide most of the calories. They eat carrion when they can find it, and small mammals when they can catch them, which isn't often. A bear would have no chance of catching a deer that wasn't sick or injured.

Q: You say they eat acorns in the winter. Don't they hibernate?

A: No. In colder climates a bear may spend most of the winter sleeping, but would probably leave its shelter on milder days. In Shenandoah, a bear might stay under cover for several days at a time in bad weather. But bears don't hibernate in the sense that groundhogs do—that is, their body temperature, pulse, and respiration never drop far below normal.

Q: Do bears have any natural enemies?

A: Outside the Park boundary, there's a bear-hunting season every fall. Inside the Park their only natural enemies are old age and other bears.

Q: Bears attack each other?

A: You bet. And there's one thing more I want to get on record. I once saw a bear's nest.

Q: You're kidding.

A: No. It was in the Big Meadows Swamp, in winter. There was nearly a foot of snow on the ground. The bear had scooped out a hollow in the snow, about four feet in diameter. And he had dug up dry grass from under the snow, and used it to line the nest.

Q: How do you know a bear did it?

A: The nest was surrounded by bear tracks and droppings, and had obviously been used for several days.

Q: You took pictures, of course?

A: I made a number of exposures. I have regretted, since, that there was no film in the camera.

The Mountain Lion

Officially, the mountain lion (or cougar, catamount, or puma) is extinct in this area. In the Blue Ridge they were wiped out well before the Civil War. In the wilder parts of Virginia a few of them lasted into the twentieth century, but barely.

Nevertheless, reports of cougar sightings in the Park keep coming in. Several visitors each year report seeing a cougar on a trail or fire road. When asked to describe it, one of the first things they mention is the long, thick tail; which means for sure that it wasn't a bobcat they saw. Many of the observers have had enough training in zoology to make them reliable witnesses. A reliable witness has heard the scream of a mountain lion. Reliable witnesses have found and measured its tracks. I have twice found a deer kill that was almost surely the work of a mountain lion. A south-district ranger recently told me that, in any given year, half the rangers in the south district will see a mountain lion while on patrol.

But no hunter in Virginia has shot a mountain lion; no one has found a dead one; and no one has taken a recognizable picture of one. Officially, the mountain lion in Virginia is still extinct. To me the evidence that it lives in Shenandoah, or at least passes through from time to time, is overwhelming.

The Deer

There are probably more than a thousand deer in the Park, and possibly two thousand—all of the same species, the Virginia white-tail. The tail is broad, and white underneath; when held aloft it's a signal flag that means "follow me". A fawn can follow its mother at a fast pace through broken cover without getting lost—by following the white flag. I once saw a couple of hound dogs chasing a buck and two does through Milam Gap, and all three were showing their white tails. Suddenly the two does veered off to one side and lowered their tails. The buck continued straight ahead, his "follow me" flag waving. And the hound dogs followed the buck.

Your chances of seeing a deer on the trail are good, especially in fairly open woods near the top of the mountain. If you walk slowly and quietly you may suddenly become aware that a deer is watching *you*. If you now stand still and make no sudden movements the deer will probably stay put, and may even resume feeding. If you move closer it will bound away, springing over brush and fallen trees with such grace that it almost seems to float slow motion through the air.

Deer like semi-open places, rather than meadows or deep woods. It's hard to drive any distance on Skyline Drive without seeing one, especially near the developed areas. When you see one ahead, beside the Drive, please slow down; the deer may become alarmed and bound away when your car gets close, and it will often choose to bound across the road in front of you.

In the developed areas deer are sometimes surprisingly tame, especially those in the Loft Mountain campground. But it's better to keep your distance. Making wild animals dependent and trusting is not doing them a favor. Besides, any food you might have to offer is, for a deer, junk food.

Foxes

Two kinds, red and gray. The red fox is uncommon in the Park. It prefers open spaces and, apparently, lower altitudes. The gray fox, which does well in the woods, is common. In my opinion the gray is the more attractive of the two, with delicate shadings of gray, white, and rusty red. They're shy, and move about mostly at night, so that seeing one requires a little luck. But in many places, such as the Big Meadows area, if you're out just before dark and watching the road or trail well ahead, you may be lucky.

Skunks

Two species, striped and spotted. The striped skunk is larger and much more common—the one you're probably familiar with. You may occasionally see a skunk in the daytime, but they prefer darkness. You're most likely to see one in the light of your headlights on the Drive, or in the campgrounds. Skunks are not at all shy, for several reasons: they're near-sighted, they're moderately stupid, and they're formidably armed.

But skunks are inoffensive and slow to anger. Several times, as a test, I've walked to within a foot or two (slowly, of course) of a feeding skunk; every time, he ignored me completely. A skunk will spray only if a larger animal actually seizes it or seems about to do so, or if it's hit by a car. But a skunk will often threaten a possible enemy, and that's sometimes as effective as spraying. There are four ways to threaten. First, by snapping the teeth, like a terrier. Second, repeatedly striking the ground with both front feet. Third, flicking the tail. Finally, raising the tail, spinning around, and backing toward the enemy.

Here are some incidents that I've observed, most of them dozens of times, that tell something about the character of the striped skunk.

1. Skunk No. 1 is feeding. Skunk No. 2 approaches. Skunk No. 1 threatens by snapping. No. 2 turns and walks away. ("Walks" doesn't quite describe it. A moving skunk somehow resembles a giant caterpillar.)

2. Skunk No. 1 is feeding. Skunk No. 2 approaches, and threatens by striking the ground repeatedly with his front feet. No. 1 ignores him. No. 2 turns and walks away.

3. A skunk is feeding, and a fox approaches. The skunk threatens by snapping, or by flicking his tail. The fox walks away.

4. A fox is feeding. A skunk approaches and threatens. The fox leaves, and the skunk begins to feed.

5. (I saw this only once.) A possum is feeding. A skunk approaches and threatens, and the possum ignores him. The skunk turns around and raises his tail. The possum ignores him. The skunk backs up and sticks his behind in the possum's face. The possum opens his mouth and takes a big bite. The skunk shrieks with pain and runs off.

In none of the encounters that I've observed has the spray been released. If you're camping at Big Meadows in late winter you may hear squeals in the night, often followed by a strong smell of skunk. Late winter is the mating season. When two males meet, they may engage in a good rough-

and-tumble fight, snapping and biting, and squealing with anger. But what you smell, I'm convinced, is just leakage due to excitement, rather than deliberate spraying.

The spotted skunk is rather uncommon, and much smaller—about the size of a large squirrel—black, irregularly spotted with white, and irresistibly attractive. (I'm tempted to say "cute", but I won't.) It can spray, and it gets as much respect from foxes as the larger striped skunk. Its threatening gesture consists of a handstand; it actually balances on its two front paws, and can hold that position for some time. The spotted skunk is a southern animal; the Park is the northern limit of its range. (The Park is the southern limit for other things. If you show me a picture of a spotted skunk under a gray birch tree, I'll tell you where you took it. Big Meadows. It couldn't happen anywhere else.)

Inoffensive though skunks may be, I suggest that you keep your distance. Fifteen feet is close enough. If you watch through binoculars from fifteen feet, it's like having a skunk in your lap. On the other hand, if you find yourself unexpectedly very close to a skunk, don't be alarmed. Just hold still, and wait for it to go away.

And Other Mammals

Bobcat. Fairly common, but shy. You may see one from your car at night. They are sometimes seen on the trails, especially in later winter; that's mating season, and they get bolder.

Raccoon. Fairly common. The best place to see one is beside the Drive after dark. They sometimes pass through the campgrounds during the night.

Beaver. I'd call this an endangered species in the Park. There are, at present, three beaver colonies, one on each branch of the Thornton River and one on the Rapidan, all near the Park boundary.

Groundhog (or Woodchuck). Quite common in clearings and beside the Drive. They often eat within a few feet of the pavement, and pay no attention to passing cars. (As long as they keep moving, that is. If you slow down or stop, the goundhog will disappear down its hole.)

Chipmunk. Very common. On a long summer hike you'll probably see dozens of them; they'll scold you with a chittering sound that could be mistaken for a bird call. In late summer you may hear a slow, steady "chock, chock, chock . . . ." at some distance in the woods. That, too, is a chipmunk.

More About Mammals

If you'd like to know more about the mammals, check the sales literature at either Visitor Center.

A Field Guide to the Mammals, by William H. Burt and Richard P. Grossenheider. (Peterson Field Guide Series.) 284 pages. Color plates and range maps. Useful.

A Field Guide to Animal Tracks, by Olaus J. Murie. (Peterson Field Guide Series); 376 pages, pen-and-ink drawings. Tracks are less interesting than

the animals that make them, but they're sometimes a lot easier to find—
especially when there's snow on the ground.

The Birds

Shenandoah National Park is a moderately rewarding place for
birdwatchers; we have about 200 species. The checklist is too long to
reproduce here, but you can get a copy on request, free, at Headquarters or
one of the Visitor Centers. For serious birdwatching you'll need a field book,
a pair of binoculars, and, if possible, a tendency to get up early in the
morning. I can help you with only the first of these requirements. The sales
outlets have the following:

Audubon's Birds of America Coloring Book. Drawings by Paul E.
Kennedy. 46 plates to color. Audubon's original plates serve as a guide.

Birds of North America, by Chandler S. Robbins, Bertel Brunn, and
Herbert S. Zim. (A Golden Field Guide.) 360 pages. Range maps and color
illustrations. For each bird, the description and the picture are on facing
pages, which makes the book easy to use.

A Field Guide to the Birds, by Roger Tory Peterson. (Peterson Field Guide
Series.) 384 pages. This book covers all the birds of eastern and central
North America, and all of them are illustrated in color. The illustrations
have distinguishing field marks indicated, which makes identification
easier.

Following are some brief notes, from my personal observation, on a few
birds that might come to your attention here even if you're *not* a serious
birdwatcher.

The Soaring Birds

The soaring birds float on currents of air, rarely flapping their wings.
You're sure to see them if you climb to a peak or a cliff and then sit quietly
for a while. Hightop and Stony Man are especially good. Vultures and
ravens sail by in front of you, sometimes surprisingly close. Here's how to
tell them apart:

Turkey vulture (or "buzzard"). Wingspan up to six feet; tail rather long
and narrow. The wings, as seen from below, are two-toned: black and dark
gray. When an adult flies close you'll see its red head. (The head of the
young is black.) It has two habits that distinguish it from other soaring birds
in the Park. First, it soars with its wings forming a flattened "V", rather than
straight out from the body. Second, it rocks and tilts as it soars, as if trying to
keep its balance.

Black vulture. Less common than the turkey vulture, and a little smaller
and heavier, so that it flaps more and soars less. And whereas the flapping
of the turkey vulture seems slow and easy, that of the black vulture seems
quick and labored. Its tail is rather short and square. Its best distinguishing
mark is a whitish patch on the underside of each wing, near the tip.

Both vultures are useful scavengers, and contrary to superstition they do not spread disease. Neither vulture, as far as I know, makes any vocal sound except a grunting noise when it's disturbed. Some day, when you're hiking after a rain, you may be treated to an unforgettable sight—a flock of vultures perched in a tree with wings spread out to dry.

Raven. Smaller than the vultures, and pure black; its tail, as seen from below, is large and wedge-shaped. Its soaring ability is limited: it alternately soars and flaps. Except, that is, near the steep western slopes of the mountain, where strong updrafts are common. There, all three birds can soar for long minutes without a single flap.

From a distance, a raven looks very much like a crow. When you see the two together it's obvious that the raven is nearly twice as big; when you see only one, there's room for doubt. The call of the crow is a high-pitched *caw* or *cah*. The raven has a lower-pitched call, a hoarse croak: *cr-r-r-uck,* or possibly *gr-r-ronk*. That's an early warning call; you're not likely to hear it on the cliffs where the birds are soaring. But as you hike through the woods, a raven may fly over so low that you can hear the air whistling through its wingtips, and it will croak to spread the word of your presence. (The raven language has at least a dozen words, but the early warning call is the only one you're likely to hear.)

The Wild Turkey

This is by far the largest bird in the Park. Except for a few minor details it looks just like the domestic turkey. Although it's fairly common in all parts of the Park, it's reported most often from the North Section. The turkey is not very good at flying, and except when it's in immediate danger it prefers to walk or run. You may occasionally see a single turkey, or a flock of them, on the trails. If you hold still you'll be able to watch them for quite a while as they run, or walk, away from danger. They are said to travel in flocks of from six to fifteen birds. But I've often seen single birds, and twice I've seen a flock of more than thirty.

During breeding season—early spring—a flock consists of the dominant male in the area plus his harem. In April, in the early morning, you may hear the male turkey gobble to assemble his flock, just before or just after he leaves the roost for the day.

The Ruffed Grouse

The grouse is a large, reddish-brown relative of the chicken. And it looks like one, especially when you see it crossing the Skyline Drive, where it tends to be a rather careless pedestrian. In the woods, it usually stays under cover. When a grouse is hidden near the trail it will wait till you get close, then take off suddenly with a loud whir of wings that can be truly startling. In late spring and early summer, when the chicks are still small, the mother puts on a skillful "broken wing" act; as you approach she flops pitifully ahead, hoping to lead you away from the chicks.

Some day, as you walk a mountain trail in spring, you may suddenly become aware of your own heartbeat, and note with mild alarm that it's beating faster and faster. But it isn't your heart, it's the drumming of a male grouse. He drums to attract a female, or to announce possession of territory, or both. The grouse mounts some favorite low perch, grasps it firmly so as not to fly away, and then beats the air with his wings, faster and faster; thump . . . . . thump . . . . thump . . . thump . . thump, thump thump-rup-rup-rup-rrrrrrrrrr.

The Woodcock

The woodcock, a relative of the snipe, is one of the first migratory birds to return to Shenandoah in the spring. It has a chunky body, a large head, short neck and legs; and a ridiculously long beak, which it thrusts into soft moist earth in search of worms. The tip of the upper mandible moves independently, so that the woodcock can grasp a worm under ground and pull it out. The plumage is barred and mottled with buff, brown, gray, and black—the color of leaves and duff of the forest floor. The bird is so well camouflaged that he seems to think he's invisible. You can sometimes get close enough to touch him before he will fly.

From mid-March to the end of April, in the partly open places such as Big Meadows, the woodcock does his sky dance, a courtship ritual. The light has to be just right. When the sun is down, and the evening star first appears, that's the time to start. The dance will go on for half an hour, until it gets too dark. (Unless there's a full moon, when it may go on all night.)

The dance begins with the male woodcock on the ground, where he will periodically give a call that's been variously represented as *peent,* or *beezp,* or "a Bronx cheer under water". I'd call it a loudly-voiced *bzzzzp.* Then the woodcock springs into the air and spirals upward, the wind whistling through his wings, his windsong getting louder and shriller as he reaches the top of his flight, some 300 feet above the ground. A pause; then he dives, darts, and zig-zags quickly downward, now with a clear warbling whistle added to the windsong. Then silence, and you know he's on the ground. Then *bzzzzp* again, in preparation for another flight.

The Herps

"Herps" is a slang term for reptiles and amphibians—which is to say lizards, snakes, turtles, frogs, toads, and salamanders—the subject matter of the science of herpetology. The best available checklist of the Park's herps was prepared by William L. Witt (1971, manuscript).

If you'd like to pursue this subject further, there's a good field book of herps for sale at the Visitor Centers:

A Field Guide to Reptiles and Amphibians of Eastern and Central North America, by Roger Conant. (Peterson Field Guide Series.) 361 pages, plus 48 plates and 311 range maps. This is a very useful book, loaded with information. For each species you have to look in three separate places for text, picture, and map, which you may or may not consider a drawback.

Invertebrates

Invertebrates other than insects are of interest to so few people that I won't discuss them here. Shenandoah is not rich in insect species, compared with the more varied habitats in the Valley. Nevertheless there's enough here to keep you busy if entomology is your hobby. The Visitor Centers offer only one book on the subject:

A Field Guide to the Insects of America North of Mexico, by Donald J. Borrer and Richard E. White. (Peterson Field Guide Series.) 404 pages, with black-and-white drawings and color plates. A good, useful introduction to entomology.

A Note on Collecting

The Park rule against collecting applies to everything—including insects. An exception might be made for a professional entomologist associated with a university or a government agency. If that describes you, write to Headquarters for information about a collecting permit.

I recommend that you collect insects as I do—on Kodachrome film, using a 35 mm camera and macro lens. Chasing butterflies with a net may be good exercise for your legs; getting closeup pictures of them is a perfect exercise for your patience.

ORCHIDS AND TOADSTOOLS
(and some plants in between)

Wildflowers are the Park's third most popular attraction, after scenery and hiking. Our checklist of vascular plants includes about 1,100 species. A few of these are ferns and clubmosses; many are grasses, sedges, or rushes; possibly a hundred and fifty are trees or shrubs. Of the remainder there are quite a few—ragweed for example—that are hard to think of as wildflowers. That leaves two or three hundred species worth the attention of a wildflower hobbyist.

But remember that you can't collect, pick, or eat the flowers. *Please* don't pick a flower and take it to the Visitor Center to be classified. Better: make an accurate drawing, *write down* an accurate description, and take those to the Visitor Center. Best: buy a flower book and take it to the flower. The Visitor Centers have several books on wildflowers, including:

A Field Guide to Wildflowers of Northeastern and North-central North America, by Roger Tory Peterson and Margaret McKinney. (Peterson Field Guide Series.) 420 pages. 1,344 illustrations, mostly pen-and-ink, but some in color. Flowers are arranged by color and form, which makes the book easy to use.

Wildflowers of the Shenandoah Valley and Blue Ridge Mountains. 208 pages. Color photographs and short descriptions of 200 species, arranged by color. Most of these species occur in the Park. This is a useful book for beginners.

Newcomb's Wildflower Guide, by Lawrence Newcomb. 490 pages, with black-and-white drawings and color plates. A new key that uses easy-to-see features.

Wildflowers in Color, by Arthur Stupka. 144 pages. Descriptions and color photos of 266 species of wildflowers of Shenandoah and Great

Smokies National Parks, and the Blue Ridge Parkway. The flowers are arranged by family.

The Wildflower Calendar is a chart that shows the usual blooming dates of the Park's more common wildflowers. It's FREE for the asking at Headquarters and the Visitor Centers.

So, Where Are the Orchids?

Shenandoah National Park has about eighteen species of orchids. Most of them are either rare or inconspicuous; none are big and gaudy like the ones you find on trees in the tropics, or in your florist's refrigerator. But, here are five attractive species that you'll see in Shenandoah if you're in the right place at the right time. All of them are locally common: you might walk for hours without finding one, then come on a small area with dozens of them.

Showy orchis, *Orchis spectabilis.* The flowers are up to an inch long, purple above and white below; from three to twelve flowers on a terminal spike. They bloom in May, in woods at lower elevations, often beside the trails and fire roads.

Purple fringe orchid, *Habenaria fimbriata.* Numerous small flowers, lilac-pink or lilac-purple, on a spike. Lower lip deeply fringed. They bloom in late June and early July, in fairly wet places, at all elevations.

Yellow ladyslipper, *Cypripedium calceolus.* The "slipper" is pure yellow and usually about an inch long (two inches in the larger, less common variety.) It blooms in May, in woods and semi-open areas, at all elevations.

Pink ladyslipper, *Cypripedium acaule.* The "slipper" is purplish pink, veined with a darker red, and up to two inches long. Blooms in May, in woods, mostly at lower elevations.

Nodding ladies tresses, *Spiranthes cernua.* The small white flowers are arranged spirally on the spike, and have an odor of vanilla. In open and semi-open places. One of our latest wildflowers; it blooms in October.

Trees

Practically the entire Park consists of trees, nearly all of them deciduous (meaning not evergreen), and most of them oaks and hickories. Other trees may predominate in specialized areas:

Black locust, a pioneer species, is usually the first tree to grow up in abandoned fields and meadows.

Evergreens, mostly hemlocks, which occur in the cooler and moist parts of the Park. Pines are common on dry slopes in the South Section.

Cove hardwoods, including yellow and black birch, basswood, tulip poplar, red and sugar maples, may be the predominant species along streams at lower elevations.

Because of the heavy timbering that occurred here before the Park was created, most of our trees are young second growth. In a few places you can find very large, old trees. The most notable are the hemlocks in the Limberlost (Mile 43.0). Here and there throughout the Park are big trees that escaped cutting because they grew in a rugged area where timbering would have been difficult. The great hemlocks and tulip poplars along Doyles

River (Mile 81.1) may have been spared for that reason.

The sales outlets at the Visitor Centers have three useful books on trees:

Trees of Shenandoah National Park, by Peter M. Mazzeo. Pamphlet, 80 pages, inexpensive. Keys and descriptions of about a hundred species, illustrated with pen-and-ink drawings.

Field Guide to Trees and Shrubs, by George A. Petrides. (Peterson Field Guide Series.) 428 pages. Descriptions of 646 species, with keys and pen-and-ink drawings. Rather comprehensive and detailed, which might make it somewhat difficult for beginners.

Trees of North America, by C. Frank Brockman (A Golden Field Guide.) 280 pages, covering about 730 species. Descriptions, range maps, and color illustrations, conveniently arranged. Less technical and easier to use than the other two.

Ferns and Clubmosses

This is a small but interesting group of plants, represented in the Park by about 47 species. References:

Ferns and Fern Allies of Shenandoah National Park, by Peter M. Mazzeo. Pamphlet, 52 pages, inexpensive. Keys and descriptions; the illustrations are pen-and-ink drawings.

Fungi

This is a large, varied, and fascinating group of plants that occur in all parts of the Park. They depend heavily on rainfall, so that in dry years they're scarce, and in wet years very abundant. I can't tell you how many species we have; probably several hundred. The only checklist is out of date and incomplete.

Mushrooms, like nuts and berries, can be legally gathered and eaten in the Park. But, a word of caution. Eating wild mushrooms is safe only if you know, for sure, what you're doing. There are various superstitions about how to distinguish between edible and poisonous mushrooms:

I've heard that you should cook mushrooms with a silver spoon. If the spoon turns black, the mushrooms are poisonous; if it doesn't, they're edible. DON'T BELIEVE IT.

I've heard that you can test a mushroom by eating a very tiny piece; then wait an hour and eat a bigger one; then wait another hour and, if you're still feeling no pain, eat all you want. DON'T BELIEVE IT. Some of the most poisonous mushrooms produce no symptoms at all during the first six to fifteen hours after you eat them.

There is no characteristic of a mushroom (color of gills, ring around the stem, cup at the base, etc.) that can tell you whether it's poisonous. There is no alternative to knowing the species of each mushroom you propose to eat, and knowing whether or not *that particular species* is edible.

A WALK IN THE WOODS

To a large extent, walking in the woods is what this Park and this book are about. Walking is a pleasure, physically and emotionally. Walking is your

means of access to the 290 square miles of Shenandoah National Park that
you can't get to by car.

The hikes I describe will take you on several kinds of trails:

The *Appalachian Trail* runs for about 2,000 miles, from Mt. Katahdin in
Maine to Springer Mountain in Georgia. For information on the trail as a
whole, see the pamphlet (not sold in the Park) called *The Appalachian Trail*,
Publication No. 5, issued by the Appalachian Trail Conference, Inc., P. O.
Box 236, Harpers Ferry, W. Va. 25425. About 90 miles of the A.T. are within
the Park, where it more or less parallels the Skyline Drive. The trail is
marked with *white blazes*; it is graded, fairly smooth in most places, and
rarely steep.

Horse Trails are marked with *yellow blazes*. You're free to use them, with
or without a horse. But remember that horses have the right of way. If you
meet a horse, or are overtaken by one, please step aside and stand quietly
until it passes.

Blue-blazed Trails include all the rest, except a few short ones that can
be followed without the help of blazes. Condition of the blue-blazed trails
varies. Most are clear and smooth; but some are steep, and some are rough
and rocky. In the descriptions of recommended hikes, I will tell you which
ones are steep or rough.

Fire Roads. I use this term rather loosely to refer to any unpaved road in
the Park, including what the Park calls fire roads, administrative roads, and
service roads. Most of these begin at the edge of Skyline Drive, and are
blocked by a chain to keep out unauthorized vehicles. Most of the fire roads
are also designated horse trails, and are therefore marked by yellow blazes.
You may hike on any of the fire roads, if you wish.

On the maps in this book, I've shown unpaved roads with a line of
dashes, and foot trails with a line of dots. There's room for some confusion
here. Where unpaved roads enter a wilderness area, they have been
blocked with boulders to keep out all vehicles, and they have been reclassified as trails. These trails get only trail-width maintenance; but they will
look like roads for a number of years, nevertheless. In all such cases I'll go
along with Park policy and refer to such routes as trails. When the old roads
actually look like trails, I will show them on the map with a string of dots. If
they still look like roads, I will show them with a string of dashes.

In a few cases, trails are marked with blazes of two different colors. This
shows that two different trails are using the same route; they will later
diverge. An example: north of Compton Gap, the A.T. coincides with a fire
road for nearly two miles, and the route has both white and yellow blazes.

Note: red or red-orange blazes mark the Park boundary—not a trail.

On older maps you may find some trails marked "fire foot trail". This
classification has been discontinued. The fire foot trails were mostly old
mountaineer trails that received little or no maintenance. They were
intended primarily for use by Park Rangers during emergencies. Some of
them have been upgraded into regular blue- or yellow-blazed trails; the
others have been abandoned. If your map shows fire foot trails, you need a
newer map.

Shelters, Cabins, and Huts

The *shelters* are open-faced structures with a table, fireplace, pit toilet, and spring. They once had bunks for long-distance hikers. But more and more people camped in the shelters, or beside them. The environmental impact was severe, so the bunks were removed. You may not spend the night in a shelter, or within sight of one, unless a *severe storm* makes it unsafe to camp elsewhere.

A few of the former shelters have been removed; others have been reclassified as *Huts* or *Maintenance Buildings* (see below). The five remaining shelters are: Byrds Nest Shelter No. 4, Mile 28.5; Byrds Nest Shelter No. 3, Mile 33.9; Old Rag Shelter (at the foot of Old Rag Mountain); Byrds Nest Shelter No. 1 (on the saddle of Old Rag Mountain); and Byrds Nest Shelter No. 2, Mile 45.6.

The *cabins* are log structures built or restored by PATC. They have a table and fireplace, bunks for up to twelve people, a spring, and a pit toilet. Both cabin and toilet are locked. If you're hiking near an unoccupied cabin, feel free to look it over. If the cabin is in use, please respect the occupant's privacy. To rent a cabin for yourself, get advance reservations and keys by mail from PATC. Write to Potomac Appalachian Trail Club. 1718 N. St., N. W. Washington, D.C. 20036.

Five locked cabins are close to the Drive: Rangeview Cabin, Mile 22.1; Corbin Cabin,, Mile 37.9; Rock Spring Cabin, Mile 48.1; Pocosin Cabin, Mile 59.5; and Doyle River Cabin, Mile 81.1.

Seven of the former shelters have been reclassified as *Appalachian Trail Huts.* These have been provided with bunks, and are intended only for overnight camping by long-distance hikers on the A.T. Each hut has a Resident Hutkeeper, who charges a small fee for spending the night. When the hutkeepers are absent, huts operate on the honor system. The seven huts are: Gravel Springs A.T. Hut, Mile 17.6; Pass Mountain A.T. Hut, Mile 31.6; Rock Spring A.T. Hut, Mile 48.1; Bearfence A.T. Hut, Mile 56.8; Hightop A.T. Hut, Mile 68.6; Pinefield A.T. Hut, Mile 75.2; and Blackrock A.T. Hut, Mile 87.2.

Three of the former shelters are now *PATC Maintenance Buildings,* which are used for tool storage, and sometimes provide overnight shelter for trail workers. The three Maintenance Buildings are: Indian Run, Mile 10.4; South River, Mile 63.1; and Ivy Creek, Mile 79.4.

Recommended Hikes

Below is a catalog from which you can choose a hike and then look up its description in the text. To avoid unpleasant surprises, please read the whole description before you start hiking. The catalog needs some explanation.

Start, mile, is the point on the Drive where you will park your car. Some hikes start from a campground or other developed area; for those I've given the mile point of the entrance road.

Description. Note that I've mentioned three different kinds of hikes. A *round trip* hike proceeds to its destination and then returns by the same route. If your main reason for walking is to see things, this kind of hike is as rewarding as any other; on the way back you'll see things that you overlooked before. A *circuit* hike proceeds to its destination and then returns, all or most of the way, by a different route. A *one way* hike proceeds to its destination and does not return at all. How can you do that? There are several ways:

1. A friend drives you to the starting point, and picks you up at the end.

2. You get out at the starting point, and your friend drives to the other end. The two of you walk the same hike in opposite directions. If he remembers, he will give you the car keys when you meet.

3. With two cars: you drive to the start, and your friend drives to the finish; walk in opposite directions, and exchange keys when you meet.

4. Drive both cars to the finish point. Both drivers return in one car to the start, and walk the trail together.

Distance. Measured by pushing a measuring wheel along the trail. Recorded to the nearest tenth of a mile.

Climb. This includes not only the net change in elevation, but also all the ups and downs in the trail. Measured with an altimeter. Accurate, I think, to within five percent.

Difficulty. This is a rough indication of how tired you'll get. Hikes are rated from "1" (very easy) to "8" (very difficult). The rating is based not only on distance and amount of climbing, but also on steepness, roughness, stream crossings, etc. But don't take my ratings too literally. A young athlete in training will find all of the hikes easy. An overweight, sedentary, chain-smoking senior citizen will find all of them difficult or impossible.

Time required. I assume that you'll look at rocks and scenery and wildflowers. If your destination is a waterfall, or a viewpoint on a mountain peak, I assume that you'll spend a little time there. The figure is based on a formula: 1.5 miles per hour, with one minute added for each 20 feet of climb, and arbitrary additions for viewing the scenery, for rough or steep trails, and for rock scrambles. After testing a couple of the recommended hikes, you can adjust the listed times in accordance with your own pace.

Start, mile	Description	Dist. miles	Climb feet	Diffi- culty	Time req'd	Page
0.05	Dickey Ridge Trail. Overgrown fields, small stream. *Round trip.*	2.7	440	2	2:10	81
4.6	Fox Hollow Trail. Homesites, cemetery. Self-guiding. *Circuit.*	1.3	310	2	1:20	84

Start mile	Description	Dist. miles	Climb feet	Diffi- culty	Time req'd	Page
5.1	Snead homesite. Orchard, barn. *Round trip.*	1.4	190	1	1:25	85
9.2	Lands Run Gap to Hickerson Hollow. Homesites. *Round trip.*	2.2	940	3	2:30	88
10.4	Compton Gap to Fort Wind- ham Rocks. *Round trip.*	0.8	130	1	0:55	90
10.4	Compton Gap to Indian Run Spring. *Round trip.*	1.0	165	1	1:00	90
10.4	Compton Gap to Indian Run Spring and Fort Windham Rocks. *Circuit.*	2.6	340	2	2:20	90
10.4	Compton Gap to Compton Peak. Views, geology. *Round trip.*	2.4	835	3	2:45	91
12.5	Mt. Marshall trail to The Peak. *Round trip.*	9.8	2160	7	8:20	93
15.95	North Marshall. Views. *Round trip.*	1.3	295	2	1:15	94
15.95	South Marshall. Views. *Round trip.*	1.6	295	2	1:20	95
17.6	Gravel Springs Gap to Gravel Springs Hut. *Circuit*	0.8	190	1	0:50	96
17.6	Big Devils Stairs. Spec- tacular canyon, stream, cascades. *One way.*	3.6	210	4	2:55	96
17.6	Bluff Trail and A.T. Views. *Circuit.*	12.8	2495	7	10:30	97
19.4	Keyser Run Road, Piney Branch, A.T. Views. *Circuit*	6.8	1145	5	5:30	100
19.4	Keyser Run Road, Little Devils Stairs. Canyon, stream, cascades. *Round trip.*	4.8	1585	5	5:15	100
19.4	Keyser Run Road, Little Devils Stairs. Canyon, stream, cascades, ceme- tery. *Circuit.*	7.7	1845	6	7:15	101
20.4	Hogback Summit. View. *Circuit.*	1.0	250	2	1:00	103
20.9	Hogback Overlook. *Circuit.*	0.7	100	1	0:35	104
21.1	Overall Run Falls. *Semi- circuit.*	6.5	1850	5	6:00	104
22.1	Piney Ridge, Piney Branch. Cemetery, homesite, stream and falls. *Circuit.*	8.3	1725	6	7:25	107

Start, mile	Description	Dist. miles	Climb feet	Diffi-culty	Time req'd	Page
22.2	Mathews Arm Campground to Overall Run Falls. *Round trip.*	3.8	1140	4	3:40	110
	Thompson Hollow to Overall Run. Stream, cascades, pools. *Round trip.*	2.6 to 4.2	480 to 640	3	2:40 to 4:30	111
22.2	Mathews Arm Campground, Traces Trail. Evidence of former inhabitants. Self-guiding. *Circuit.*	1.7	335	2	1:40	109
22.2	Mathews Arm Campground, Knob Mountain, Elkwallow. *Circuit.*	5.8	1130	4	4:30	110
24.1	Elkwallow Picnic Area, Knob Mountain, Jeremys Run. Stream, cascades, falls. *Circuit.*	11.7	2615	7	10:00	113
24.1	Elkwallow Picnic Area, Jeremys Run, Neighbor Trail, A.T. Stream, falls. *Circuit.*	14.0	2765	8	11:40	113
28.5	Beahms Gap to Byrds Nest Shelter. Views. *Round trip.*	1.7	485	2	1:50	118
28.5	Beahms Gap, A.T. *Circuit.*	0.4	60	1	0:20	117
28.5	Beahms Gap to viewpoint on Pass Mountain. Views. *Round trip.*	1.6	495	2	1:40	117
30.1	Pass Mountain Overlook. *Circuit.*	0.25	50	1	0:15	119
31.6	Panorama to Pass Mountain A.T. Hut. *Circuit.*	3.4	670	3	3:00	122
31.6	Panorama to Marys Rock. Views. *Round trip.*	3.7	1210	4	3:40	120
33.5	Buck Hollow Trail. Stream. *One way.*	3.1	45	3	2:40	124
33.5	Hazel Mountain Trail, falls, "cave" *Round trip.*	5.3	1070	4	4:45	128
33.5	Marys Rock via Meadow Spring Trail. Views. *Round trip.*	2.9	830	3	2:55	129
35.1	Hannah Run. Mountaineer cabins (ruins). Stream. *One way.*	5.7	315	4	4:25	130
35.1	Hannah Run, Hot-Short, Catlett Mountain. Mountaineer cabins (ruins). Stream. *Circuit.*	9.1	2755	7	8:50	131

Start, mile	Description	Dist. miles	Climb feet	Diffi-culty	Time req'd	Page
36.4	Jewel Hollow Overlook to The Pinnacle. Views. *Round trip.*	2.1	460	2	1:55	132
36.4	Jewel Hollow Overlook to Panorama via The Pinnacle and Marys Rock. Views. *One way.*	5.3	805	4	4:30	132
37.9	Corbin Cabin. Mountaineer cabins, cemetery. *Round trip.*	2.9	1095	3	3:10	134
37.9	Corbin Cabin. A.T. Moun-taineer cabins, cemetery. *Circuit.*	4.3	1350	4	4:20	136
38.4	Nicholson Hollow. Moun-taineer cabins (ruins). Stream, cascades, pools. *One way.*	5.8	130	4	4:20	136
	Weakley Hollow to Old Rag. Rock scramble. Views. *Circuit.*	7.2	2380	6	7:30	138
	Berry Hollow to Old Rag. Views. *Round trip.*	5.4	1760	4	5:20	141
39.1	Little Stony Man. Views. Geology. *Round trip.*	0.9	270	2	1:00	137
41.7	Stony Man Nature Trail. Self-guiding. Views. *Circuit.*	1.6	340	2	1:40	142
41.7	Passamaquoddy Trail. Views. *Circuit.*	3.5	770	3	3:10	144
42.5	Millers Head. Views. *Round trip.*	1.6	450	2	1:35	145
42.6	White Oak Canyon. Spec-tacular gorge, stream, waterfall. *Round trip.*	4.6	1040	4	4:15	148
43.0	Limberlost Trail. Giant hemlocks. *Circuit.*	1.2	130	1	0:55	149
44.4	Crescent Rock to Bettys Rock. Views. *Round trip.*	0.7	150	1	0:45	151
44.4	Crescent Rock. Limberlost. Giant hemlocks. *Semi-circuit.*	3.3	495	3	2:40	152
44.4	Crescent Rock, A.T. Limber-lost. Giant hemlocks. *Circuit.*	4.6	780	4	3:45	152
45.6	Cedar Run Falls. *Round trip.*	3.5	1556	4	4:00	153
45.6	Cedar Run, White Oak Canyon. Two rugged can-yons, nine waterfalls. *Circuit.*	7.3	2495	6	7:30	154
45.6	Hawksbill summit. Views. *Round trip.*	1.7	690	3	2:00	155

Start, mile	Description	Dist. miles	Climb feet	Diffi- culty	Time req'd	Page
45.6	Hawksbill summit via A.T. Views. *Circuit.*	2.9	860	3	2:50	155
46.7	Hawksbill Summit. Views. *Round trip.*	2.1	520	3	2:00	156
46.7	Horse trail, Rose River, A.T., Hawksbill summit. Homesite, stream, falls, views. *Circuit.*	9.7	2465	7	8:45	157
49.4	Fishers Gap to Rose River Falls. *Round trip.*	2.7	720	3	2:35	161
49.4	Rose River, Dark Hollow. Cascades, falls. *Circuit.*	4.0	910	4	3:45	161
49.4	Fishers Gap to Davids Spring. Hemlock grove, homesite. *Round trip.*	1.8	470	2	1:40	162
49.4	Fishers Gap, Davids Spring, horse trail. Hemlock grove, homesite. *Circuit.*	3.2	590	3	2:45	162
50.7	Dark Hollow Falls. *Round trip.*	1.4	440	2	1:25	163
50.7	Big Meadows Swamp. Wildflowers. *Round trip.*	0.5	90	1	0:30	163
51.0	Big Meadows. Stroll through the meadow. Wildflowers.	0.2 to 5.0	20 to 100	1 to 3	0:10 to 4:30	164
51.0	Big Meadows Visitor Center. Nature Trail. Self-guiding. *Circuit.*	1.8	290	2	1:30	167
51.2	Big Meadows Lodge to Blackrock. Views. *Round trip.*	0.4	60	1	0:25	166
51.2	Big Meadows Amphi- theater to Lewis Falls. Views. *Circuit.*	3.3	990	3	3:10	167
51.4	Lewis Falls. View. *Round trip.*	2.5	795	3	2:25	168
51.6	Tanners Ridge. Homesite, cemetery. *Round trip.*	1.1	160	1	1:15	169
52.8	Milam Gap, Camp Hoover. Historic site. Stream, cascades. *Round trip.*	4.1	870	4	3:50	170
52.8	Camp Hoover, Laurel Prong, Hazeltop. Stream, cascades, historic site. *Circuit.*	7.4	1520	5	6:30	171
56.4	Bearfence Mountain. Rock scramble, geology, views. *Round trip.*	0.8	275	3	1:05	175
59.5	Upper Pocosin Mission (ruins). *Round trip.*	1.9	425	2	1:55	178

Start, miles	Description	Dist. miles	Climb feet	Diffi- culty	Time req'd	Page
59.5	Pocosin Mission, South River, A.T. Ruins, cemetery, falls. *Circuit.*	8.5	1830	6	7:30	179
62.8	South River Falls. *Round trip.*	2.6	850	3	2:25	181
62.8	South River Falls. *Circuit.*	3.3	910	3	3:05	182
62.8	South River Trail Maint. Bldg. *Round trip.*	1.7	225	2	1:30	182
66.7	Hightop summit. Views. *Round trip.*	3.0	935	3	2:55	184
68.6	Hightop summit. Views. *Round trip.*	3.7	950	4	3:25	187
75.2	Pinefield Gap to Pinefield A.T. Hut. *Circuit.*	0.6	125	1	0:35	190
76.2	Rocky Mount Summit. Views. *Round trip.*	6.9	2065	5	6:40	191
76.9	Rocky Mountain saddle. Views. *Round trip.*	3.9	1140	4	3:40	192
76.9	Big Run Portal via Brown Mountain. Views. Stream. *Circuit.*	9.9	2465	7	9:05	193
77.5	Ivy Creek Overlook to Ivy Creek. *Round trip.*	2.8	695	2	2:30	194
77.5	Ivy Creek Overlook to Loft Mountain summit. Stream, views. *Round trip.*	6.4	1455	5	5:30	194
79.5	Loft Mountain Wayside: Deadening Trail. Self-guiding. *Circuit.*	1.4	455	2	1:35	197
79.5	Loft Mountain Wayside: Loft Mountain summit via A.T. Views. *Circuit.*	2.7	570	3	2:25	197
79.5	Loft Mountain Campstore to Loft Mountain summit. Views. *Round trip.*	3.5	515	3	2:50	197
79.5	Loft Mountain Amphi-theater; Big Flat Mountain Hike. Views. *Circuit.*	1.8	265	2	1:15	198
79.5	Loft Mountain Amphi-theater to viewpoint on A.T. Views. *Round trip.*	1.5	260	1	1:15	199
81.1	Doyles River upper falls. *Round trip.*	2.7	850	3	2:45	199
81.1	Doyles River Trail. Three waterfalls. *One way.*	4.8	1410	4	4:35	200
81.1	Doyles River Trail and A.T. Three waterfalls. *Circuit.*	7.8	1825	5	7:00	201

Start, mile	Description	Dist. miles	Climb feet	Diffi- culty	Time req'd	Page
81.2	Head of Big Run. *Round trip.*	4.4	1250	4	4:00	202
81.2	Big Run Loop Trail. A.T. *Circuit.*	5.8	1365	4	5:00	203
83.0	Browns Gap: Doyles River, upper falls, A.T. *Circuit.*	5.3	1000	4	4:30	205
83.0	Browns Gap: fire road, Doyles River Trail, A.T. Three waterfalls. *Circuit.*	6.5	1400	5	6:45	205
83.0	Browns Gap, Rockytop, Big Run Portal. Views. *Circuit.*	14.6	2900	8	12:20	206
84.1	Jones Run Falls. *Round trip.*	3.6	915	3	3:15	207
84.8	Blackrock summit. Views. *Round trip.*	1.0	175	1	1:10	208
87.2	Blackrock A.T. Hut. *Round trip.*	1.3	555	2	1:25	209
87.4	Blackrock Springs. Historic site. *Round trip.*	2.2	425	2	2:10	210
90.0	Chimney Rock. Views. *Round trip.*	3.4	830	3	3:10	211
90.0	Chimney Rock, Riprap Hollow to park boundary. Views, stream, cascades, pool. *Circuit.*	4.9	620	4	4:15	212
90.0	Chimney Rock, Riprap Hollow, Wildcat Ridge. Views, stream, cascades, pool. *One way.*	7.1	2000	6	6:45	213
90.0	Chimney Rock, Riprap Hollow, Wildcat Ridge, A.T. Views, stream, cascades, pool. *Circuit.*	9.8	2365	7	8:50	213
92.1	Wildcat Ridge, Riprap Hollow. Stream, cascades, pool, *Round trip.*	6.8	1670	5	6:15	215
96.8	Jarman Gap. *Circuit.*	0.5	135	1	0:25	218
96.8	Jarman Gap to Beagle Gap. Views. Open pasture. *One way.*	2.7	825	3	2:25	218
99.5	Beagle Gap to Calf Mountain summit. Views. Open pasture. *Round trip.*	2.1	495	2	1:45	220
99.5	Beagle Gap to summit of Bear Den Mountain. Views. Open pasture. *Round trip.*	1.2	355	1	1:05	220

Suggestions for Hikers

The short and easy hikes, especially in summer, require no preparation. For the longer ones, planning ahead may save you some inconvenience or discomfort.

Most of our hikes start near the top of the mountain; they take you down into a hollow and back again. Some of the downhill trails are deceptive, so that you can quickly descend a thousand feet without realizing it. Then, when you turn around and start back, comes the unpleasant surprise. You should know, first, your own strength and capabilities; and second, what you're getting into. In the above catalog of recommended hikes, the distance, climb, and difficulty figures tell you what you're getting into. If you don't know your own capabilities, test them by taking a few short hikes first.

The "Time required" figure in the above list doesn't include time for lunch, or a nap, or birdwatching. You may want to revise your time estimate to include these things.

Plan to get back well before dark. On June 21 it's dark at nine o'clock, daylight time. On December 21 it's dark at five, standard time.

Many of the trails have rough stretches where you walk on rocks that vary in size from smaller than your fist to bigger than a basketball. With thin-soled shoes, the small rocks hurt your feet; with any low shoes, walking on rocks is tiring. Sturdy hiking boots that cover your ankles are the best solution to both problems. The boots should be well broken in. If you hike with new ones, be sure to carry adhesive tape. When a boot begins to rub, stop at once. Tape your foot at the rubbing point, so that the boot rubs tape, rather than skin. Don't wait for a blister to develop.

For the longer hikes, a knapsack is almost essential. Hikes start on the ridgetop, where it's relatively cool. As you descend, and as you exercise, you'll feel warmer and begin to shed sweaters and jackets. You'll need a knapsack to put them in. And in the bottom of the knapsack should be extra clothing to take care of a sudden drop in temperature, or an unexpected night in the woods.

Take a hat. It does a lot to keep you warm if the temperature drops unexpectedly. When the weather's hot, a sun-stopping hat helps keep you cool. Gnats and small flies, buzzing around your face, can sometimes be a nuisance. I've found that a broad-brimmed hat helps keep them away from your eyes and out of your ears.

Carry rain gear. Plastic pants, jacket, and hood are light and take up little space. Standing under a tree won't keep you dry, and it can be dangerous in a thunderstorm. You'd think that with all the cliffs and ledges beside the trail, there would be overhanging rocks where you could find shelter from the rain. And there are—about one such rock in every ten miles of trail. In summer, raingear can save you some discomfort. In cooler weather *it can save your life*.

At any temperature below 50 degrees F (10 degrees C), if your clothes get wet and the wind blows, you're in serious danger of *hypothermia*. That's a condition in which your body loses heat faster than it can produce it. The only remedy is to quickly get into a warm place and out of those wet clothes.

On a long hike, that's impossible. But preventing hypothermia, by using the extra sweater and raingear in your knapsack, is easy.

Besides food, extra clothing, and raingear, here are a few other things that you might want to tuck into your knapsack:

A *first aid kit* with antiseptic, bandaids and bandages, salt tablets, adhesive tape to prevent blisters, and scissors to cut it with.

A *knife.*

A *snake-bite kit.*

Matches, in a waterproof container. (As you know, you're not permitted to build a fire in the Park, except in designated fireplaces. But in an emergency, when you *must* have a fire to keep warm, the rules are off.) You may some day need to start a fire in the rain, with wet wood. Camping stores sell a flammable gel that makes fire starting easier.

A *flashlight,* with fresh batteries.

Map and compass. For most of the hikes described in this book, the maps in the book are all you'll need. For those that I've labeled "for experienced hikers only", or for backcountry exploration, you'll need a compass and a topographic map (the kind with contour lines.) And of course you should practice reading the map and using the compass *before* you start exploring.

Drinking water. Take it with you, in a canteen. The springs and streams may or may not be contaminated by the excrement of hikers, or by drainage from a developed area. The risk is small, but it's not negligible. If you must drink water from a spring or stream, boil it first.

Don't Get Lost

Because the Park is so narrow, you will never be more than a few miles from either the Skyline Drive or an inhabited area outside the Park. In summer you can't get seriously lost, though you may be inconveniently misplaced for a while—possibly overnight.

As I've said, if you go exploring off the trails you should be prepared (and willing) to get lost, and able to find your way back. If you stay on the main trails, and follow my directions, and read all the bands on the trail marker posts, you can forget the whole subject. But nearly everybody wants to get a little way off the trail from time to time, to watch a bird, or to follow a shrew, or to photograph an orchid, or for more personal reasons. When you're ready to return to the trail, you may come on a patch of brambles and have to walk around it. And then you come to a hawthorn thicket, and make another detour. Suddenly you're aware that the trail is not where you thought. Clearly, you're going in the wrong direction. The trail is close by, but which way?

No matter; you're equipped for anything. You have extra food and clothing, water, map and compass, and even a flashlight. They're all in your knapsack, of course. You say you left your knapsack back beside the trail? Then you have a problem.

The best time to solve that problem is before you take your first step off the trail. Note the position of the sun. For example, if it's directly behind you when you leave the trail, it will be directly in front as you return. In cloudy weather, take a compass reading, and know the compass direction that will bring you back to the trail. And of course the map and compass belong in your pants pockets, not in your knapsack or jacket. For maximum safety, take the knapsack with you when you follow that shrew into the woods.

Explorers sometimes get lost in spite of precautions. When you know you're lost, your natural tendency is to walk faster. If it's nearly dark, or if the weather's getting bad, you may even be tempted to run. Don't do it. Panic is your enemy. Although the Park is narrow, there's plenty of room to walk or run in circles until you're exhausted.

Sit down and think. Look at the map. Try to figure out where you left the trail, and approximately where you are now. Plot a compass course that will take you back to the trail, and then follow it. If your sense of direction tells you the compass is wrong, believe the compass anyway.

Now suppose you've lost the compass, or for some other reason can't get back to the trail, and darkness is coming on. Then prepare to spend the night as comfortably as you can. You'll have a better chance of survival than if you hurry along until you're exhausted, and then spend the night. If someone knows you're overdue, and if the weather is such that spending the night in the woods might be dangerous, then wait for the search party to find you. It will come, sooner or later.

When all else fails, there's one last resort. If you started at the Drive and walked downhill, then you'll find the Drive again by walking uphill. Or, if you walk downhill, preferably following a stream, you will eventually come to civilization.

That's enough advice for summer hikers. Winter hiking is a separate subject, which I'll take up a little later.

Backpacking

Camping in the backcountry, carrying your own food and shelter, is a rewarding experience. Doing it successfully is a complicated art, and I won't go into it here. Before you buy your equipment, get some expert advice—preferably from a friend who's an experienced backpacker. Second best is to read a book on the subject. Worst is to follow the advice of a salesman who would like to sell you equipment. After you buy your outfit, test it thoroughly by camping in your back yard, or in a campground, before you start out into the wilderness.

The Park's sales outlets have three books on hiking:

Circuit Hikes in Shenandoah National Park, published by the Potomac Appalachian Trail Club. 86 pages, describing 22 circuit hikes of from three to 21 miles. I have described most of these hikes in *this* book, but from a somewhat different viewpoint. The Circuit Hikes book is small enough to tuck into a pocket. It has a two-color contour map for each hike.

Guide to the Appalachian Trail and Side Trails in Shenandoah National Park, also published by the Potomac Appalachian Trail Club. 263 pages.

Describes the trails in both directions. A lot of information about trails, but with little or no interpretation of what you see. Primarily a book for Walkers.

Appalachian Hiker II, by Edward B. Garvey, 429 pages. In 1970, Garvey walked the entire 2,000 miles of the Appalachian Trail, from Georgia to Maine. In this book he describes his hike. There is a lot of information about the trail itself, and valuable suggestions on backpacking equipment and techniques.

SEASONS AND WEATHER

Let's start off with the most-asked questions: When will the rain stop? When will the fog lift?

Tell Me When . . . .

If it's raining on the mountain, you can be 90 percent sure it's raining throughout the surrounding area. In summer, look for a Washington or Richmond paper at one of the lodges, and check the weather forecast. Or try to get a local station on your car radio at news time. As I write this, the weather forecast is posted on a bulletin board at the front door of the Byrd Visitor Center at Big Meadows. I hope that service will continue and even expand, so that during the summer season the forecast will also be posted at the campground entrance stations.

The fog is different; its coming and going can't be predicted. On the average, you can expect fog on the mountaintop two or three times a month in winter, and once or twice a week in mid-summer. The problem is that, to a large extent, the mountain *causes* fog. Moving air masses must rise to get over the mountain. As the air rises, it expands and cools; if the air is moist, cooling may cause moisture to precipitate as tiny droplets, and produce the clouds that we call fog. As the air descends the eastern slopes it warms, and the fog dissipates.

How long will this go on? A morning fog will often lift before noon, as the air grows warmer. But "often" can't tell you when *this* fog will lift. I have no statistics on fogs and how long they last. The following figures are guesses, based on my own experience as I remember it.

The chances are between five and ten percent that the fog will be gone within an hour.

The chances are better than 50 percent that it will be gone within 24 hours.

The chances are better than 90 percent that it will be gone within three days.

The chances are better than 99 percent that it will be gone within a week.

When the mountains are covered by fog, and your time is limited, my guesswork statistics are not much comfort. But visitors have found several things to do about fog:

1. Sit in the car and sulk.

2. Complain to a ranger. You'll feel better afterward, though the ranger may feel worse.

3. Go to the Visitor Center, sign your name in the registration book and,

under "Remarks", write your complaints about the fog. This is harmless, and gives your morale a temporary boost.

4. Go to the lodge and have a champagne cocktail. Maybe two.

5. Relax and enjoy it.

The fourth alternative may help you advance to the fifth, which requires a slight change of outlook. There are no views from the overlooks, or from the mountain peaks. But the streams and waterfalls still work. Wildflowers still bloom, and the flowers and leaves are more attractive with water droplets on them. (I've heard of wildflower photographers who carry atomizers to spray their subjects with.) The rocks are still there, and their subdued colors seem brighter on a gray day. Wildlife are less timid in fog, so that you're more likely to see a fox or a deer on a foggy day. And finally, if it's a really damp July or August, mushrooms are popping up all over.

You say you can't take pictures in the fog? Sure you can. This is the time for closeups. Wildflower pictures are better with a soft and subtle background than with spotty sun and shadows. And pictures of trees in a foggy woods have a certain fascination. A couple of hints: Look for moderately open woods. Compose your pictures with one or two trees in the foreground, fairly well defined, and others at various distances, fading by steps into invisibility. To record the scene as you see it, trust your exposure meter. But you might want to experiment with a one- or two-stop underexposure, for a "spooky" effect.

Half a dozen times a year, an atmospheric inversion may produce a strange effect: fog lies like a soft white blanket on the Valley and the Piedmont, while the mountaintop is clear. Then we look down on a "fog ocean", with the lower peaks rising above it like islands. Several times, from the "Z" loop of the Big Meadows Campground, I've watched a thrilling sight: a fog ocean rises on the Piedmont side of the mountain, then flows through Fishers Gap and spills down the western slope like a giant Niagara half a mile high.

The Climate

Because of its elevation, the mountaintop has from fifteen to twenty percent more precipitation than the surrounding lowlands. The average temperature is about ten degrees cooler at Big Meadows than in the Valley, and fifteen degrees cooler than downtown Washington or Richmond. The following table gives the average temperature (in degrees F.), and precipitation (in inches), at Big Meadows (elevation 3535 feet) for a recent twelve-year period.

Month	High	Low	Rain	Snow
Jan.	35.9	18.6	3.1	12.7
Feb.	35.2	18.3	3.3	10.4
Mar.	45.0	26.1	3.7	6.8
Apr.	55.0	34.9	3.1	2.6
May	63.6	44.5	5.0	0.
June	72.0	53.8	4.8	0.
July	74.8	57.9	4.4	0.

Month	High	Low	Rain	Snow
Aug.	73.6	56.7	4.4	0.
Sept.	67.9	50.4	5.3	0.
Oct.	57.7	39.2	6.2	0.2
Nov.	47.1	30.3	4.1	7.2
Dec.	39.1	23.2	3.6	8.2
		TOTALS	51.0	48.1

There you have the averages. But few days, and fewer years, are average. The weather seems to go in cycles, so that several dry years are followed by several wet ones, and several cool years by warmer ones. At Big Meadows, the highest temperature during the twelve-year period was 89 degrees, and the lowest 20 below zero. Most winters are "open", which means that snow falls only occasionally and soon melts, so that the ground is bare during most of the season. But every five or ten years comes a snowy winter that raises the average. I've seen almost four feet of snow on the ground at Big Meadows, with drifts higher than your head.

The Spring

Spring comes late on the mountain. If you visit the Park at the end of March, you'll drive through springtime in the lowlands and ascend into winter on the mountain. The trees and grass are brown. Only if you look closely, and in the right places, will you see signs of hope: willow catkins opening; coltsfoot and hepatica blooming tentatively. Not until April, when you see flowers of bloodroot and marsh marigold, will you know that springtime is irreversibly here.

In May, the *green line* glides up the mountain. From high points you can look down the slope and see that trees below a certain level are a pale new green, while those higher up are still brown. Some people say that the green line comes up the mountain at a hundred feet a day. By which they mean, of course, that it gains a hundred feet of altitude a day. (A hundred is such a nice, round number. I've never heard anyone say that the green line comes up the mountain at 30.48 meters a day.)

Summer

Summer is the time for camping, for weekend crowds, for conducted walks and campfire programs. And an unending succession of wildflowers: those with leading roles stay all summer, while bit players come and go. The days are warm, but nights can be nippy. You'll need a sweater or jacket at the evening campfire program, and a warm blanket if you're camping out. The air, which was fairly clear in springtime, is now hazy, and visibility is often limited. At times, my sketches of views from the overlooks will be worthless: they show what you might have seen if you'd come on a clearer day.

The haze has two causes. One is dust in the air combined with water vapor and, I've been told, organic compounds given off by the trees. That's the haze that makes the Blue Ridge blue, and it's been here for a long time. The earliest descriptions of views from the mountains begin, "On a clear day . . . ."

But now the Blue Ridge haze has a second ingredient: smog from industry and automobile exhaust. Summer smog used to be a dirty purplish blanket that lay on the lowlands, so that we could look down on the top of it. Just as the green line creeps up the mountain day by day, the summer smog line crept up year by year, and in 1976 it reached the top. I'm hopeful that during the 1980's, as various anti-pollution programs take effect, the smog line will recede downward. Then once again we can say, even in midsummer, "On a clear day . . . ."

Fall

In September, the wildflowers still in bloom are goldenrod, asters, white snakeroot, and gentians. Fall colors begin to appear: first the Virginia Creeper, and toward the end of the month the black gum — both a rich, deep red. In an "average" year the peak of fall colors comes, so they say, between the tenth and twenty-fifth of October. By then the leaves of the maples are yellow, gold, and red, and maybe a little beyond their best color. But along the Drive you see only an occasional maple, for this is primarily an oak-hickory forest. The oaks and hickories turn dark brick-red, or a modest dull yellow-orange, soon fading into brown. The cove hardwoods, at lower elevations, produce a more colorful display. The crowds who come to Shenandoah from Washington and Richmond pass brilliantly colored trees near home before they see the subdued colors along the Drive. But I've heard no complaints. Skyline Drive is famous for fall color and, to a large extent, people see what they expect to see.

Winter in Shenandoah

Winter is special. The air is cold, and sometimes so clear that only the curvature of the earth limits your visibility. The wildflowers are dead, but real aficionados can identify their dry remains. The leaves are down, so that all the trails offer views, through bare brown branches, that you could never see in summer. The fair-weather visitors are gone; if solitude is what you came for, you needn't look very far.

You have to be lucky to arrive just after a fresh snowfall, but you can depend on ice. There are rock faces along the Drive that develop spectacular masses of icicles — for example at Mile 39.5 in the Central District, and Mile 10.8 in the North. A trip to a waterfall is a different experience now; you may find it frozen solid. Columns of hoarfrost here and there lift the surface of the trail, and crunch underfoot as you walk.

A winter phenomenon that only the luckiest visitors will see, depends on a combination of special conditions. First we must have a thick fog, moving in a slow breeze at below-freezing temperature. The fog freezes on everything it touches, building up a thin, white, icy feather on the upwind side of every twig and every blade of grass. Then, if the fog lifts and the sun comes out while the temperature stays below freezing, you'll see a mountain range covered not with snow, not with ice, but with a brilliant white frosting of sugar.

Equally spectacular, and equally rare, is a major ice storm. Aggie Crandall, in her campfire program "White on Blue", describes it better than

I can. Here's Aggie:

"Rain, too, can be different in winter. The gentle rain that precedes a warm front sometimes falls into below-freezing air at the earth's surface. So, instead of soaking in or running off, it freezes as clear ice. If it rains long enough under such circumstances, thick deposits of heavy glaze ice are built up on trees and shrubs and anything else the rain touches. For a long time the forest is a fairyland of crystal branches that tinkle against one another in the gentle wind. But slowly, despite the fairy charm of the landscape, a sense of impending danger begins to seep into your awareness. As the gentle rain falls and falls and freezes and freezes a limit is reached. Either the load of ice gets too great or the faint wind gets a little stronger, and branch after branch breaks off and falls with a crash like a huge crystal chandelier dropping onto a pile of glasses.

"Long after the forest has struggled against a severe ice storm the scars of the conflict remain. Gnarled and twisted trees, like the Imagination Tree on the A.T. at Big Meadows, are the result of freezing rain. They are usually oak trees—strong, but brittle. The gray birch, on the other hand, survives undamaged because of its flexibility. As the burden of ice increases it bends lower and lower until it lets the ground help support the weight. Then, when the ice melts, it stands up straight again."

If you really want to know yourself and test your capabilities, winter is the time for it. In January and February you'll find no food, or lodging, or gasoline in the whole 105 miles of Skyline Drive. Even water is hard to get. I've said that there are frostfree faucets in some, but not all, of the picnic areas; but, for one reason or another, you may find some or all of them turned off. Rangers will still help you when you need help, provided they know about it. But the temporary summer rangers are gone; the Park is down to its permanent staff, which is small. Self-reliance is expected of you in winter. Come with a full tank of gas. Use snow tires or carry chains. Bring food, water, and proper clothing.

There's always a chance, however small, that your car will break down, or get stuck in the snow, or that its gas line will freeze. Be prepared to survive a breakdown without help. I've mentioned a temperature of 20 below zero. With a strong wind that could have a chilling effect equal to still air at 60 or 70 below. If you have a breakdown it's safer to stay with the car, which will protect you from the wind. Don't depend on the car heater, because the danger of carbon monoxide is too great.

For a safe visit to the mountaintop in the coldest part of winter, I recommend down-filled pants and parka, and insulated boots. For camping out you should also have a mountain tent and a down-filled sleeping bag. Many of the larger cities have stores that sell such things. They are often listed in the yellow pages of the phone book under "Expedition Outfitters."

Here's Aggie Crandall again:

"Because the wintertime staff of the Park is limited, the winter visitor must be ready to depend on his own resources. The ice and cold have created a uniquely beautiful world that often seems like fairyland. But it's not fairyland, because the ice and cold are real — and real ice is slippery and hard, and real cold freezes.

But, for anyone who makes the extra effort and takes the extra precautions, the rewards of a winter visit to Shenandoah can be very, very special."

STORIES IN THE ROCKS

To those who have learned to read their language, the Blue Ridge rocks tell of momentous events. But their story as written here, in English, is like the story of the mountain people: both are based on educated guesses. Experts study the evidence, then decide, "It must have been like this . . ." The guesses of geologists are highly educated, and geologists all agree on what happened here. Only when you get down to details, such as *why* it happened and exactly *when*, are there differing opinions.

The oldest rocks in the Park are the ancient granites that form the core of the mountains. In most places they lie hidden under more recent rocks. But they are exposed on some of the higher peaks, such as Hogback, Marys Rock, and Old Rag, and in road cuts along the Drive. Geologists divide this granite core into two categories:

Old Rag granite, which is exposed on Old Rag, and on the crest of Oventop, and on a rather narrow strip of land that connects the two.

Granodiorite of the Pedlar formation, which is far more extensive, exposed in many places along the main Blue Ridge.

The two differ somewhat in chemical composition. Old Rag granite is a little lighter in color than the granodiorite. Both have been somewhat changed from their original structure by what happened later.

Q: What's a "Pedlar" formation?

A: The dictionary says that a "formation" is a mass of rock that's considered as a unit for the purpose of geological mapping. We can assume that all the rocks in a given formation were formed by the same process and at roughly the same time. A formation is named for the place where it was first described.

As we've seen, the human history of the Blue Ridge spans eleven thousand years. The history of the rocks is a hundred thousand times that long. The granite that forms the core of these mountains is a fourth as old as the earth itself. It crystalized from molten magma 1,100,000,000 years ago. That date can be fixed, with a reasonably small percentage of error, by measurement of radioactive elements and their decay products.

There's a certain satisfaction in assigning dates to events, even though we can't appreciate their meaning. Eleven hundred million years, in human terms, is an inconceivable span of time. We might try to grasp its magnitude by analogy: if the age of the oldest Blue Ridge rocks were twelve hours, then all the time that has elapsed since the birth of Christ would be considerably less than a tenth of a second. But such comparisons don't really work. Let's get on with the story, assigning dates as best we can, without trying to understand them in human terms.

Evidence tells us that the ancient rocks cooled and crystalized very slowly, for the different minerals form an interlocking mosaic of moderately large crystals. Such a structure forms only when the rocks solidify slowly, at high temperature and under great pressure. Thus we know that the granite core of the mountain was more than a mile underground when it solidified from molten magma. What lay on top of it we'll never know. Over a period of three hundred million years, the land was slowly lifted upward. And as it rose, the higher rocks weathered, disintegrated, and washed into the sea.

With a little effort we can picture the landscape as it was eight hundred million years ago. Hills and low mountains of bare granite, from a few hundred to perhaps two thousand feet high, covered the land. Streams flowed down the hollows and through the valleys. Here and there on a wet shaded rock, there may have been a green film of algae; but there was no other life outside the oceans. As the granite hilltops weathered, the streams carried sand and gravel to the lowlands, and spread them in a layer up to 200 feet thick over the valleys.

Then to this bleak landscape came the lava flows. The granite, strained by the forces that were lifting it upward, cracked and split. The lava that surged up through the fissures was so hot that it spread out in the valley and formed a smooth flat sheet before it hardened. Where the eruptions were especially violent, clouds of volcanic dust and ash poured through the fissures and settled on the land, and were covered by the lava.

Now the landscape was different. The low mountains of bare granite were still there, but a sheet of lava covered the valley floor. The streams still flowed down the hollows, and began to carve channels through the lava. They carried more sand and pebbles from the eroding granite hills, and spread them here and there over the lava on the valley floor.

The lifting force continued, until at last the rocks split again. More dust and cinders spewed out, and more lava flowed, forming a new and higher floor in the valleys. And this was repeated at least a dozen times, for we find evidence of a dozen separate lava flows in the Park. With each new eruption, the lava reached higher on the granite hillsides, and eventually covered all but the highest peaks.

The valley sediments that were covered by the first lava flow were cemented by mineral fluids from the lavas, and compacted by heat and pressure. These sediments now form the rocks of the *Swift Run* formation, which is exposed at several places along the Drive.

The lava flows, collectively, comprise the *Catoctin formation,* consisting mostly of *igneous* rocks (which hardened from a molten state.) But in places the lava flows are separated by *sedimentary* rock (formed of sediments laid down by water, and later hardened by pressure.) These relatively thin layers of sedimentary rocks were the sand and pebbles that washed down onto each new lava surface before the next flow occurred. In many places, soil that had formed on top of a lava flow was torn up and churned into the base of the next flow. There's a good example of this at Little Stony Man.

Near its upper surface, newly hardened lava is porous and filled with gas bubbles. We can assume that in many places the pores and voids were filled with ground water when a new flow of white-hot lava covered them. Minerals crystalized from the superheated solutions. Bubble cavities filled with concentric shells of minerals such as *epidote* (bright yellow green), *chlorite* (dark green); *feldspar* (bone white); and *quartz* (glassy, milky white to nearly transparent.)

The epidote that filled the lava pores served as a cement; when this lava was later compacted by the pressure of overlying rocks it became *greenstone,* which makes up nearly 80 percent of the Catoctin formation within the Park. Greenstone caps our highest peaks, and forms nearly all our waterfalls. Where rock surfaces are old and weathered and covered by lichens, the green color may be hidden under shades of gray; on freshly broken rock it's very evident.

As each flow of lava cooled it contracted, and cracks traced polygons on its surface as they do on the surface of drying mud. As cooling continued the cracks spread downward, forming long prismatic columns of five, six, or seven sides — from a few inches to more than two feet across. This *columnar jointing* is evident at many points in the Park, and I'll point out examples in the log of the Drive.

The fissures through which the lava poured are now filled with *dikes* of solidified lava. Within the Park more than a hundred greenstone dikes in the granite rock have been found and mapped. The best example beside the Drive is at the north portal of the Marys Rock tunnel, Mile 32.2.

Just how long the intermittent volcanic activity lasted, no one can say. It had probably ended entirely by the beginning of the Cambrian period, something less than 600 million years ago. After the last lava flow a few hilltops of granite were still exposed, and it's likely that there were higher granite hills or mountains to the west. New streams cut channels through the lava beds, and deposited sand and pebbles that washed down from the granite mountains. These deposits became the rocks that now constitute the *Weverton formation.*

Now the land was sinking. As it neared sea level, the streams stopped flowing and became bogs. The sea came nearer. The land that is now the Park was covered by shallow lagoons, separated by sand bars from the open ocean. Sandy mud and clay washed into the lagoons and, as the land continued to sink, built up to a depth of hundreds of feet. This material later became the sandstone and shale of the *Hampton formation.*

The land sank farther. The sea advanced, and the Blue Ridge area became a sandy shore. The white beach sands later became the white quartzite of the *Erwin formation.*

And then the land sank beneath the sea. The sediments now were carbonates — some precipitated by chemical action in the sea water, and some consisting of shells of marine animals. The land continued sinking for perhaps another eighty million years, while the sediments built up limestone and dolomite deposits two or three miles thick. Then the land rose again, and the limestone emerged from the sea. That must have been roughly 450 million years ago.

The story of the rocks during the next 225 million years is somewhat garbled, or maybe it loses something in translation. The details are uncertain. We know that a number of things happened, though we can't put them in exact sequence, or assign exact dates. The rocks we now see in the Park were *metamorphosed,* which means their physical nature was changed by the pressure of rocks above them. Second, the uplift of the land continued. Third, tremendous forces thrust against the land, pushing toward the northwest. The rocks buckled and broke; fault lines developed; great masses of rock were thrust on top of others; formations in some places were tilted, and in others turned on their sides. But this didn't happen in one great, literally earth-shaking event. It must have resulted from continued thrust, and intermittent slippage along the fault lines, spread out over nearly all of the 225 million years.

The final chapter brings us from 225 million years ago to the present. During most of this time uplift continued, and during all of it the land eroded. The miles of sediments that lay above the granite and greenstone of the Blue Ridge crest were washed away. But granite and greenstone are more resistant than the sedimentary rocks, and when they were exposed the erosion slowed. To the west, the softer carbonate rocks had been pushed downward by the buckling of the land that shaped these mountains. The limestone eroded rapidly, forming what is now the Shenandoah Valley.

Uplift of the land may still be going on: if so, it's too slow to detect. Erosion of the Blue Ridge speeded up during the ice ages when, most likely, the talus slopes that we now see along the western slopes of the mountain were formed. Erosion is slower now, but it continues nevertheless.

Q: Why should the surface of the land rise and fall?

A: Questions that begin with "why" are hard to answer. Each answer leads to another question beginning with "why", and the conversation spirals outward toward infinity.

Q: Give it a try.

A: The earth has a solid outer crust maybe fifty miles thick, floating on hot plastic material. "Plastic" in this sense means capable of flowing. But it's not a liquid. It can flow very slowly, in response to great pressure. A sideways pressure can make the crust buckle, so that it rises in some places and sinks in others. That's a simplified version of one theory. There are others.

Q: Why should there be sideways pressures on the earth's crust? What caused the "tremendous forces" that pushed the land toward the northwest and made it buckle and break?

A: Again, we have a choice of theories. Here's a simplified version of one of them. The earth's crust is not a continuous mass; rather, it consists of a number of separate "plates". Hugh Crandall, in *Shenandoah, the Story Behind the Scenery,* aptly compares the plates to ice floes that are loosely frozen together at their edges. Currents in the sea can break the floes apart and grind one floe against another, or crush two floes together. In much the same way, plates in the earth's crust can be moved by slow but powerful convection currents in the hot plastic material underneath. The forces that thrust one plate against another can cause earthquakes and, over a period of time, can build mountains.

Q: Remind me once more: what has all this got to do with me?

A: As you tour the Drive and hike the trails you'll see rocks belonging to all the formations I have mentioned. You will see how one lava flow rests on another, sometimes separated by the sediments of ancient streams. You will see the prismatic columns into which the lava cracked as it cooled, and you will see dikes of cooled lava in the granite. I find satisfaction in knowing how these things came about. I hope you will too.

What I've given is no more than a simplified outline of the story of the rocks. To fill in some of the details, look for these books at one of the Park's sales outlets:

Rocks and Minerals, by Herbert S. Zim and Paul R. Shaffer (Golden Guide Series). 160 pages; small and inexpensive. Color illustrations help identify the most common rocks and minerals.

Geology of the Shenandoah National Park, by Thomas M. Gathright II. 93 pages. An excellent treatment, not too technical. The price may seem a little high until you look at the three maps in the pocket of the back cover. If you have more than a passing interest in the geology of the Park, this book is a bargain.

IF YOU WANT TO KNOW MORE

Rangers will answer your questions if they can. You can learn a great deal about the Park from campfire programs and conducted walks, and from the exhibits in the two Visitor Centers.

For more detailed information on a specific subject, you'll need a book. The *Shenandoah Natural History Association* is a non-profit organization. It sells books at Dickey Ridge Visitor Center (Mile 4.6), and at Big Meadows Visitor Center (Mile 51.0). The "profits" are used to publish other needed books, to pay for the color slides that are used in the campfire programs, to buy audiovisual equipment, etc.

I've already listed the books that apply to the subjects I've discussed. Here are some others:

Shenandoah, the Story Behind the Scenery, by Hugh Crandall. Photographs by William Bake Jr. 32 pages. Crandall covers about the same range of subjects that I've dealt with in this book up to now, but more concisely. The color photographs are beautiful.

Shenandoah National Park, by Ruth Radlauer, 48 pages, 55 color photos. A children's book, but informative nevertheless. Some oversimplification, as you might expect. A few small errors.

National Parks Recreation Directory, by Rand McNally. 160 pages. Concise facts about Shenandoah; and points of interest, food, and lodging in the surrounding area—from Baltimore, Md. to Little Switzerland, N.C.

National Parks: The American Experience, by Alfred Runte. 240 pages, black-and-white photos. A scholarly history of the national park idea in general, with barely a mention of Shenandoah. This is not light reading, but it's well worth while.

The Earth-Man Story, by Darwin Lambert. 200 pages. This is *not* science fiction, as the title might suggest, but a Shenandoah-based study of man and his environment. This book is so packed with information and ideas that it's not easy reading, but it will repay whatever time you put into it. Black-and-white photographs.

Herbert Hoover's Hideaway, by Darwin Lambert. 143 pages. This is the story of President Hoover's summer retreat at the head of the Rapidan River. (Camp Hoover is now a part of the Park; it's a fairly easy hike from Milam Gap, Mile 52.8). Black-and-white photographs.

Shenandoah Heritage, by Carolyn and Jack Reeder. 87 pages. A brief account of some of the mountain people, based largely on interviews, Park documents, and PATC records. Black-and-white photos.

Shenandoah Vestiges, by Carolyn and Jack Reeder. 71 pages. Black-and-white photographs of mountaineer homesites, cemeteries, and artifacts which the authors have found at more than 300 sites within the Park. The authors do not reveal the location of any of these sites.

Skyland, by George Freeman Pollock. 283 pages. Reminiscences of the founder and owner of the Skyland resort. Black-and-white photographs.

Dean Mountain Story, by Gloria Dean. 80 pages. The story of James and Sarah Dean and their family. The Deans lived on Dean Mountain, which is now a part of the Park.

Lost Trails and Forgotten People, by Tom Floyd. 152 pages. Life on Jones Mountain before the Park was created.

ANY MORE QUESTIONS?

Here are a few questions that Park visitors often ask the rangers. They don't seem to fit elsewhere in the book.

Q: Why must I pay to get into the Park?

A: Entrance fees are required by the Land and Water Conservation Fund Act. The money is used to buy land for new parks, and to preserve threatened natural environments.

Q: It's been raining ever since I got here. Can I get my money back?

A: No.

Q: How can I get a job as a Park Ranger?

A: For either permanent or seasonal employment, write to the National Park Service, Washington, D.C. Few jobs are available, and competition is lively.

Q: How can I get a job with the concessioner?

A: Write to ARA Virginia Sky-line Co., Inc., P.O. Box 727, Luray, Virginia 22835.

Q: Where is Walton's Mountain?

A: In the television series, the Walton family lives at the foot of Walton's Mountain, which is clearly in the Blue Ridge and somewhere near Charlottesville. The Mountain is fictitious, of course. The author's home is in Schuyler, Virginia, about 30 miles south of Charlottesville. Therefore Walton's Mountain, as conceived by the author, must be south of the Park, near Rockfish Gap.

Q: Why do the Park signs have barbed wire around them?

A: For some reason, bears like to chew the signs. Barbed wire keeps them off.

Q: The tree trunks have gray-green stuff all over them. Are the trees sick?

A: The gray-green stuff is lichen, which does no harm. Lichens grow where the air is cool, clean, and damp, which explains why they are common at higher elevations in the Park.

Q: (In May.) Down in the Valley, the trees are covered with leaves. Up here they're bare. Are the trees sick?

A: The leaves will come. On the mountaintop, spring is three or four weeks later than it is in the Valley.

Q: (August to October.) Trees beside the Drive have bare branches covered with cobwebs. Is something killing the trees?

A: What you saw is the work of the fall webworm, *Hyphantria cunea*. It's not killing the trees. The webworms don't come until late in the growing season, when the tree has enough nutrients stored in its roots to last through the winter. A tree would have to be completely stripped for several years in a row to be seriously damaged.

Q: Why doesn't the Park spray the trees?

A: Park policy is to rely on natural controls — birds and frost, not chemicals — to keep webworms under control.

Q: But the webs are ugly.

A: Take a look when they're backlit by the afternoon sun.

Q: Has the gypsy moth reached Shenandoah?

A: Yes. There has been major defoliation in some areas.

Q: Every few miles along the Drive I see a brown post with two brown cylinders on it. What's that?

A: That's part of the "grapevine" — an old telephone system used by the rangers before they developed the present system of radio communication.

Q: Where are the caverns?

A: There are a number of caverns in the Shenandoah Valley, but none in the Park. Caverns occur in limestone. There is no limestone in the Park, except at a few points near the boundary. The largest and most famous caverns in the area are at Luray, nine miles west of Panorama (Mile 31.5).

Q: I saw two hound dogs beside the Drive. Why doesn't the Park do something about that?

A: The Park is narrow, and dogs come in from the nearby farms. Rangers round them up as quickly as possible, put them in a pound at Big Meadows or Park Headquarters, and notify the owner.

Q: Why doesn't the Park re-introduce the bison, elk, and cougar?

A: Their populations would have to reach a certain level for the species to be self-sustaining. The Park isn't big enough for a self-sustaining number of bison, elk, or cougars. Even if it were, the animals would drift out onto surrounding farmland and cause problems.

Q: Where are the fire towers?

A: We have none. In the 1940's the Park had nearly a dozen fire towers, but they've all been taken down. Fires are detected by rangers patrolling the Drive, and by Fire Wardens outside the Park.

This was asked by a visitor at Big Meadows:

Q: Do you mind if I jump off Franklin Cliff?

A: You're speaking of hang-gliding. The Superintendent has authorized three launch sites. One is on Millers Head, near Skyland. The others are on Hogback Mountain and Dickey Hill, in the North Section. But the rules are strict. Write to Park Headquarters for information: Shenandoah National Park, Luray, Virginia 22835.

So, now you're loaded with background information and receptive attitudes and fieldbooks. You're qualified to find maximum profit and enjoyment in your Park experience. Let's travel.

LOG OF THE DRIVE, NORTH SECTION

MILE 0.0 Skyline Drive begins at U.S. Highway 340 near the south edge of Front Royal. You can find food and lodging in Front Royal, mostly at the far end of town.

Going south from the Drive, U.S. 340 passes through an especially attractive part of the Shenandoah Valley. Skyline Caverns is 1.1 miles south of the Drive on U.S. 340. The "anthodites" — small but pretty clusters of long white crystals — are its principal attraction.

MILE 0.05, PARKING AREA. Elevation 590 feet. *Dickey Ridge Trail.* As you enter Skyline Drive from U.S. 340, you come immediately to a parking area on the west (right) side of the road. Pull off and stop for a minute. This is the lowest point on the Drive, and the only place in the Park where the basement rock is limestone. But you can't see it, because it's covered by soil and broken rock that have washed down from the Catoctin formation on the ridge.

From this point the Drive climbs steadily on Dickey Ridge, finally reaching the Blue Ridge at Compton Gap, Mile 10.4. The Dickey Ridge Trail begins just to the south of where you are parked. It goes more or less parallel to the Drive for 9.2 miles, then joins the A.T. (Appalachian Trail) near Compton Gap. I recommend a short walk up the Dickey Ridge Trail, and return by the same route. (Note: the terms "Dickey Ridge" and "Dickey Hill" are synonymous.)

HIKE: *Dickey Ridge Trail. Round trip* 2.7 miles; total *climb* about 440 feet; *time* required 2:10. A pleasant, easy walk beside a small stream.

The trail starts at the marker post on the west side of the Drive. The first half of your walk goes through an area that, when the Park was created in the 1930's, was pasture with only an occasional tree. Now it's grown up with spindly black locusts and other pioneer trees, and it's carpeted and festooned with Japanese honeysuckle. This area shows what your front yard may look like if you forget to mow the lawn for fifty years.

The stream is dry where you first see it, but there's water after you walk about 0.4 mile. Beyond that point, look for tall young sycamores on the right.

Sycamores are not common in the Park; they occur only near streams at low elevations.

About half a mile from the start, a side trail goes left for 200 yards, and reaches the Drive just south of the Entrance Station. A little more than a hundred yards farther, another side trail (actually an old road) also goes left to the Drive. Just beyond, you cross the stream on a small but sturdy bridge.

Throughout the rest of your hike you'll see evidence of the mountain people who once lived here: stone piles, stone walls, and traces of old roads. At about 0.4 mile beyond the stream crossing, look for the remains of a stone chimney, now filled in, to the left of the trail. This is all that remains of a mountaineer homesite.

About three quarters of a mile beyond the bridge the trail leaves the stream and, at a concrete marker post, switches back sharply to the right. I suggest that you return to your car from this point. Ahead, the trail climbs rather steeply for half a mile to the Drive crossing at Mile 2.1.

Mile 0.3, ROAD, east side. This goes into the Park Service residential area. Use it as an emergency exit if you want to leave the Drive but find the normal exit closed.

MILE 0.6, FRONT ROYAL ENTRANCE STATION. Elevation 705 feet. There's a parking area just south of the Entrance Station. Beside it, on the west side of the Drive, are a buckeye (horse-chestnut) and several Kentucky coffee trees. Both species are rare in the Park.

Geology: The Front Royal fault crosses the Drive here, separating the limestone and dolomite of the Rockdale Run formation from the lava flows of the Catoctin formation.

MILE 1.4, PARKING AREA, west side. Elevation 970 feet. There are two modest attractions here:

Waterfall: Cross the Drive and walk south (uphill) about a hundred feet, then look to your left. There, directly in front of you, is a charming cascade of water some 60 feet high. This is the only waterfall that's visible from Skyline Drive. And like all our falls, this one is at its best in spring or after heavy rains. It may be completely dry in summer.

Geology: The rocks across the Drive from the parking area are basalt of the Catoctin formation; they were molten lava about 800 million years ago. In a fresh break the rock is mostly gray-green—the green color caused by the mineral epidote (calcium aluminum iron silicate). Here, weathering has produced a variety of colors: gray-green, light brown, and dark gray-purple.

In the downhill half of the rock cut you can see, if you look closely, small dark spots—from 1/8 to 1/2 inch in diameter—on the purplish rocks. These were once gas bubbles in the lava, which were later filled by minerals. At no point do the Catoctin lavas have the porous appearance of recent lava; they have been metamorphosed by the pressure of other rocks above them, so that no bubble spaces remain except where the minerals that filled them were later lost by weathering.

MILE 2.0, PARKING AREA, west side. A gravel parking pulloff, about 100 feet north of the milepost, with room for several cars. Park here if you want to hike on the Dickey Ridge Trail from the crossing at Mile 2.15.

MILE 2.15, DICKEY RIDGE TRAIL CROSSING. Elevation 1,155 feet. There's no marker or sign here, and the trail is hard to see from your car.

Use the parking area at Mile 2.0 if you want to hike. On the west side, the trail goes 1.9 miles to its origin at Mile 0.05 on the Drive. On the east side it goes 2.6 miles to the Fox Hollow Trail, across the Drive from the Dickey Ridge Visitor Center. There's an offset in the trail as it crosses the Drive here; on the east side it goes steeply up the bank from a point 100 feet south of the trail on the west side.

MILE 2.8, SHENANDOAH VALLEY OVERLOOK. Elevation 1,390 feet. The view here is quite worthwhile, and if the air is fairly clear I recommend that you give it a little time. Use binoculars, if you have them. You look across the Valley, 800 feet below, and a stretch of the Shenandoah River, to the two ridges of the Massanutten Mountain, with Signal Knob at their right-hand end. The Massanutten divides the Shenandoah Valley, separating the north fork of the Shenandoah River, on the far side of the Massanutten, from the south fork on this side. The two meet at Riverton, a few miles north of Front Royal.

Front Royal is toward the right of your view, and two to three miles away. The tall smokestacks belong to a synthetic fibers factory. When the wind blows toward the overlook from Front Royal there's a strong medicinal smell in the air, but that may be just a coincidence. After dark, the lights of Front Royal make this overlook a very worthwhile stop.

Legend: Front Royal got its name because at one time it lay on the frontier of the land occupied by the Royal (British) troops.

Legend: "Front", in the language of the mountain people, meant "foothill". The foothills here were occupied by Royal troops.

Legend: When the town consisted principally of a tavern, and Royal troops were stationed there, the sentry's challenge was "front", and the password was "royal".

Legend: Front Royal was originally called Lehewtown. In frontier times it had so many brawling and disorderly inhabitants that the name was changed, informally at least, to Helltown.

MILE 4.6, DICKEY RIDGE VISITOR CENTER. Elevation 1,940 feet. Information, publications, an orientation movie, exhibits, telephone, rest rooms, water; Fox Hollow self-guiding trail; access to Dickey Ridge Trail. From near the north end of the building, a side road goes down to a group of mobile homes where rangers live during the summer season.

The Visitor Center was built in 1938 as a dining hall, and the concessioner had cabins for rent in the area now occupied by the mobile homes. They closed the dining hall during World War II, and did not re-open it when the war ended. It was converted to a Visitor Center in 1958.

There's a view of sorts from the far side of the building. If you walk down to the edge of the grassy area you can look across the Valley to the Massanutten. To the far left is Hogback Mountain, with four separate bumps along its crest. Between Hogback and here is the Browntown Valley.

The Dickey Ridge Trail is about 80 yards to the east of the Drive, on the side across from the Visitor Center. From here the trail goes 2.6 miles north to the Drive crossing at Mile 2.15; and 2.5 miles south to the Drive crossing in Low Gap, Mile 7.9.

HIKE: *Fox Hollow Trail. Circuit* about 1.3 miles; total *climb* about 310 feet; *time* required 1:20. This is a pleasant self-guiding trail through two old mountaineer homesites. The trail is easy; no part of it is steep or rough. See map below.

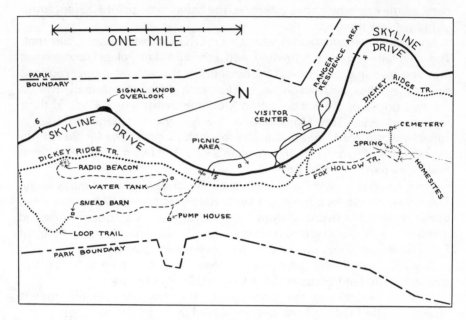

Map of Dickey Ridge — Fox Hollow area.

Ask at the Visitor Center for the self-guiding pamplet. If you should happen to find the Visitor Center closed, the following summary should be helpful.

The trail begins in the grass across the Drive from the Visitor Center. Where the trail forks, a few feet from the Drive, keep left. In less than 100 yards you'll reach the Dickey Ridge Trail. Keep to the left here; continue another 0.2 mile, then turn right at the junction. You will pass piles of stones that several generations of the Fox family cleared from their fields and pasture. The trail turns sharp right when it reaches the walled cemetery. The vine that grows inside the wall is periwinkle, *Vinca minor,* which has blue flowers in the spring. Periwinkle was sometimes called "cemetery plant". It was used in cemeteries because it makes a good ground cover, and doesn't have to be mowed.

Continue past the site of the Fox family garden and house, then turn sharp left at a concrete-enclosed spring (which was built to supply water to the Dickey Ridge development when the building there was a restaurant, rather than a Visitor Center.) Pass an old millstone near the site of the Fox family barn. (There was no mill here; the stone was brought into the hollow for ornamental purposes.) Cross the stream and continue to a dirt road. Edgar Merchant had his home here: the house was on the flat area to your left; the barn covered the rock-bordered hole on your right.

Turn right on the old road. Follow it uphill for a little more than 0.4 mile, then take the trail that goes uphill to the right. Cross the Dickey Ridge trail and continue uphill to your starting point.

MILE 4.7, DICKEY RIDGE PICNIC AREA. Elevation 1,935 feet. Entrance is at the south end of the Visitor Center parking lot. A one-way road takes you through the Picnic Area, and rejoins the Drive at Mile 5.0. There are tables, fireplaces, several drinking fountains (turned off in winter), and a comfort station. For winter use there's a frostfree faucet in front of the comfort station, and pit toilets behind it.

MILE 5.0, EXIT ROAD, west side, from the Dickey Ridge Picnic Area. Do not enter.

MILE 5.1, SNEAD FIRE ROAD, east side. This road leads to an old homesite; the hike is interesting and easy. There's limited parking in the grass on the west side of the Drive. For better parking, or to make the hike a little longer, start from the Picnic Area or the Visitor Center.

HIKE: *Snead homesite. Round trip* 1.4 miles (from the edge of the Drive); total *climb* about 190 feet; *time* required 1:25. See map, page 84. Take the fire road; cross the Dickey Ridge Trail and then, a tenth of a mile from the Drive, come to a fork in the road. The right-hand fork climbs to the highest point on Dickey Ridge, which is occupied by a *Vortac* radio beacon belonging to the Federal Aviation Authority. This facility is an aircraft navigation aid. For that reason, F.A.A. is a little nervous about the possibility of sabotage or vandalism. I suggest that you not use the road, nor go to the summit by other means.

Take the left fork. Walk a tenth of a mile through an old apple orchard to a second fork; keep to the right here. The other road goes down to the pumphouse, a part of the Dickey Ridge water system. The Snead homesite is 0.7 mile from the Drive. The house has been torn down, but the barn is in fairly good condition. In front of it are the remains of a water tank. The small structure in back may have been a root cellar.

The road continues beyond the barn to the site of the Snead house, on the right, where a wall and steps still remain. As you might guess, the owners of this property were not typical mountaineers. Originally it belonged to the Carter family, who were farmers and fruit growers in comfortable circumstances. They owned extensive orchards; and the land now occupied by the Visitor Center was, in 1930, Carter's cornfield. This property is now called the Snead place, although Snead, a Rappahannock County judge, owned it for only a few years. The Park bought the 200-acre property in 1962, in order to develop and protect the Dickey Ridge water supply.

You can go back the way you came, or continue on the Snead Farm Loop Trail. That goes 0.7 mile to the Dickey Ridge Trail. Turn right, and go 1.2 miles back to the Snead Farm fire road.

MILE 5.3, PAVED PARKING PULLOUT, west side. Elevation 1,985 feet. Room for about six cars. This is obviously an overlook, though it has no name and does not appear on the Park's list of overlooks — probably because it has only a part of the view that you'll see from Signal Knob Overlook, Mile 5.7. From here you look westward across the Shenandoah Valley, and several loops of the Shenandoah River, to the Massanutten. To the far right is a part of Dickey Ridge; Front Royal is hidden behind it. Here, as at many of the overlooks in the North District, I like to study the farms, roads, and ponds through binoculars. The barn that you see at the foot of the ridge is about eight hundred feet below you.

MILE 5.7, SIGNAL KNOB OVERLOOK. Elevation 2,090 feet. To the far left you can look up the Browntown Valley to the two peaks of Mt. Marshall and, farther right, the four humps of Hogback. Below you is the Shenandoah Valley, with the south fork of the Shenandoah River meandering through it. The first two ridges on the far side of the Valley are the Massanutten, with the Fort Valley between them. The Massanutten divides the Shenandoah Valley for a distance of nearly fifty miles.

Legend: Massanutten is an Indian word meaning "three-topped."

Legend: Massanutten is an Indian word meaning "old field" or "potato field" (though I've been told that the Indians who lived in this area did not grow potatoes).

Legend: Massanutten is an Indian word meaning "Indian basket", referring to the supposedly basket-shaped Fort Valley.

History: In 1726 a group of Germans moved into the Valley from Pennsylvania, and established a settlement, which they called Massanutten, to the west of the present town of Luray. They called the ridge to the west of the settlement not Massanutten, but Peaked Mountain. (That name is still used locally for the peak at the southern end. It's pronounced with two syllables: PEAK-id.) The Massanutten colony survived in peace until about 1754; then followed a dozen years of Indian attacks. Homes in the area, some of them still standing, were built like forts.

Sometime before 1750, the name of Peaked Mountain changed to Buffalo Mountain. The deep gap near the middle, now called New Market Gap, lay just to the west of the Massanutten settlement, and was therefore called Massanutten Gap. The name of the gap was later applied to the whole 50-mile ridge.

Signal Knob is the high point at the right-hand end of the Massanutten. Although there was no Civil War action on the mountain itself, there were battles on both sides of it. Signal Knob was a Confederate Army signal station. (It may or may not have been used briefly by Union troops.) Signals were relayed to another knob farther south on the Massanutten, and from there to Stony Man, on their way to Richmond.

Geology: Cross the Drive at a point a little south of the middle of the overlook, and look at the rocks from the edge of the Drive. At about eye level is a band of sandstone, two-and-a-half to three-feet thick. It separates a dark lava flow (below) from a later, lighter-colored lava flow above.

The sandstone is banded with colors varying from tan to reddish to reddish-purple, showing that it was formed from various kinds of sand and mud. We can conclude that many years, or more likely many centuries, elapsed between the two lava flows. During that time streams eroded higher ground, depositing sand and mud here. The reddish color of the sandstone is probably the result of mineralization by the upper lava flow.

MILE 6.8, GOONEY RUN OVERLOOK. Elevation 2,085 feet. There is no view from the middle of the overlook. Looking to the right from the north end, you have a view across the Valley, with several meanders of the Shenandoah River in sight. Signal Knob is at the far end of the Massanutten. Farther right, on the near side of the Valley, is a part of Dickey Ridge, with the white tower of the radio navigation beacon on its highest point. Gooney Run, which drains the Browntown Valley, passes about a mile straight out from the overlook, and about 1,300 feet down.

Legend: Gooney Run was originally called Sugar Tree Creek. When Lord Fairfax went hunting there his favorite hound, Gooney, was accidentally drowned. His Lordship changed the name of the creek to Gooney's Run in honor of the dog.

Geology: The overlook rests on the contact between the Pedlar granodiorite, below, and the Catoctin lava flows above. With very little walking you can see both. First cross the Drive. In the road cut are layers of basalt, separated by a layer of tuff (compressed volcanic ash.) The layers are rather hard to make out because the rocks are weathered and crumbling. Now return to the other side of the Drive, and look for a trail near the middle of the overlook.

If the trail is not too badly overgrown, follow it for about 250 feet to a ledge of granodiorite, which looks like fine-grained granite.

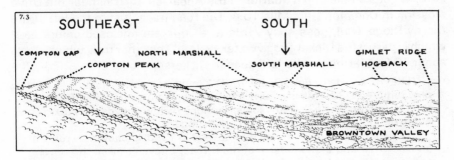

View from Gooney Manor Overlook.

MILE 7.3, GOONEY MANOR OVERLOOK. Elevation 1,930 feet. (See sketch). Hogback Mountain is more or less straight ahead across the Browntown Valley, which is drained by Gooney Run and its tributaries. Many of the homes in the valley belong to people who were displaced when the park was created. Browntown itself is about halfway between here and Hogback, just outside the sketch to the right. Descending to the right from Hogback is Gimlet Ridge, which breaks up into the three small hills that enclose the Browntown Valley on the west.

To the left of Compton Mountain (at the left of the sketch) is Carson Mountain, from which the Blue Ridge descends, still farther left, toward Chester Gap. If you have binoculars, look at a point a little way down the left slope of Compton Peak. The rock ledge you see there has a good view in this direction. It's one of the objectives of the Compton Peak hike, page 91. As you can imagine, it's not a difficult climb.

History: As I told you earlier, the Northern Neck became the property of Thomas, sixth Lord Fairfax. Fairfax sold most of the land, but set aside several "manors" over which he kept seignorial rights. Two of these included land that is now within the Park — both of them in the North Section. The Manor of Leeds was on the east side of the mountain, and I'll mention it later. Gooney Manor, consisting of about 13,000 acres, included a large part of the Browntown Valley below the overlook, as well as land farther north (toward Front Royal) on both sides of Dickey Ridge. Note that the term "manor" refers to the whole property; there was no mansion.

MILE 7.9, LOW GAP. Elevation 1,790 feet. *Dickey Ridge Trail Crossing.* Parking in the grass on both sides of the Drive. There's a concrete trail marker, but it's hard to see from a moving car unless you're looking for it. On the east side, it's 2.5 miles by trail to the Snead fire road, and 3.0 miles to the Fox Hollow Trail near the Dickey Ridge Visitor Center. On the west side it's 1.0 mile to Skyline Drive in Lands Run Gap, Mile 9.2.

MILE 9.2, LANDS RUN GAP. Elevation 2,015 feet. *Dickey Ridge Trail* crossing; fire road; *hikes.* Ample parking space beside the fire road, on the west side.

There are two trails and an unpaved road trace on the east side of the Drive. Farthest right is the Dickey Ridge Trail (which is also a horse trail here). It goes a mile and a quarter to the Appalachian Trail near the Drive crossing in Compton Gap, Mile 10.4. The road trace, just to the left of the Dickey Ridge Trail, goes sixty yards to a concrete-enclosed chlorinator, which is part of the Dickey Ridge water system. The other trail, which starts about 40 feet farther to the left, goes to Hickerson Hollow.

HIKE: *Hickerson Hollow, Round trip* 2.2 miles; total *climb* about 940 feet; *time* required 2:30. This is a fairly easy walk on a horse trail that descends through Hickerson Hollow, and joins Harmony Hollow outside the Park. The above figures apply to a hike to the Park boundary.

This yellow-blazed horse trail was opened in 1980. It follows the route of an older trail and a still older mountain road. I haven't hiked the newest version, so I can't offer any details. The old road trace is easy to follow. There were several mountaineer homesites along this route, but the evidence is now hard to find. Explore the whole hollow, if you wish. You aren't likely to get lost, even without a compass.

Trivia: Harmony Hollow is drained by Happy Creek. Both names are more than 200 years old. I don't know whether they reflect former conditions in the hollow, or whether the names were used sarcastically.

The Dickey Ridge Trail goes north from the small parking area on the west side of the Drive. It's 1.0 miles by trail to the Skyline Drive in Low Gap, Mile 7.9.

HIKE: *Lands Run Falls. Round trip* 1.3 miles; total *climb* about 325 feet; *time* required 1:30. This is an unrewarding experience for most people, so please read the whole description before you start. See map, page 89.

On the west side of the Drive, follow the fire road downhill for about 0.6 mile. (The road is rough — covered with fist-sized rocks — and fairly steep.) Look for a low point where a small stream flows under the road. Follow the stream about 25 yards to the right, to the top of the falls.

The falls are a series of small cascades that descend a total of about 80 feet in a narrow gorge. Except in spring, when the snows are melting, there isn't much water. There is no point from which you can see all the cascades at once. To see the first one, cross the stream to its left bank and cautiously work your way down through the rocks. If you've become attuned to small and subtle pleasures, this place has a great deal of charm. The rocks are covered with mosses, lichen, and polypody. But the hillside is very steep. The ground is carpeted with needles of pine and hemlock, and sometimes dead leaves, so that the footing is treacherous and the descent must be classified as difficult. As I said, this trip is not for everyone. We have bigger falls that are easier to see. This is for the very few hikers who are willing to go to a lot of trouble to find solitude beside a small pool on a mountain stream.

The fire road continues beyond the falls, descending another 560 feet in 1.4 miles, to the Park boundary. But there's nothing to see or do down there, unless you're botanizing: several species of plants grow at low elevation, near the boundary, that you won't find on the mountain.

MILE 9.5, UNPAVED PARKING PULLOUT, west side. *Rock lovers only:* Park here and walk south (uphill) a little more than a hundred yards, to the rocks exposed on the east side of the Drive. These are "migmatitic, granitic gneiss" of the Pedlar formation. The bands of lighter-colored rock "define plunging folds." The nearly vertical bands are thickest, and easiest to see, near the downhill end of the exposure.

MILE 10.4, COMPTON GAP. Elevation 2,415 feet. Parking for several cars on the east side of the Drive. *A.T. crossing; Dickey Ridge Trail* access; *hikes.* See map below.

Dickey Ridge, on which the Drive has ascended to this point, joins the Blue Ridge here. The rest of the Drive follows the Blue Ridge near its crest. The Dickey Ridge Trail ends where it meets the Appalachian Trail, about a quarter of a mile to the north. The Compton family, for which the gap and Compton Peak were named, had its home near the present site of Indian Run Spring.

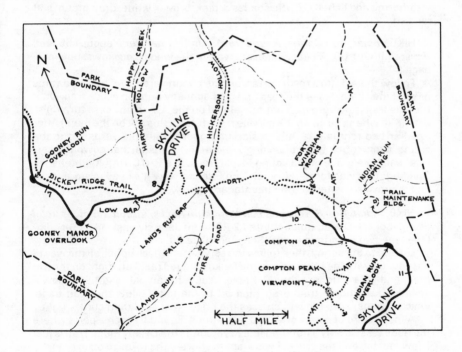

Map of Lands Run — Compton Gap Area

An old road crossed the mountain here. On the east side of the Drive it goes 2.2 miles north to the Park boundary; it serves as both fire road and, for most of this distance, as the A.T. On the other side of the Drive the old road turned right and descended into Lands Run; it has been abandoned for many years, and has nearly disappeared. The A.T. goes 2.0 miles south to Jenkins Gap, where a short side trail leads to Skyline Drive at Mile 12.35.

HIKE: *Fort Windham Rocks. Round trip* 0.8 mile; total *climb* about 130 feet; *time* required 0:55. An easy hike to an interesting rock formation. See map, page 89. Follow the A.T. (fire road) north for about a quarter of a mile, to its junction with the Dickey Ridge Trail, on the left, and a service road, on the right. Turn left on the Dickey Ridge Trail and walk 300 yards to Fort Windham Rocks.

At the left-hand edge of the trail is a large boulder, with a vertical split through the middle. Most of the rocks are on the right, but about a hundred feet from the trail and rising 45 to 50 feet above it. They are deeply split, and weathering rapidly. These rocks are all that remains of the Catoctin lavas here on the summit of Carson Mountain. A short distance from here, in any direction, the Pedlar granodiorite is exposed.

If you'd like a closer look at the rocks, continue past them on the trail, then go around behind them on the far side. Around back, where the rocks are crumbling, you'll see a fine display of the subtle colors that result from weathering and lichen growth: shades of pink, brown, white, gray-green, and reddish.

HIKE: *Indian Run Spring. Round trip* 1.0 mile; total *climb* about 165 feet; *time* required 1:00. An easy, pleasant walk in the woods; no views. See map, page 89.

Follow the A.T. (fire road) north from the parking area; two hundred yards beyond the chain, leave the road and go diagonally right on a side trail. Or, if the side trail is overgrown, continue ahead on the A.T. In any case turn right, downhill, when you get to the service road. (Check this out on the map.) After another two tenths of a mile, a side trail goes a hundred yards left to the spring. (Don't drink without boiling.) About 150 yards farther down the service road, in a grove of tall young locust trees, is a PATC Trail Maintenance Building. This was formerly Indian Run Shelter. Now it's used to store tools, and to provide shelter for trail maintenance workers.

HIKE: *Indian Run Spring* and *Fort Windham Rocks. Circuit 2.6 miles; total climb* about 340 feet; *time* required 2:20. A moderately easy hike that combines the two described above. See map, page 89.

Go first to the spring; then follow the service road back uphill, all the way to its junction with the fire road and the Dickey Ridge Trail. Turn right on the fire road, and go a little less than 0.3 mile. Watch for an old road trace (now a yellow-blazed horse trail) branching off to the left. Follow the road trace, which swings far to the left, crosses the ridge crest, and then curves right.

About a third of a mile after you leave the A.T., you'll reach a point where the ridge crest is only a hundred feet to your left. The Dickey Ridge Trail is just a few feet beyond the crest; if you want to shorten the hike, go on over to the trail and turn left. To walk the full distance, continue another 0.3 mile on the horse trail, to a point where it intersects the Dickey Ridge Trail.

Turn left on the Dickey Ridge Trail and go about a third of a mile to Fort Windham Rocks. (To climb them, leave the trail on the near side of the rocks and go around to the left; they're easy to climb from the side opposite the trail.) From Fort Windham Rocks, continue another 0.2 mile in the same direction on the Dickey Ridge Trail. Turn right on the A.T. (fire road) and go a quarter of a mile to your starting point.

HIKE: *Compton Peak. Round trip* 2.4 miles; total *climb* about 835 feet; *time* required 2:45. Views, and an outstanding example of columnar jointing. Most of the trail is fairly easy; but part of it is rather rough and rocky, and in one place it's quite steep. See map, page 89.

Take the Appalachian Trail on the west side of the Drive (the side opposite the parking area.) At the beginning, the exposed rocks are granodiorite. But 0.2 miles from the Drive you'll pass a large basalt boulder at the left of the trail — the first conspicuous evidence of the Catoctin lava that forms the crest of Compton Peak. In the next tenth of a mile you'll pass more boulders, in successively more advanced stages of disintegration, until you reach a point where the whole area, including the trail, is strewn with broken rock. This is the roughest part of the hike, but it's only about a hundred yards long.

The high point on the A.T. on Compton Mountain is 0.8 mile from the Drive. You'll see a concrete trail marker post there, and a side trail to right and left. Each goes about 0.2 mile to a viewpoint. Take the right-hand side trail first. After crossing the crest of Compton Peak, the trail goes a short distance down the northwest slope. The trail is rough and rocky here. Toward the end it's a little hard to follow, so watch the blue blazes. The viewpoint ledge is marked with a blue cross, meaning "this is it".

To the right of your view, the sharp crest in the distance is on the Blue Ridge outside the Park. To the left of it, and much closer, you can see Skyline Drive on the near side of Dickey Ridge, which takes a sharp turn to the right at Gooney Manor Overlook, near the left end of your view. On the highest part of Dickey Ridge is the tower of the F.A.A. radio beacon. From there the ridge descends to the right, toward the town of Front Royal. From a second, lower ledge, you can see farther to the right — including a part of the Piedmont.

Now return to the marker post, where the other side trail is directly across the A.T. It leads to a rather limited viewpoint; it's rather rough and rocky, and the last part of it is quite steep. If you skip it you can shorten the hike by 0.4 mile, and reduce the total climb by 230 feet. But I recommend that you go anyway, to see a fine example of columnar jointing. (This particular rock raised my interest in geology from near zero to the threshold of enthusiasm. Maybe it will do the same for you.)

Follow the blue blazes downhill to a boulder that rises ten or fifteen feet directly in front of you. Climb to the top. There's a view directly ahead, out into the Piedmont. The Blue Ridge goes to the right, with a good stretch of Skyline Drive, including Jenkins Gap Overlook, in view. Straight out from this rock, The Peak rises beyond the near ridge. At the right of your view are the two summits of Mount Marshall.

The blue blazes continue down the left side of the rock you're standing on, but I consider that route a little dangerous. To be cautious, climb down the rock the way you climbed up, and then go around it. You'll promptly pick up the blue blazes again. Follow them for about 50 yards, steeply downhill, to the base of the cliff. Then look up. The lava cracked into these prismatic columns when it cooled, some 800 million years ago. The thrusting force that formed these mountains tilted the columns to their present angle. During subsequent erosion, the downhill side of the cliff crumbled away, so that you now look up at the lower ends of the giant prisms.

MILE 10.8, INDIAN RUN OVERLOOK. Elevation 2,400 feet. You're looking across the hollow formed by Indian Run and, to the right, out into the Piedmont. The house and clearing on the opposite ridge are outside the Park. (To your right, down the hollow, the boundary is less than a quarter of a mile away.)

In winter, after a long cold spell, the rocks in the road cut across the Drive build up impressive displays of icicles and cascades of ice.

Geology: The rocks across the Drive from the overlook are a part of the first (oldest) lava flow of the Catoctin formation. They're worth a closer look. Even if you don't care for geology you can enjoy the subtle colors of the rocks, which vary from medium gray, tan, and rusty rose, to various shades of gray-green.

Near the north end of the rock cut, about 50 yards beyond the north end of the overlook, is a good display of columnar jointing that extends for about 50 feet along the Drive. The lava, when it cooled, cracked into 4-, 5-, or 6-sided prisms from four to ten inches across — some nearly vertical, some fanning outward. Near the south end of this display (nearest the overlook), stop and look up. Fifteen or twenty feet overhead are inclined columns that have broken off, so that you view them endways. This is the same effect that you see on a much larger scale under the ledge on Compton Mountain. (See Compton Peak hike, above.)

MILE 11.75, ROAD TRACE, east side. In winter, this could be mistaken for a trail head. It goes into the woods, curves left, parallels the Drive for 0.1 mile, and then disappears.

MILE 12.35, JENKINS GAP. Elevation 2,350 feet. *A.T. access; Bluff Trail* circuit hike. Plenty of parking space in the grass on the west side. An old road that went down the west side of the mountain to Browntown starts here. The first part is now a service road: 80 yards from the Drive is a dirt and gravel storage area on the right. The A.T. is less than 70 yards farther. Beyond the A.T. the road is now a yellow-blazed horse trail, which descends rather steeply to the Park Boundary.

Distances on the A.T., from its junction with the road trace: To the right (north) it's 2.0 miles to Compton Gap, Mile 10.4. To the left (south) it's 1.7 miles to the Drive crossing at Hogwallow Flats, Mile 14.2.

> HIKE: *A.T. and Bluff Trail. Circuit* 12.8 miles; total *climb* about 2,495 feet; *time* required 10:30. (See map, page 96; you're at the upper right corner of the map.) Because of its length and the amount of climbing, I've classified this hike as "difficult"; but no part of it is very steep, and it's only moderately rough. The route goes from the grassy parking area in Jenkins Gap, via the service road to the A.T., and then to the left, across both summits of Mount Marshall, to Gravel Spring Gap. Return via the Bluff Trail to the Mount Marshall Trail. Turn left, return to the Drive, turn right, and return to your starting point. As the map shows, you could start this hike at any of five points on the Drive. I've chosen to describe it only once, starting at Gravel Springs Gap, Mile 17.6. See page 97.

MILE 12.4, JENKINS GAP OVERLOOK. Elevation 2,355 feet. The gap is named for one of the early settlers. When the Park was created, sixteen families named Jenkins, owning a total of 850 acres, were displaced from this area. Most of them were descended from Timothy Jenkins, who was born about 1735.

From the overlook you have a narrow V-shaped view into the Piedmont. The hollow below the overlook is drained by the Burgess River, which divides just outside the Park boundary and flows off in two different directions. The high point to your left is Compton Peak. If you have binoculars, look a little way down and to the right from the highest point. The rock ledge there is one of the objectives of the Compton Peak hike, page 91.

MILE 12.5, MOUNT MARSHALL TRAIL, east side *Hikes.* You may park at Jenkins Gap Overlook (Mile 12.4) or on the grassy shoulder beside the Drive, between the overlook and the trail head. The Mount Marshall Trail is a former fire road, which is now closed to vehicles. Nevertheless it will look like a road for some years to come, and I have shown it as an unpaved road on the map, page 96.

HIKE: *The Peak. Round trip* 9.8 miles; total *climb* about 2,160 feet; *time* required 8:20. Parts of the trail are very rough and very steep. This is a difficult and not very rewarding hike. But if you collect trails the way some people collect postage stamps, you'll need this one for your collection. (See map, page 96. You're near the upper right corner of the map; The Peak is near bottom center.)

Follow the Mount Marshall Trail, mostly downhill, to Thorofare Gap in the saddle between Mount Marshall and The Peak, 3.9 miles from the Drive. There, on your left, are the yellow-blazed Jordan River Trail and the blue-blazed Peak Trail. Take the Peak Trail, which climbs steeply. A third of a mile from the Mount Marshall Trail, the Peak Trail forks, so as to form as a loop (see map). But the left-hand fork is steeper, and parts of it are dangerous because of loose rock. I suggest that you keep to the right-hand fork.

About half a mile beyond the fork, the trail turns sharp left, uphill. After another hundred yeards, look for a short side trail on the right; it leads to the "south lookout", with a view out through Harris Hollow to the Piedmont. The summit of The Peak is a little more than a tenth of a mile farther. There a second side trail on the right leads to the "north lookout", with a view along the Blue Ridge toward Compton Peak, and farther right to the Piedmont.

Note: Both "lookouts" were cleared by members of the Potomac Appalachian Trail Club. But vista clearing here had to be discontinued in 1976 when The Peak was included in the Wilderness Area. By the time you read this, both views may be completely blocked by trees.

On your return, you can save about two tenths of a mile by completing the loop. But it's safer to return to Thorofare Gap the way you came.

MILE 13.8, HOGWALLOW FLATS OVERLOOK. Elevation 2,665 feet. From here you have a wide view of the Piedmont, which extends 70 miles east to the coastal plain. The small town you see is Flint Hill — one of the seven resettlement areas into which mountain people were moved when the Park was created in the 1930's. The high point toward your right is The Peak.

Piedmont is from an Italian word meaning "foothill". It applies to any foothill region, but especially to the plateau between the Appalachian Mountains and the coastal plain — including parts of Virginia, the Carolinas, and Georgia. Waterfalls and rapids occur where rivers cross the *fall line* — the contact between the rocky, resistant Piedmont and the

softer, more easily eroded soils of the coastal plain. A number of major
cities were developed along the fall line, for two reasons: first, it was as far
inland as ships could navigate; second, the falls served as a source of
power.

Most of what you see from the overlook is in *Rappahannock County.*
About a fifth of the county's 274 square miles are within the Park. This is
the only county near Washington D.C. that has remained completely rural.
Its total population is considerably less than 6,000. It has no railroad, no
industry, no mobile homes, and no rural property of less than 25 acres. The
residents intend to keep it that way.

MILE 14.2, HOGWALLOW FLATS. Elevation 2,745 feet. *A.T. crossing.*
There's a grassy parking pullout on the west side of the Drive. Distance on
the A.T.: North (on the west side) it's 1.6 miles to Jenkins Gap, where an old
road leads a short distance to the Drive. South (on the east side) it's 2.1
miles, via the north summit of Mount Marshall, to the Drive crossing
between the two Marshalls at Mile 15.95.

MILE 14.9, BROWNTOWN VALLEY OVERLOOK. Elevation 2,890 feet.
Drinking fountain (turned off in winter.) To the left of your view is Hogback,
with a notch where the Drive crosses it at Hogback Overlook. Descending to
the right from Hogback is Gimlet Ridge. The view looks straight out across
the Browntown Valley to the Massanutten, with Signal Knob at its right-
hand end.

To the right you can see a part of Dickey Ridge. Browntown is visible from
the north end of the overlook, near the center of the view.

This overlook, and the Drive for a half mile or more to the south, lie on a
shelf formed by one of the many lava flows that now cap the two summits of
Mount Marshall.

MILE 15.95, A.T. CROSSING. Elevation 3,075 feet. *Hikes* to both peaks of
Mount Marshall, with a pleasant view from each. Distances on the A.T.:
North (on the east side) it's 2.1 miles to the Drive crossing at Hogwallow
Flats, Mile 14.2. South (on the west side) it's 1.6 miles to the Drive crossing
in Gravel Springs Gap, Mile 17.6.

HIKE: *North Marshall.* To the viewpoint, *round trip* 0.75 miles; total *climb*
about 105 feet; *time* required 0:45. To the summit, *round trip* 1.3 miles; total
climb about 295 feet; *time* required 1:15. An easy walk; the trail is mostly
smooth, and not steep.

Take the A.T. on the east side of the Drive, less than a hundred yards north
of the milepost. The trail is nearly level at the start, then climbs gradually with
a couple of switchbacks. Less than 0.4 mile from the start, the trail turns 90
degrees to the right. There, on your left, is a fine view from an open ledge with
a sheer drop of about 60 feet. To your left you can look over nearby Pignut
Mountain to higher, more distant peaks: the Pinnacle, Marys Rock, Stony
Man, Millers Head, and Pass Mountain. (If you'd like to identify them for
certain, see the right-hand end of the Range View Overlook sketch, page 95.)
Farther right and nearby you see a stretch of the Drive on south Marshall, with
Hogback beyond it. Continuing to the right: Browntown Valley, the
Shenandoah Valley, and then Dickey Ridge, with the Drive and two overlooks
in sight.

If you like, continue to the summit of North Marshall; there's no view from
the summit, but the trail is easy. A hundred yards beyond the first viewpoint is

a second, just off to the left. This view is not as wide as the first; but from late August to early October, the view is framed on the right by the bright red berries of mountain ash.

HIKE: *South Marshall.* To the viewpoint: *round trip* 1.6 miles; total *climb* about 295 feet; *time* required 1:20. A fairly easy walk; the trail is smooth, and not very steep.

Take the A.T. on the west side of the Drive, 200 feet north of Milepost 16. The trail climbs easily to the summit, where it flattens out for a while. There's no view from the summit. Keep going, and begin the descent on the far side. You'll pass several narrow, somewhat overgrown viewpoints on the right. Keep going. A hundred feet beyond the point where the trail jogs right, then left, (and a quarter of a mile beyond the summit), the trail turns left, and a side trail on the right goes 25 yards to the viewpoint ledge.

The view is not quite as wide as that from North Marshall. but I find it more exciting because the treetops below the ledge are a long ways down, so that the view includes a lot of pure mountain air. What you see from here is practically the same as what you see from North Marshall, except that you can't see South Marshall because you're standing on it.

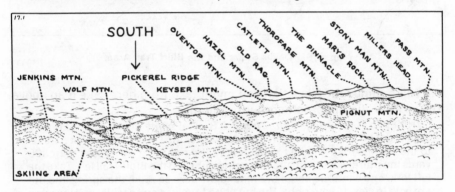

View from Range View Overlook.

MILE 17.1, RANGE VIEW OVERLOOK. Elevation 2,810 feet. Unless it's a very hazy day, be *sure* to stop here; this overlook is the superstar of the North Section. Toward the south-southwest you're looking lengthwise down the Blue Ridge, all the way to Stony Man, fourteen miles away. The sketch shows only about half the view. To the right of Pass Mountain, and considerably nearer, you can see Skyline Drive at Mount Marshall Overlook. Farther right, the high point with the radio towers is Hogback, from which Gimlet Ridge descends to the right. Beyond Gimlet Ridge you can see two ridges of the Massanutten and, sometimes, the Alleghenies far beyond.

MILE 17.6, GRAVEL SPRINGS GAP. Elevation 2,665 feet. *Hikes: A.T. crossing.* There's a small parking area on the east side of the Drive, with space for about six cars. Distances on the A.T.: North (on the west side of the Drive) it's 1.6 miles to the Drive crossing at Mile 15.95, on the saddle between the two peaks of Mount Marshall. South (on the east side) it's 1.3 miles to the Drive crossing at Mile 18.9.

The old Browntown-Harris Hollow Road crossed the mountain here. On the west side it's now yellow-blazed and classified as a horse trail. On the east it's used as the service road for Gravel Springs Hut.

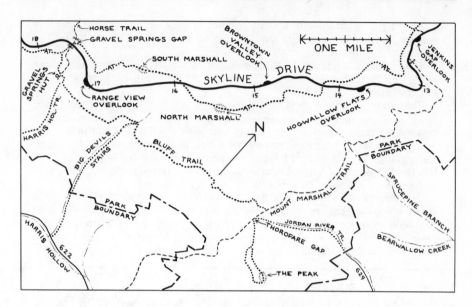

Map of Big Devils Stairs and the Bluff Trail Area.

I will outline four hikes that you might take from here. See map above. You're near the upper left corner of the map.

HIKE: *Gravel Springs Hut. Circuit* 0.8 mile; *climb* about 190 feet; *time* required 0.50. Take the A.T. on the east side of the Drive; it starts out parallel to the service road and just a few feet to the right of it. After less than 300 yards the trail divides, with the A.T. going right and the Bluff Trail left. Take the left fork, and continue about 0.2 mile to the service road; the spring and hut are both in view to your right. The hut has a fireplace and a table, and there's a pit toilet a short distance beyond it. The old Browntown-Harris Hollow road used to continue downhill beyond this point, in what is now an overgrown ditch in front of the hut.

Unverified report: The spring was the scene of considerable social activity in mountaineer days. Travellers crossing the mountain on the Browntown-Harris Hollow road could buy moonshine whiskey here. Water from the spring, or from another not far away, was used to make moonshine in the head of a nearby hollow.

You can return to your car the way you came or, for variety, make it a circuit hike by returning on the service road. It rejoins the A.T. at the parking area.

HIKE: *Big Devils Stairs. One way* 3.6 miles; total *climb* about 210 feet; *time* required 2:55. You can avoid the very strenuous return trip if you have a two-car hiking party, or a driver willing to meet you at the bottom. To reach the bottom of the trail: from Thornton Gap, Mile 31.5 on the Drive, take U.S. 211 east toward Washington. Pass through Sperryville, continue about 2.4 miles, and turn left on Va. 622. Go about five and a quarter miles on Va. 622 to Rush River Lodge, at the foot of the Big Devils Stairs Trail. They'll let you use their parking lot, which has room for about 25 cars.

From Gravel Springs Gap, start out as above (Gravel Springs Hut Hike.) Continue across the service road on the Bluff Trail, which from this point follows an old road trace. About 250 yards from the service road, the road trace makes a sharp switchback to the right. Leave the old road here and continue ahead, following the blue blazes down a rough, rocky, 75-yard shortcut. Rejoin the road trace, and turn left on it.

From here, the Bluff Trail continues through the disintegrating lava flows on the side of South Marshall. There were fine views along the trail when the Park was young, but now they're overgrown. About 0.4 mile beyond the shortcut, there's a ledge on the right; in the winter, when the leaves are down, there's a view through the bare branches, of a part of what you can see from Range View Overlook, which is more or less straight uphill from here. Continue 0.8 mile farther to the junction with the Big Devils Stairs Trail, about 1.4 miles from Gravel Springs. Turn right onto the trail, which follows an old road for a short distance and then turns left into the canyon.

The canyon is spectacular and steep, with cascades, waterfalls, and huge boulders between high sheer walls of rock. The original trail followed the stream. The present trail follows along the top of the gorge, on the left side of the stream. It's not as exciting as the old one, and not quite as strenuous; but it's a lot safer. And at several points the trail offers exciting views down into the canyon.

I think you'll enjoy this hike, even though you may be tired at the end of it. Because the canyon is deep and narrow it tends to be deeply shaded, with spotty sunlight, which makes photography difficult. For best results choose a light-overcast day, and use high-speed film.

After you cross the Park boundary, the trail is not steep. It continues for more than half a mile across private land. To keep the natives friendly, I suggest that you not wander far off the trail.

HIKE: *Big Devils Stairs,* to the bottom of the canyon and return. *Round trip* 5.7 miles; total *climb* about 1,850 feet; *time* required 6:50. As above, to the Park boundary; then return by the same route. As I said, this is an exhausting hike. But if there's only one driver in your party, I can't think of any other way to see the canyon.

HIKE: *Bluff Trail* and A.T. *Circuit* 12.8 miles; total *climb* about 2,495 feet; *time* required 10:30. This is a difficult hike because of its length and amount of climbing. Parts of the Bluff Trail are moderately rough. See map, page 96.

Unconfirmed report: "The Bluff" is the local name for Mount Marshall.

Follow the A.T. and Bluff Trail to the head of Big Devils Stairs, as described above. Continue on the Bluff trail for a little more than two miles, to the Mount Marshall trail (a former fire road). Turn left and follow the Mount Marshall trail, mostly uphill, to the Drive. Turn right on the Drive; pass Jenkins Gap Overlook, and go another hundred yards to a fire road and grassy area on the West side. Follow the fire road for less than 150 yards to the A.T., and turn left. The A.T. crosses the Drive (at Mile 14.1) and then climbs the north crest of Mount Marshall. There's no view from the top; but as you descend you reach a ledge on the right side of the trail, less than 0.3 mile beyond the summit, with a fine view. (See page 94.)

Cross the Drive (at Mile 15.95) and ascend the south peak of Mount Marshall. Again, there's no view from the summit. But after you descend a quarter of a mile on the far side, the trail turns to the left, and a side trail on the right leads 25 yards to a good viewpoint. Continue downhill until the A.T. joins another fire road. Turn left, cross the Drive, and you are at your starting point.

MILE 18.4, GIMLET RIDGE OVERLOOK. Elevation 2,675 feet. The view is straight out toward Signal Knob, at the right-hand end of the Massanutten. Farther to the right you can look across the Browntown Valley and the Shenandoah Valley. The sketch shows the right-hand end of the view, beginning just to the right of Browntown. The cliff on South

Marshall, shown at the right end of the sketch, has a very worthwhile view, and it's an easy walk from Mile 15.95 on the Drive. (See page 95.)

To your left, the high peak with the radio towers is Hogback, with Gimlet Ridge descending to the right of it. Gooney Run, which drains the Browntown Valley, flows away from you — past Browntown and out through the notch between Dickey Ridge and the last of the three small

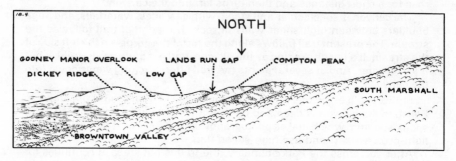

View to right from Gimlet Ridge Overlook.

hills that enclose the Browntown Valley on the left. These hills, with nearly the same elevation and almost equally spaced, are, from left to right, Round Mountain, Long Mountain, and Buck Mountain.

MILE 18.9, A.T. CROSSING. Elevation 2,805 feet. There's parking space in the grass, on the east side. Distances on the A.T.: North (on the east side of the Drive) it's 1.3 miles to Gravel Springs Gap, Mile 17.6. South (on the west side) it's 0.6 mile to Little Hogback Overlook, Mile 19.7.

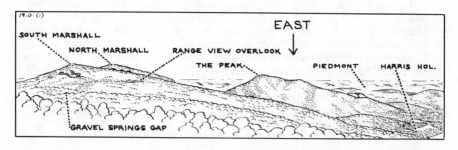

View from Mount Marshall Overlook. (No. 1)

MILE 19.0, MOUNT MARSHALL OVERLOOK. Elevation 2,850 feet. The view is wide, and I've used two sketches to show it. The first one shows the left part of the view, from the Marshalls to Harris Hollow, which is a little to the left of straight out from the overlook. The cliffs on both Marshalls provide fine views, and can be easily reached from Mile 15.95. The hike to The Peak from Mile 12.5 is more strenuous and less rewarding.

Report: People who live in the Piedmont near here call Mount Marshall "Big Bastard", and The Peak "Little Bastard."

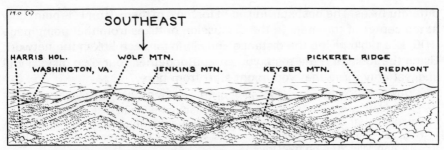

View from Mount Marshall Overlook. (No. 2.)

In the second sketch, the hollow between Jenkins Mountain and Keyser Mountain is locally called Gib Brown Hollow, though I can't find that name on the maps. In both Gib Brown and Harris hollows you can see trees in rows. These are some of the apple orchards for which Rappahannock County is famous.

Geology: Note that The Peak, Wolf Mountain, Jenkins Mountain, and Keyser Mountain, all of which you can see from here, are separated by gaps from the main Blue Ridge. From overlooks farther south you can see that Pignut, Fork Mountain, and Oventop are similarly separated from the main ridge. A fault line passes through the gaps that separate these mountains from the ridge. It was not movement along the fault that caused the separation; but such movement shattered and weakened the rocks, and made them more susceptible to erosion.

History. As I've mentioned, Lord Fairfax kept seignorial rights to several huge estates in this area. One of these was the Manor of Leeds, which consisted of 119,927 acres, including the two peaks of Mount Marshall and lands to the east and north.

Lord Fairfax must have seen the American Revolution coming, for in 1767 he "conveyed" his estates to his nephew, who promptly "conveyed" them back. Thus Fairfax acquired a private title, as well as a seignorial title, to his lands. After the revolution the seignorial title was worthless, but the private title remained valid.

Fairfax died in 1781. His heir later sold the estates to a syndicate of speculators, who divided the land among them. The speculator that got the Manor of Leeds was John Marshall, who was Chief Justice of the United States from 1801 to 1835. The two Mount Marshalls are named for him.

MILE 19.4, KEYSER RUN FIRE ROAD, east side. *A.T. access,* west side. *Hikes.* There's a small parking area beside the fire road, a few feet from the Drive. *Note:* This is the former Jinney Gray fire road. The name was changed in 1980 on the grounds that nobody knows who Jinney Gray was.

Legend: Jinney Gray was a mountain girl who was so friendly that mountain men beat a path to her door. In the late 1930's the Civilian Conservation Corps made the path into a road, even though Jinney was no longer there.

Look at the map on page 107, and note that I've given a separate letter of the alphabet to each trail junction. You're at point "A", at right center of the map, at one end of a network of trails and roads that offer a dozen or more different hikes. The best starting point for most of them, I think, is point "L", at top center of the map. In the discussion of hikes from that point, page 106, is a table giving the distance and climb for each link in the network. Using the table and the map, you can put together your own hikes. I will suggest only three that you might start from here.

HIKE: *Keyser Run, Piney Branch, A.T. Circuit* 6.8 miles; total *climb* about 1,145 feet; *time* required 5:30. This is a medium-difficult hike. None of it is very steep, and only a few stretches are rough. (The only views are from Hogback and Little Hogback Mountains, which are easily reached from Mile 19.7 and Mile 20.4 on the Drive.)

Follow the Keyser Run Road, mostly downhill, for exactly a mile to *fourway*. Here the Little Devils Stairs Trail goes left, and the Pole Bridge Link goes right. Turn right. The Pole Bridge Link is nearly level, following an old road trace most of the way; it goes exactly one mile to point "J". Turn right here, onto the Piney Branch Trail, and cross the stream at the site of the former 'pole bridge'. (Note on the map, page 107, that you have the option of a "shortcut" via another old road trace.)

From "J" the trail is steep and rather rough for a short distance, until it joins the old road trace. From there to point "K" it's mostly smooth, and gently uphill. At "K" the Piney Branch Trail and the A.T. meet at the edge of the service road for Range View Cabin. Turn right, doubling back onto the A.T. Cross and the Drive at point "M" on the map, with Rattlesnake Point Overlook in view to the right. Ascend easily past the summit of Sugarloaf; pass the junction with the Big Blue Trail on the left, and then cross the first of the four humps of Hogback.

Cross the Drive and climb the second hump. A short side trail on the left leads to some large granite boulders above Hogback Mountain Overlook, with a view down the crest of Gimlet Ridge and, to the right, Browntown Valley and Dickey Ridge. Descend, cross the Drive, and climb the third and highest hump of Hogback. On the summit are antenna towers of various radio systems, including the one used by the Park rangers. There's no view from here; but descend about 150 yards on the far side of the summit, and watch for a short side trail leading to a viewpoint at the left. (This point has been used as a hang-glide launching site, because the slope is abrupt.) Straight ahead you can look down the Browntown Valley to Front Royal, with Dickey Ridge ascending to the right. On your left, Gimlet Ridge descends from the high point on Hogback.

Continue across the fourth hump of Hogback, and descend to Little Hogback Overlook. About 125 yards beyond the overlook, with the summit of Little Hogback on your right, the A.T. takes a sharp right turn; straight ahead a side trail leads to a ledge with a view similar to that from the hang-glide launch site. Continue on the A.T. for another quarter of a mile, and watch for the side trail that will take you back to your starting point.

HIKE: *Little Devils Stairs. Round trip* 4.8 miles, total *climb* about 1,585 feet; *time* required 5:15. This hike takes you to the bottom of the canyon, and back again by the same route; it requires a fairly strenuous effort. (There is a small parking area at point "D" on the map. If you can get some one to meet you there, you can make this a one-way hike and save a lot of climbing.) Little Devils Stairs is very much like Big Devils Stairs (page 96), and not a great deal smaller.

Take the Keyser Run Road, mostly downhill, for one mile to "Fourway" (point "B" on the map). Turn left onto the Little Devils Stairs Trail, which descends and curves right, down to the stream. Just to your left at this point is a small waterfall. The trail turns right and descends beside the stream, crossing it many times (more than I've shown on the map.) The next mile is pure rock scramble, with no relief. You climb over boulders in a narrow gorge between high rock walls, beside an almost endless series of cascades. The going is a little easier if you watch for and follow the blue blazes, but it doesn't really matter. There is no trail, only a suggested route for your rock scramble. and there's no way you can get lost while you're hemmed in by sheer rock walls.

The stream crossings aren't difficult because the stream is small. But the rocks can be deceptively slippery, even when they're dry. Use caution, especially on the way *down* the gorge. (For some reason the footing seems a little more reliable on the way up.) If it's raining, or if there's snow or ice on the rocks, I suggest that you call the whole thing off.

At the bottom of the gorge (point "C" on the map), the trail flattens out and swings to the right, away from the stream. Turn back here.

HIKE: *Little Devils Stairs. Circuit* 7.7 miles, total *climb* about 1,845 feet; *time* required 7:15. This hike goes down the gorge and then returns by fire roads. Because of its length and the amount of climbing, it's a fairly difficult hike.

As above, to the foot of Little Devils Stairs, at point "C" on the map, page 107. The trail swings to the right, away from the water. Look for evidence of the mountain people who once lived here: a split rail fence, an old stone wall, and rock abutments where a bridge once crossed the stream. (I have a report that the bridge was built by the CCC, not the mountain people.) Continue to point "D" on the map, where you will find a small parking area beside the Keyser Run Road.

Turn right on the road; pass the posts and chain at the Park boundary, and continue to the junction at point "E", 1.4 miles from "D". Turn right. The Bolen cemetery is now in sight, diagonally ahead on your right. As you can imagine, it once was fairly elegant; but now the wall is crumbling, and the gate is off its hinges. Inside the wall are 21 inscribed markers of marble or granite, and a dozen fieldstone markers. No one has been buried here since the Park was created. The Bolens were relatively prosperous farmers, millers, and blacksmiths. Two Bolen families, owning a total of 795 acres, were displaced from this area when the Park was established.

Continue on the Keyser Run Road, mostly uphill, another 3.3 miles to your starting point. Note on the map that, about half a mile before you get to Fourway, the road makes a 90-degree turn to the left. After you make the turn, if you're not too tired, look off to the right for a view of the cliffs that border Little Devils Stairs.

NOTE: You can, of course, take this circuit hike in the opposite direction. As I've said, it's a little safer to climb *up* the canyon than down, and going up gives you a better view of the cascades. The clockwise circuit, as I've described it, has the advantage of doing the hard part first, before you get too tired.

MILE 19.7, LITTLE HOGBACK OVERLOOK. Elevation 3,035 feet. *A.T. access.* Short walk to *viewpoint.* The overlook itself provides a narrow view down the Browntown Valley. At your left, the crest of Hogback Mountain rises above the treetops. The summit of Little Hogback is out of sight in the woods, about 500 feet to your right. The A.T. passes below the overlook, 25 yards beyond the wall. And 25 yards beyond the A.T., the slope drops off steeply into the Browntown Valley.

Access to the A.T. is via a 25-yard trail at the north end of the overlook (that's the right-hand end, as you face the Valley.) Distances on the A.T.: North (straight ahead from the end of the access trail) it's 0.6 mile to the

Drive crossing at Mile 18.9. South (a sharp double-back to the left from the end of the access trail) it's 1.2 miles to the Drive crossing at Mile 20.8, at the north end of Hogback Overlook.

The *round trip* to the *viewpoint* is a little less than 0.2 mile, with a *climb* of about 80 feet. Take the connecting trail at the north end of the overlook and continue in the same direction on the A.T. to where it makes a sharp right turn. A side trail goes straight ahead here, fifteen yards to the viewpoint. The view is straight out through the Browntown Valley to the north end of the Massanutten. Dickey Ridge ascends to the right; Browntown is in a line between you and the high point on Dickey Ridge. Hogback is at your left, with Gimlet Ridge descending from it to the hills that close off the Browntown Valley on the west.

MILE 20.1, LITTLE DEVILS STAIRS OVERLOOK. Elevation 3,120 feet. There's a wide view here; the sketch shows only a part of it. At your left are the two Marshalls, visible over the top of Little Hogback. Farther right is The Peak, then a view over the mouth of Harris Hollow to the town of Washington, Va., and then Jenkins Mountain, where the sketch begins.

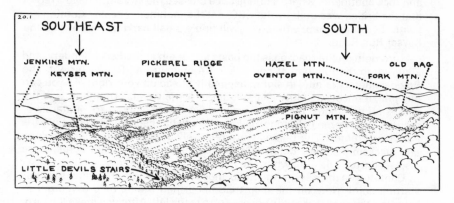

View from Little Devils Stairs Overlook.

To the right of Old Rag (at the right-hand edge of the sketch) are several peaks in the Central Section that are better seen from Rattlesnake Point Overlook, Mile 21.9. They are identified in the sketch on page 105.

Little Devils Stairs is in the gorge directly in front of the overlook. You can't see the bottom of it, but with binoculars you can make out some of the ledges at the top of the cliff that forms the left wall of the gorge. Little Devils Stairs is a very rewarding, if somewhat strenuous hike from Mile 19.4.

Geology: Note that, as I mentioned earlier, Keyser Mountain, Pignut Mountain, Fork Mountain, and Oventop are all set off from the main Blue Ridge by low gaps. These gaps, like those that mark off Jenkins Mountain and The Peak farther north, are the result of relatively rapid erosion along a geological fault.

The rocks in the road cut across the Drive are granodiorite, which is well exposed here.

MILE 20.4, SPRING; HIKE TO HOGBACK SUMMIT. Plenty of parking in the grass on the west side of the Drive.

HIKE: *Hogback Summit. Circuit* 1.0 mile; total *climb* about 250 feet; *time* required 1:00. A fairly easy short hike, with a view. The trail is somewhat rocky in places. It starts into the woods from the marker post at the edge of the grass. About a hundred feet from the Drive it passes a boxed-in spring on the left. (This is the source of Piney River.) The trail curves left around the spring, then makes a sharp right turn and climbs the ridge. When you reach the A.T. on the ridge crest, turn left. Less than 50 yards from the junction, a short side trail on the right leads to a viewpoint at the top of a very steep slope, where the powerline (which provides power for the radio transmitters on Hogback summit) descends steeply into the Valley.

There's a better view farther on: less than 100 yards from the trail junction, a side trail on the right leads to a ledge where a clearing was made for a hang-glide launch site. The ridge descends very steeply into the Browntown Valley, with an exciting, open view. Straight ahead in the distance is Front Royal, with Dickey Ridge ascending to the right. On the left, the ridge that descends from Hogback splits into Gimlet Ridge, on the right, and Mathews Arm, on the left. Return to the A.T. and, if you wish, go back the way you came; there are no more views.

To complete the circuit continue on the A.T., and reach the summit of Hogback by a short, easy climb. The summit, elevation 3,474, is the highest point in the North Section. There are radio transmitters of several State and Federal Government Agencies: GSA, the Virginia Division of Forestry, Virginia State Police, and Shenandoah National Park. You will also see the four concrete piers that once supported a fire tower. On the far side of the summit descend, on either the A.T. or the service road, to the Drive at Mile 20.8. Turn left and walk 0.4 mile beside the Drive to your starting point. The grass is fairly wide, so that you can walk a safe distance from the pavement.

MILE 20.8, A.T. CROSSING. On the west side of the Drive is the service road for the radio installations on Hogback summit. Don't park here; continue to the overlook, just a few feet to the south.

MILE 20.8 to 21.0, HOGBACK OVERLOOK. Elevation 3,385 feet. This overlook offers a couple of short, easy *hikes*, as well as a view. It's the longest overlook in the Park; to see the whole view you have to stop somewhere near the middle of it; or stop twice — once at each end.

From the middle of the overlook you look down on the crest of Gimlet Ridge, which curves to the right as it descends. Splitting off to the left from Gimlet Ridge is Mathews Arm. And in the hollow on the near side of Mathews Arm is Overall Run, which has the highest waterfall in the Park. It's a moderately strenuous hike from the A.T. crossing at Mile 21.1, just to the south of the overlook, or from Mathews Arm Campground, Mile 22.2.

Beyond Gimlet Ridge, across the Valley, are the two ridges of the Massanutten, with Fort Valley between them. Beyond the Massanutten, if the air is very clear, you can make out at least three ridges of the Alleghenies. It's said that, on a clear day, you can see eleven bends of the Shenandoah River, though I've never counted that many. The nearest bend of the river is a little more than half a mile lower than the overlook.

The view to the right is similar to that from Gimlet Ridge Overlook (see sketch, page 98), except that from here you can see the radio towers on the crest of Hogback Mountain.

If you have binoculars, and it's a clear day, relax and spend time on details of the view. This is especially enjoyable in late afternoon, when the slanting light makes each object stand out in sharp relief.

Geology: The rocks exposed across the Drive are coarse-grained granodiorite of the Pedlar formation. The grain is best seen near the north end of the overlook, where the rocks are less weathered. *Rock lovers only:* go to the north end of the paved walk that runs along the wall. Turn around, walk 150 feet, then cross the Drive. There you'll find a boulder with a network of purple veins. These are iron-oxide stains caused by weathering in ancient cracks, nearly a billion years ago. The cracks have since been "healed" by heat and pressure.

HIKE: *Hogback Overlook* and *A.T. Circuit* 0.7 mile; total *climb* about 100 feet; *time* required 0:35. An easy, pleasant walk. On the paved walkway at the overlook, walk south (i.e. with the view on your right.) Continue to the A.T. crossing, about 200 yards beyond Milepost 21. Cross the Drive and take the A.T. uphill. From the edge of the Drive it's a little more than 200 yards to the summit — the crest of one of the four humps that make up Hogback Mountain. A hundred feet beyond the summit is a side trail that goes a hundred feet to the left, to the boulders above the overlook. There's a view from the boulders, but not as good as the view from the overlook.

Continue downhill on the A.T. and cross the Drive (with caution, because of the blind curve on your left.) If you wish, continue ahead on the service road (see Hogback Summit Hike, below.) If not, turn left and walk in the grass, back to the overlook and your starting point.

HIKE: *Hogback Summit. Round trip* 0.4 mile; total *climb* about 115 feet; *time* required 0:25. If you're curious about the radio towers on the summit of Hogback, up to the right of your view from the overlook, the walk to the top is short and easy. (You can get there by a slightly longer circuit route from Mile 20.4.)

From the north end of the overlook, continue north on the Drive for a short distance, then turn left on the service road. The road and the A.T. are more or less parallel, and you can take your choice. On the summit are radio transmitting towers of various State and Federal Government agencies, including the Park. There is no view from the summit. If you want to lengthen the hike a little, continue on the A.T. down the far side of the crest for about 160 yards, to a side trail on the left that goes 25 yards to a hang-glide launch site. There, at the top of a very steep slope, you have a view out into the Browntown Valley, with Gimlet Ridge to the left and Dickey Ridge to the right. If you go to the launch site, the total *round trip* from the edge of the Drive will be 0.6 mile, and the total *climb* about 195 feet.

MILE 21.1, A.T. CROSSING. *Hike to Overall Run Falls.* There is parking space in the grass on the west side of the Drive. Distances on the A.T.: South (on the west side of the Drive) it's one mile to the Drive crossing at Mile 22.0, with Rattlesnake Point Overlook in sight to the left. North (on the east side) it's 1.5 miles to Little Hogback Overlook, Mile 19.7.

HIKE: *Overall Run Falls. Semi-circuit* 6.5 miles; total *climb* about 1,850 feet; *time* required 6:00. This is a fairly difficult hike; part of the trail is moderately steep, and part is rough and rocky. (If you're staying at Mathews Arm Campground, you might prefer the shorter and easier hike from the campground. See page 110. The access road to the campground is closed in winter.)

Take the A.T. south, on the west side of the Drive. (See map, page 110; you're near the right-hand edge of the map, a little above center.) About a third of a mile from the start, turn right onto the blue-blazed Big Blue Trail, which after a short distance becomes moderately steep and rocky. At 0.7 mile from the A.T., at a concrete marker post, the Big Blue Trail turns 90 degrees to the right. (The trail that continues ahead goes about a hundred yards, then connects with the "Traces" nature trail that encircles the campground.)

From the junction, the Big Blue trail continues 1.6 miles to the Mathews Arm fire road. Turn right on the fire road, go less than a hundred yards, then turn left onto the Big Blue/Overall Run Trail. The trail descends and, after about a tenth of a mile, a short side trail branches off to the left. It leads fifty yards or so to a small overlook with a close view of the upper falls, which has a total drop of 29 feet. Like nearly all of the waterfalls in the Park it's a cascade down the face of the rock, rather than a sheer plunge.

Return to the main trail and continue downhill, less steeply now. The trail goes close to the edge of a steep gorge. Watch for one or more short side trails on the left. They lead to viewpoints at the top of the gorge, from which you can see the big falls — the highest in the Park. Like the smaller one, it's a cascade down the face of the rocks; the total drop is 93 feet. When there's plenty of water it's a beautiful sight. In an unusually dry summer there's little or no water here.

From one of the viewpoints a blue-blazed trail descends to the base of the falls. This trail is extremely rough going, hazardous in wet or icy weather, and infested with rattlesnakes. Not worth the risk and effort.

Return uphill to the fire road, and turn right. To add a little variety and make this hike a semi-circuit, continue on the fire road for a little more than 1.1 miles, to where the Traces Trail crosses. (Take another look at the map, page 110.) Turn left on the Traces Trail and walk 0.6 mile to the junction with the connecting link. Turn left and go about a hundred yards to the junction with the Big Blue Trail, which comes in from the left. Continue straight ahead, uphill. Turn left when you reach the A.T., and go another third of a mile to your starting point.

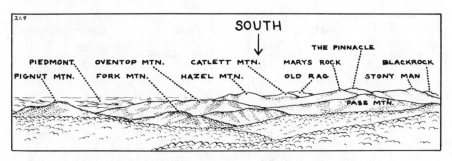

View to Right from Rattlesnake Point Overlook

MILE 21.9, RATTLESNAKE POINT OVERLOOK. Elevation 3,105 feet. There's a wide view from here; the sketch shows only the right-hand half of it. At the far left of the view is Hogback Mountain, with its radio antennas. The Peak appears over the ridge that descends to the right from Hogback. Pignut Mountain, where the sketch begins, is a little to the right of straight out from the overlook. About halfway between The Peak and Pignut is Jenkins Mountain. You're not likely to see Blackrock (at the right-hand edge of the sketch) except in winter; it's near Big Meadows Lodge, nearly 18 miles away.

Geology: Across from the north (uphill) end of the overlook, and extending north from there, is a good exposure of the Catoctin basalt. Weathering and lichens have created a muted display of color, from pale tan and green to dark green and brownish purple. The rocks nearest the overlook are vesiculated. Bubble cavities in the lava were later filled by other minerals: white, light and dark green, and even pink. This is easy to see at the lower levels where the rock is freshly broken.

MILE 22.0, A.T. CROSSING. The crossing is about a hundred yards north of the milepost. Don't park here; you can't pull a safe distance off the pavement. There's ample safe parking in the grass across from the entrance to the Piney River ranger area, a tenth of a mile to the south.

MILE 22.1, SERVICE ROAD, east side; entrance to *Piney River Ranger Station. Hikes.* If you need ranger help, turn into the road on the east side of the Drive and go about a tenth of a mile to the junction; the ranger office is in the trailer diagonally ahead on your right. If you're going to hike, park in the grass on the west side of the Drive.

Look at the map on page 107; you are at point "L", near top center of the map, on the edge of a network of trails and fire roads. A dozen or more circuit hikes are possible, I'll describe only one of them — the Piney Ridge and Piney Branch circuit — here. (See page 100 for hikes to Little Devils Stairs.) If you'd like to plan your own hike, use the following table to calculate the total distance and climb. Note that the amount of climbing between two trail junctions depends on which way you're going; it includes the net change in elevation, as well as the ups-and-downs in the trail. From "A" to "M", for example, the total climb is 795 feet; while from "M" to "A" it's only 630 feet.

From	To	Dist. miles	Climb feet	From	To	Dist. miles	Climb feet
A	B	1.0	15	H	G	0.4	285
A	M	2.9	795	H	I	0.5	110
B	A	1.0	265	I	H	0.5	5
B	C	1.4	20	I	J	2.5	1095
B	F	1.9	25	I	N	3.3	1475
B	J	1.0	25	J	B	1.0	170
C	B	1.4	1285	J	I	2.5	55
C	D	0.6	5	J	K	1.5	470
D	C	0.6	235	K	J	1.5	15
D	E	1.4	715	K	L	0.3	85
E	D	1.4	20	K	M	0.4	5
E	F	0.4	95	K	N	0.4	10
E	G	0.4	0	L	K	0.3	5
F	B	1.9	730	L	M	0.2	25
F	E	0.4	0	M	A	2.9	630
F	G	0.8	10	M	K	0.4	0
G	E	0.4	205	M	L	0.2	0
G	F	0.8	310	N	I	3.3	60
G	H	0.4	0	N	K	0.4	90

HIKE: *Piney Ridge-Piney Branch. Circuit* 8.3 miles; total *climb* about 1,725 feet; *time* required 7:25. A rather difficult and tiring hike. In some places the trail is very rough. There are four stream crossings, and except in a dry season they are troublesome. Features: a woods hike, with no views; a mountaineer cemetery and homesite; a stream, with two small waterfalls and numerous cascades and pools. Since this is a circuit hike, you can go in either direction. But if you go counterclockwise, as I describe it here, there's less chance of mistaking road traces for the trail. And the steepest part of the hike will be downhill.

From point "L" at top center of the map on this page, your route will be K-N-I-J-K-L. Cross the Drive and follow the service road on the east side, swinging around to the left, past the residential area and past the chain, until you pick up the A.T. and Piney Branch trails at point "K" on the map. (You will

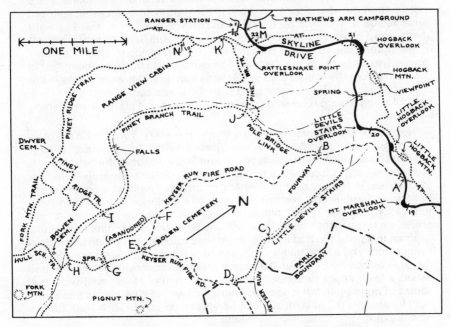

Map of Piney Branch and Little Devils Stairs area.

return to this point via the Piney Branch Trail.) Continue on the service road to point "N", the beginning of the Piney Ridge Trail. (If you follow the service road a hundred yards farther, to its end, you'll come to the locked Range View Cabin, which has a pit toilet, also locked, and a spring. Please keep your distance if the cabin is occupied. But you can occupy it yourself if you wish. Write to Potomac Appalachian Trail Club, 1718 N St., N.W., Washington, D.C. 20036.

From point "N" on the map, the Piney Ridge Trail goes along near the crest of the ridge for two miles. Its blue-blazed, relatively open, and smooth compared with what's coming later. Most of the trees are black locust, pine, and other pioneer species. When the Peak was established this area was a goat pasture, with only a few trees left for shade; views from the ridge crest, they tell me, were spectacular. There are many pine trees along the trail — all of them younger than the Park, and much younger than the name of the ridge.

A little less than two miles after you leave the service road, the Dwyer family cemetery is 200 feet off to your right. It's about 25 yards square, surrounded by a falling-down wire fence, and in the process of returning to wilderness. No effort will be made to maintain it. There are two metal markers, and eleven inscribed stones of marble or granite, plus a dozen or more uninscribed fieldstone markers. The most recent burial was in 1927. According to one of the markers, Mary G. Dwyer died in 1867 at the age of 75. Some of the graves marked with uninscribed fieldstone may be older. When the Park was established, seven families of Dwyers, owning a total of 850 acres, were displaced.

Fifty yards farther down the Piney Ridge trail is a double blue blaze (which means be alert for a change in direction). On the right, two large stones mark the former entrance road to the cemetery. (If you want to see the cemetery, but missed it, you can find it from here. Turn around, facing back the way you came. It's now 45 degrees on your left, and about 100 yards away.)

A hundred feet beyond the first double blaze is a second double blaze, and a trail junction. An abandoned trail goes to the right, with a decaying split-rail fence beside it. The Fork Mountain Trail follows an old road trace straight ahead, and a mile from the start dead-ends at the Hull School Trail (lower left on the map, page 107.) The Hull School Trail descends to meet the Piney Branch Trail at point "H" on the map. The cemetery to the left of point "H" is not visible from the trail; it's 50 to 75 yards uphill, in the woods. This is the Bowen cemetery (not to be confused with the Bolen cemetery at point "E"). It's well along toward returning to wilderness; the stone markers are leaning or fallen.

Now, back to the junction near the Dwyer cemetery. Turn left on the blue-blazed trail. In the next 300 yards you'll pass a former "ghost forest" of large chestnut trees, all of them now fallen. About 200 yards after the trail begins to descend steeply, you come to a former clearing, still fairly open, and a number of rockpiles. There was a homesite here, on the left. The rocks were cleared by hand from garden and pasture. There is still evidence of habitation here: foundations, broken brick, tile, and crockery; a walnut tree, and an old grapevine three inches thick. Explore if you wish, but don't collect souvenirs.

From this point the trail follows an old road trace for a short distance, then swings right and a little uphill, while the road trace continues ahead. Watch the blue blazes here. About 0.9 mile beyond the homesite, where the trail makes a fairly sharp switchback to the right, another rather well-worn trail comes in on the left; but it goes nowhere. Follow the blue-blazed trail to the right for another 0.2 mile, until it dead-ends at the Piney Branch Trail. You are now at point "I" on the map. Turn left.

Less than 300 yards from the junction is the first stream crossing. On the other side, the trail swings left and follows a dry stream bed for a short distance, then actually becomes a branch of the stream, so that you have to walk beside the trail rather than on it. This is very rough going, but there's only about 500 feet of it. Watch for a double blue blaze, where the trail swings right and becomes a little smoother.

The second stream crossing is 0.6 mile from the first; some 50 yards before the crossing is a waterfall on the left—a double cascade with a total drop of about 25 feet. (A guess; I didn't measure it.) Three hundred yards after the second crossing, look for a somewhat smaller waterfall down to the right. The trail follows an old road trace here, and during the rest of the hike it will repeatedly join and leave old road traces.

After another stream crossing, the trail continues for a mile and a third to the junction at point "J" on the map. During most of this distance the stream is down to your left, often out of sight. Which is too bad, because it has many attractive small cascades. Walking beside the stream is rough going, and will take more time than walking on the trail. But if you have time and energy to spare, you may enjoy it.

Turn left at point "J" and cross the stream for the last time. Join the short connecting trail that comes in on your right. Continue uphill another 1.2 miles to the service road at point "K" on the map. As you go, the trees become younger and younger, until it's obvious that you're in a former clearing. If you pass some rusting oil drums and other junk, they have nothing to do with the mountain people who once lived here. This is refuse that was abandoned when the CCC left the Park about 1942. The junk is gradually being cleaned up, and I hope it will be gone when you read this.

At point "K" turn right on the service road and follow it back to your car.

MILE 22.2, ENTRANCE ROAD, west side, for MATHEWS ARM CAMP-GROUND. (Closed in winter.) On your left as you approach the entrance station, 0.7 mile from the Drive, is the beginning of a trail to Elkwallow Wayside and Campstore. See map below. On your right you'll see a parking area, from which short walkways lead to the amphitheater where the evening campfire programs are given. The "Traces" self-guiding nature trail begins at the edge of the parking area.

After you pass the entrance station, turn right to enter the campground, or turn left to reach the trailer sewage disposal facility and the beginning of the Knob Mountain Trail.

I will describe three hikes that you can start from the campground.

HIKE: *Traces Trail. Circuit* 1.7 miles; total *climb* about 335 feet; *time* required 1:40. The trail begins at the edge of the amphitheater parking area, and encircles the campground. The hike is self-guiding; get a pamphlet from the dispenser near the trail head. This is an easy walk on a smooth trail, which

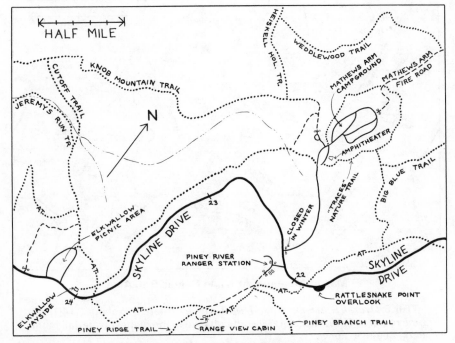

Map of Mathews Arm and Elkwallow Area

is moderately steep in a few spots. The "traces" are evidence left by the mountain people who once lived here; old roads, overgrown fields, rock piles and walls, and the remains of a mountaineer homesite. There are several junctions along the trail, but at each of them a marker post or a small sign on a tree tells you which way to go.

HIKE: *Knob Mountain,* Jeremys Run, and Elkwallow. *Circuit* 5.8 miles; total *climb* about 1,130 feet; *time* required 4:30. A moderately difficult hike through the woods; no views, but a variety of forest environments. Part of the trail is rough; another part is quite steep. See map, page 109.

The trail starts from the end of the loop at the trailer sewage dump. It was formerly a fire road all the way to the summit of Knob Mountain; but because it's in a Wilderness Area it has been closed to vehicles and reclassified as a trail. It goes along the east side of the mountain, mostly downhill. At about two and a third miles from the start the trail is on the crest of a ridge, at a low point between two knobs, in a former clearing. Turn left there, onto the cutoff trail.

The cutoff trail descends steeply at first, then less so, to the upper end of Jeremys Run. Cross the stream, reach the junction with the Jeremys Run Trail. Continue ahead, uphill. In less than half a mile join the A.T., which comes in from the right. Pass a service road on the right. After another tenth of a mile, keep left at the trail junction. (Ahead, on the right fork, it's less than a hundred yards to the Elkwallow Picnic Area.) Three tenths of a mile beyond the junction, you reach the trail that goes from Mathews Arm Campground to Elkwallow. Turn left here.

The rest of the hike, about 1.9 miles, is mostly a gentle uphill climb. For most of its length the trail follows an old woods road, and is in fairly good condition. Only the last 200 yards of it, just before you reach the campground road, are somewhat rough and rocky.

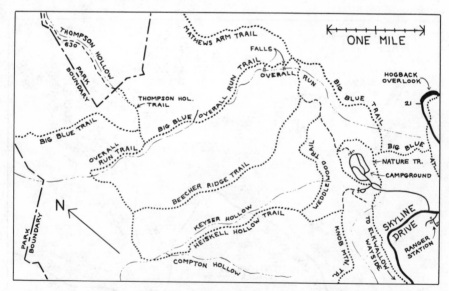

Map of Mathews Arm and Overall Run Area

HIKE: *Overall Run Falls. Round trip* 3.8 miles; total *climb* about 1,140 feet; *time* required 3:40. A moderately difficult hike to the highest waterfall in the Park. See map above.

Take the Mathews Arm fire road, which begins at the end of "B" loop in the Campground. (The road goes into the Wilderness Area and has therefore been reclassified as a trail, although it still looks like a road here.) Follow the fire road, mostly downhill, for 1.4 miles to its junction with the Big Blue Trail, which comes in on the right. Continue for less than a hundred yards. Then turn left on the Big Blue/Overall Run Trail; follow it downhill for about a tenth of a mile, and take the side trail to the left. It goes to a small overlook with a good close view of the upper falls. Like most of our waterfalls, this is a cascade down the rock face, rather than a sheer plunge. Its total drop is 29 feet.

Continue downhill on the main trail, which goes along near the edge of a steep gorge on your left. Watch for one or more short side trails going to the left, to viewpoints from which you can see the big falls. Like the upper falls, this is a cascade down the face of the rocks; the total drop is 93 feet. It's a spectacular sight in springtime, when the stream is full. In a dry summer, the stream may go completely dry.

From one of the viewpoints, a blue-blazed trail descends to the base of the falls. The trail is steep, rough, and snake-infested; and you have to clamber over a jumble of rocks from one to three feet in diameter. Not worth doing. Return to the campground the way you came. (Or, if you have surplus time and energy, read on.)

From the big falls, the trail descends steeply, then begins to level out after it crosses the stream. The lower end of the hollow is especially beautiful. Explore it if you wish, but note that it's a long hard climb back to the campground. Don't consider a one-way hike with a car posted outside the boundary at the foot of the hollow. Beyond the boundary you're on private property, and the owner is hostile. The easiest way to reach the lower part of Overall Run is from Thompson Hollow (see hike below.)

Note on the map, page 110, that a short trail goes from the lower end of Overall Run to Beecher Ridge, and from there to the upper end of Heiskell Hollow. Thus, from lower Overall Run, you might use either the Beecher Ridge Trail or the Heiskell Hollow Trail on your return trip. Either will take you through a delightfully wild area where you'll rarely meet another hiker. But be sure you have the necessary time and energy, plus a little skill at map reading.

HIKE: *Thompson Hollow to Overall Run. Round trip* from 2.6 to 4.6 miles; total *climb* from 480 to 640 feet; *time* required from 2:40 to 4:30. A fairly easy hike into lower Overall Run. Park in Thompson Hollow, outside the boundary. (See upper left corner of the map, page 110.) The length of the hike depends on where you find parking space and how much of Overall Run you want to explore.

To reach Thompson Hollow from the campground: Return to the Drive and turn left. Go 22.2 miles to the beginning of the Drive, and turn left on U.S. 340. Go about ten miles to Bentonville, and turn left on Virginia highway 613. Go less than a mile, and turn right on Virginia highway 630. From there it's a little over two miles to the Park boundary. The road is narrow, and there's almost no place to pull off. When you park be careful not to block the road, or access to private property. (That's what makes the natives hostile.)

The Thompson Hollow Trail begins at the Park boundary. Cross the ridge, joining the Big Blue Trail which comes in on the right. At the junction with the Overall Run Trail turn right, and explore at will. The lower end of the hollow is truly delightful, with large boulders, small cascades, and several pools deep enough to swim in. At last report there were still trout in the stream.

MILE 23.9, A.T. CROSSING. There is limited parking beside the Drive, but I recommend that you park at Elkwallow Wayside (in view to the south.) Distances on the A.T.: North (on the east side of the Drive) it's 1.6 miles to the Drive crossing at Mile 21.1, just south of Rattlesnake Point Overlook. South (on the west side) it's 3.9 miles to a side trail that goes to the Drive at Mile 26.8.

MILE 24.0, ELKWALLOW WAYSIDE. Usually open from May to October. Cafeteria, campstore, souvenirs, gas, oil, water, toilets. The outdoor telephone is in service all year.

MILE 24.1, ELKWALLOW PICNIC AREA. Elevation 2,420 feet. The one-way road makes a loop around the picnic area and returns to the Drive at Mile 24.2. There are picnic tables and fireplaces; and several drinking fountains, which are drained in winter. The comfort station is on the inside of the loop, near the middle. Pit toilets for winter use are just outside the far end of the loop at the second parking area. Also at this point, a connecting trail goes less than a hundred yards to join the A.T. See map below. Via the A.T., it's a short walk to the head of Jeremys Run.

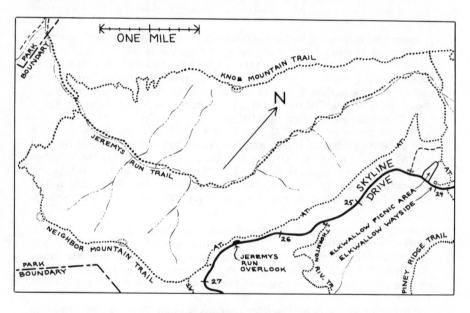

Map of Jeremys Run Area.

Jeremys Run is one of the most beautiful streams in the Park, with an endless succession of cascades, cataracts, and pools. Near its lower end is a small waterfall. The stream flows through a rather steep-sided, rocky canyon. The upper half is narrow; the lower half somewhat less so. The trail is moderately steep at each end, but has a gentle slope throughout most of its length. There are trout in Jeremys Run, but because it's very popular with fishermen, they are not always plentiful. The trail crosses the stream a dozen times — or maybe twenty. (I haven't counted the crossings, and reports vary. Don't take my map too literally on this point.) The crossings are not easy. In spring, and in rainy weather in summer, the stream is high and the trail is soggy. I recommend waterproof boots that come nearly to your knees.

Access to Jeremys Run from the bottom is uncertain. You have to cross private property. At last report the owner does not permit driving or parking on his property, though he doesn't mind if you walk across. Of course that's subject to change, for better or worse. I will describe two circuit hikes into Jeremys Run. Both begin here at Elkwallow Picnic Area, and both are rather long and difficult.

HIKE: *Knob Mountain and Jeremys Run. Circuit* 11.7 miles; total *climb* about 2,615 feet; *time* required 10:00. See map, page 112. This is a long and tiring hike; parts of the trail are steep, and there are many stream crossings. If you can cope with the difficulties, it's a delightful, highly rewarding experience.

Take the connecting trail from the second parking area, and in less than a hundred yards reach the A.T., which joins from the right. About two hundred yards from the junction a service road comes in on the left. Just beyond the road, on the left and about 60 feet from the trail, is an unprotected spring. Continue downhill on the A.T. In less than a tenth of a mile, the A.T. turns off sharply to the left; continue ahead on the blue-blazed Jeremys Run Trail. About 0.3 mile after you leave the A.T., watch for a trail junction where the Jeremys Run Trail turns sharply to the left. Continue ahead here, on the cutoff trail. Cross the stream, and climb steeply up to the Knob Mountain Trail. Turn left.

The former road ends about two miles from the cutoff trail, a hundred yards before you reach the high point on Knob Mountain. From here it's 3.3 miles to Jeremys Run. The trail descends steeply at first, then more gradually, then steeply again. At the foot of the ridge, cross the stream; turn left on the Jeremys Run Trail and pass the foot of the Neighbor Trail, on the right. Pass an attractive waterfall in less than 0.7 mile. From there it's about 4.2 miles to the junction where the cutoff trail from Knob Mountain comes in on the left. Turn right, and continue half a mile uphill to your starting point.

HIKE: *Jeremys Run and Neighbor Mountain. Circuit* 14.0 miles; total *climb* about 2,765 feet; *time* required 11:40. A rewarding, but very long and tiring hike, with a lot of climbing; part of the trail is steep. See map, page 112.

Start as above, from the second parking area of the Elkwallow Picnic ground. At the intersection with the cutoff trail, about half a mile from the start, turn left on the Jeremys Run Trail. Follow it downstream for 4.8 miles, to the junction with the Neighbor Trail on the left, and the Knob Mountain Trail a little farther on the right.

Turn left onto the Neighbor Trail, which climbs by switchbacks to the crest of Neighbor Mountain. A part of this trail is moderately steep. Along it you may see a few white birch trees, which are rare in the Park. (They're somewhat easier to spot in winter.) Some parts of the trail, especially at the top of the ridge, tend to be overgrown and hard to follow; watch for the blue blazes. From the high point on Neighbor Mountain, the trail continues near the ridge crest, with a few ups and downs, reaching the A.T. 4.6 miles from Jeremys Run. Turn left, downhill, on the A.T. In less than 0.3 mile the trail forks; keep left. (The right-hand branch goes 160 yards to the Drive at Mile 26.8.) Continue another 3.4 miles to the junction with the Jeremys Run Trail, which comes in from the left. Turn right, and continue uphill to your starting point in the picnic area.

MILE 24.2, ROAD, west side. This is the exit road from the Elkwallow picnic area. Do not enter. The entrance is at Mile 24.1.

MILE 24.3, FIRE ROAD, west side. This was the service road to Elkwallow Shelter, which was removed in 1980.

MILE 25, GEOLOGY. Here, and for more than a mile to the south, the
Drive runs close to the contact between the Catoctin lavas and the Weverton formation; often it's just above road level. In many places the bank on
the west side is made of broken purplish slate of the Weverton.

MILE 25.4, THORNTON RIVER TRAIL, east side. There is parking space
for several cars in the grass beside the Drive. This trail is the former
Thornton Hollow fire road. It descends steeply at first, then less so. About
2.5 miles from the Drive it crosses the Hull School Trail, then continues to
the Park boundary. To the right, from the junction, the Hull School Trail
climbs to the Drive at Mile 28.2. To the left it crosses the saddle of Fork
Mountain, then descends to join the Piney Branch Trail and the Keyser Run
fire road. (See the lower left part of the map on page 107.) The Thornton
River and Hull School trails are fun to explore if you have enough time and
energy.

MILE 26.4, JEREMYS RUN OVERLOOK. Elevation 2,410 feet. The
overlook provides a narrow, V-shaped view across the hollow of Jeremys
Run, with Neighbor Mountain to the left and Knob Mountain to the right.
Jeremys Run, which was formerly called Jeremiah's Run, is a delightfully
scenic place of cascades and cataracts.
I've described two circuit hikes that go into the hollow. Both are rather
difficult. They begin at Elkwallow Picnic Area, Mile 24.1 (page 113).

Across the Shenandoah Valley is the Massanutten. Its two prominent
crests are Kennedy Peak on the left and Strickler Knob on the right, both
with an elevation of about 2,600 feet. Between the two ridges of the
Massanutten is the *Fort Valley*. It's a natural stronghold, accessible
through a narrow passage between sheer cliffs. In the 1730's it was
occupied by a man named Powell, who needed its defendability because he
was in trouble with the law. For a while thereafter the valley was called
Powell's Fort Valley, and the ridge to the west of it Powell's Fort Mountain.

Legend: Powell discovered a rich silver deposit in the Fort Valley, and
became an outlaw by making counterfeit silver coins out of real silver.
According to legend the mine is still there, and still loaded with silver; but
its location is unknown.

History: In 1748, when George Washington was 16 years old, he
surveyed the Fort Valley for its owner, Lord Fairfax. Thirty years later, after
the hard winter at Valley Forge, Washington's advisors suggested that the
Continental Army might have to surrender to the British. Washington
replied that rather than surrender he would retreat to the Shenandoah and
take refuge with his army in the Fort Valley. He actually began preparations
for such a retreat.

Geology: Most of the drainage area of Jeremys Run, below the overlook, is on ancient lavas of the Catoctin formation. The higher parts of Knob Mountain, Neighbor Mountain, and the Blue Ridge between here and Elkwallow, are capped by sedimentary rocks of the Weverton and Hampton formations.

MILE 26.8. GRASSY PARKING AREA, west side. *A.T. access; hikes.* A short access trail to the A.T. begins here, but it's not visible from the Drive. Park near the north end of the grassy area. From there, as you stand with your back to the Drive, the access trail goes diagonally left, about 150 yards, to the A.T. From that point on the A.T., distances are: North (to the right) it's 3.8 miles to Elkwallow Picnic Area. South (to the left) it's 1.6 miles to the Drive crossing in Beahms Gap, Mile 28.5.

NOTE. In the first edition of this book I described a hike that began here and followed a fire foot trail straight down the mountain side into Jeremys Run, returning by the Neighbor Mountain Trail. That hike is no longer possible, because the fire foot trail has been obliterated. It was steep and rough, and eroding badly, so that it was a menace to the environment as well as to hikers.

But you can still hike to Jeremys Run from here. On page 113, I described a circuit hike using the Jeremys Run Trail, the Neighbor Mountain Trail, and the A.T. (See the map on page 112.) My description starts from the Elkwallow Picnic Area, but you could just as well begin the hike here.

MILE 26.9, GEOLOGY. The jointed sandstone beds in the road cut on the west side of the Drive are in the lower part of the Weverton formation. The blocks are eroding into roughly spheroidal form, and surface weathering has produced a variety of colors.

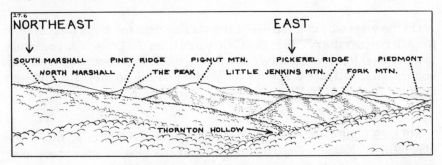

View from Thornton Hollow Overlook.

MILE 27.6, THORNTON HOLLOW OVERLOOK. Elevation 2,460 feet. There's a wide view here — more than 180 degrees. The sketch shows only a part of it, mostly to the left of center. On your left, outside the sketch, the high mountain with four bumps is Hogback; farther left, lower and closer, is Sugarloaf. To the right of Fork Mountain (which is near the right-hand end of the sketch), the distant ridge is Oventop; and farther right, nearer and higher, is the rounded top of Pass Mountain.

Down below the overlook, and about a third of a mile away, is a clearing. (It's easier to see in the winter, when the yellow dry grass makes it stand out clearly.) This is a mountaineer homesite, suitable for exploration by experienced hikers. It's fairly easy to each from Mile 28.2. (See below.)

Geology: Across the Drive from the south end of the overlook is an exposure of massive Catoctin basalt. It shows narrow veins and exposed surfaces of a greenish-white mineral that appears to consist of parallel fibers. (The best exposure covers several square feet; it's a few feet above eye level.) This is fibrous anthophyllite — a kind of asbestos.

MILE 28.2, HULL SCHOOL TRAIL, east, and **SERVICE ROAD,** west. *A.T. access; Byrds Nest Shelter* No. 4; *explorer hikes.* There's parking space in the grass.

On the east side of the Drive is the former *Hull School* fire road, which is now a trail. It descends about two miles to the site of Hull School, where it crosses the Thornton River Trail that comes down from Mile 25.4. The Hull School Trail then continues across the saddle of Fork Mountain to join the Piney Branch Trail and the Keyser Run fire road.

> To reach the old homesite below Thornton Hollow Overlook, go about a quarter of a mile down the Hull School Trail. Turn left onto an overgrown road trace, which is at first grassy and then wooded. Continue about 0.4 mile; then leave the road trace, drop down to the left, and cross the creek. On the other side you'll come to an old orchard, and beyond it the homesite. The house foundation, the well, and other signs of habitation are well preserved. The cemetery is some distance beyond the homesite and around to the left, below the overlook. Note: this is not one of the recommended hikes, because you could get lost. But it's suitable for exploration by *experienced hikers.*

On the west side of the Drive is the service road for Byrds Nest Shelter No. 4. It crosses the A.T. less than 200 yards from the Drive. You could hike to the shelter from here (*round trip* 1.0 mile; total *climb* about 396 feet), but I suggest that you take a slightly longer hike to the shelter, starting from Beahms Gap, Mile 28.5.

MILE 28.5, BEAHMS GAP. Elevation 2,485 feet. *A.T. access; hikes.* This was formerly Beahms Gap Overlook, but the treetops are now at eye level, and the view is gone. From one point in the parking area you can see the top of the Massanutten, and from another the sharp angle of Neighbor Mountain, ahead on the right. From most of the parking area you can see a nearby knob to the right; Byrds Nest Shelter No. 4 is near its summit.

When the Park was created there was a good view here, directly down Kemp Hollow; the slope below the overlook was grassy, all the way down. But now it's covered with trees, and the slope is so gradual that vista clearing is impracticable. (Across the Drive, diagonally to the left, is a rather poor view of Hogback Mountain and the Marshalls.)

Geology: The boulders on either side of the trail at the north end of the parking area, and those at the north end of the island, are epidotized basalt brecchia that shows many colors: various shades of purplish and green, with imbedded white pebbles and fragments.

The A.T. crosses the Drive about 100 feet south of the parking area. Distances on the A.T.: North (on the west side of the Drive) it's 1.6 miles to a side trail that reaches the Drive at Mile 26.8. South (on the east side) it's 3.0 miles to the Drive crossing at Mile 31.4, near Thornton Gap.

I recommend three short hikes from Beahms Gap: a loop using the A.T. in Beahms Gap; a hike south to a viewpoint on Pass Mountain; and a hike north to Byrds Nest Shelter No. 4 and two viewpoints near it.

HIKE: *Beahms Gap* and *A.T. Circuit* 0.4 mile; total *climb* about 60 feet; *time* required 0:20. A very easy hike with no views and, in fact, no particular attraction. But if you've been driving for a while, and have only 20 minutes to stretch your legs, try this. Go to the north end of the parking area and take the trail that starts toward Byrds Nest No. 4. It reaches the A.T. in a little more than 200 yards. Turn left on the A.T., and follow it for about 300 yards to the Drive, passing two or more old road traces that branch off to the right. Turn left at the Drive, and return to your starting point.

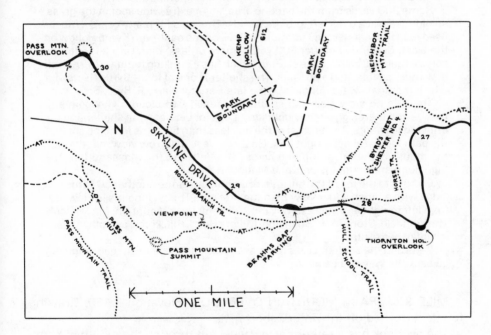

Map of Beahms Gap Area.

HIKE: *Viewpoint on Pass Mountain. Round trip* 1.6 miles; total *climb* about 495 feet; *time* required 1:40. A fairly easy hike; the trail is smooth, and only a small part of it is moderately steep. See map above.

Take the A.T. south (on the east side of the Drive) from a point a hundred feet south of the parking area. The first third of the hike goes through a former clearing; there was a homesite nearby, on the east of the trail. About three quarters of a mile from the start you'll reach a high point in the trail, beyond which it descends a few feet. There's a rock ledge on your right, but the view is overgrown. Continue another 25 yards, passing a boulder at the left edge of the trail. Turn right; leave the trail and walk directly away from it for about 50 yards. Turn right again, and go another 20 yards to a ledge with a fine, open view.

You're looking over Kemp Hollow. Straight out from the mouth of the hollow is the town of Luray, and beyond it New Market Gap in the Massanutten. To the left is Stony Man, seven miles away. To the right of Kemp Hollow is Neighbor Mountain. Near the far right of your view, Neighbor Mountain joins the Blue Ridge. The high knob at the extreme right is the location of Byrds Nest Shelter No. 4; the shelter itself is out of sight, but you can see the clearing in front of it.

HIKE: *Byrds Nest Shelter No. 4. Round trip* 1.7 miles; total *climb* about 485 feet; *time* required 1:50. This is a fairly easy walk, which goes first through the grass beside the Drive, and then uphill on the Shelter service road. It's smooth all the way, although the service road is rather steep. See map, page 117.

Follow the sidewalk to the north end of the parking area (That's to your right as you stand on the walk with your back to the parking area.) Continue northward in the grass beside the Drive; the grass is wide, so you can walk a safe distance from the pavement. I've suggested that you start this walk from Beahms Gap, rather than the foot of the service road, because of the wild-flowers that grow beside the Drive here in Spring and Summer.

Some 300 yards from the parking area, at an extra wide spot in the grass, an old road trace goes left into the woods. This was for many years a much-used road that connected Thornton Hollow, on the east, with Kemp Hollow on the west. Continue another 300 yards, more or less; then turn left onto the service road and climb to the shelter, which has a drinking fountain (turned off in winter), a table, and a pit toilet. The shelter is one of four "Byrds Nests" for which materials were donated by the late Senator Harry F. Byrd, Sr.

There is no view from the shelter. To reach two cleared viewpoints (if they're still there), go directly uphill from a point between the shelter and the drinking fountain. On the crest of the hill, less than 50 yards from the shelter, the path forks. Take the right fork. Go 20 yards to a narrow view: out through the mouth of Jeremys Run and across the Valley to the Massanutten. The high point at the right is on Knob Mountain.

Go back to the top of the hill and turn right. Continue another 60 yards to a ledge with a much wider view than the first one. The high points in view are, from left to right and successively more distant: Pass Mountain, Marys Rock, The Pinnacle, Stony Man, Bushytop, Millers Head, Blackrock, and other peaks even farther south.

Return to the shelter, cross the grass to pick up the service road, and then go back the way you came.

MILE 30.1, PASS MOUNTAIN OVERLOOK. Elevation 2,460. Drinking fountain (turned off in winter): short *hike.*

The overlook has a rather narrow view out through the mouth of Kemp Hollow and across the Shenandoah Valley to the Massanutten. The low point in the Massanutten is New Market Gap. The town that appears to fill the whole valley between the Massanutten and the mouth of Kemp Hollow is Luray. To the left of the mouth of the hollow is Pine Mountain, with divided highway U.S. 211 passing on this side of it. As the highway comes closer, it disappears between Pine Mountain and Pumpkin Hill. The ridge at the right of the hollow rises to the peak of Neighbor Mountain.

From this overlook the lights of Luray make an enchanting display after dark. Luray is the location of the famous Luray Caverns. Surprisingly, its name is pronounced with equal emphasis on both syllables, or with a slightly stronger stress on the first syllable. Origin of the name is in doubt.

Legend: One of the early settlers was a blacksmith named Louis Ramey. The town was named by taking the first syllable of his first and last name.

Legend: The first settlers were French Huguenots from Lorraine. "Luray" is a corruption of "Lorraine."

History: On August 13, 1812, the General Assembly of Virginia authorized a surveyor to lay out a town at the present site of Luray. *Legend:* The parents of the man who drafted the bill were immigrants from Lorraine, and he gave the proposed town that name to honor them. But because of his poor penmanship the name he wrote appeared to be "Luray."

> HIKE: *Pass Mountain Overlook Loop. Circuit* less than 0.25 mile. Total *climb* about 50 feet; *time* required 0:15. A pleasant, very easy walk on a smooth graded trail. Go straight out from the overlook, downhill to a rock ledge. The view here is a little wider than from the overlook. Continue downhill, following the trail around to your left, and return to your starting point via the gate in the fence.

MILE 30.2, FIRE ROAD, east side. The entrance is 125 yards south of Pass Mountain Overlook. The road goes a third of a mile up the west side of Pass Mountain, to a concrete-enclosed spring that provides water for the drinking fountain at the overlook. Just off the road, 200 yards from the Drive, is a storage area for dirt and gravel. Explore if you wish, but I don't think it's worth your time.

MILE 31.4, FIRE ROAD, east side; *A.T. crossing.* On the west side the A.T. descends, crosses U.S. 211, then passes near the Panorama restaurant (see below, Mile 31.6.) On the east is the service road for Pass Mountain Hut. The A.T. follows it for a short distance, then turns off to the left. There's no safe parking here. If you want to hike on the A.T., park at the Panorama development on the south side of the overpass.

MILE 31.5, THORNTON GAP. Elevation 2,304 feet. U.S. 211 interchange. For Luray, Luray Caverns, and I-81, exit here and turn right on U.S. 211. For Sperryville, Warrenton, and Washington, D.C., exit here and turn left on U.S. 211. Exit here if you want to climb Old Rag Mountain (see page 138.)

LOG OF THE DRIVE — CENTRAL SECTION

MILE 31.6, PANORAMA DEVELOPMENT. Telephone, restaurant, gift shop, Information station. *A.T. access. Hikes.*

The Information and Backcountry Permit Station, near the Drive, is open on summer weekends. It has a single restroom, and there's a public telephone beside it. The restaurant is open in the daytime in spring, summer, and fall, and sometimes on weekends in winter.

A.T. access is via a 35-yard trail that starts at the turnaround circle in front of the restaurant. Distances on the A.T.: South (to the left) it's 4.9 miles to Jewell Hollow Overlook, Mile 36.4. North (to the right) it's 2.9 miles to the Drive crossing in Beahms Gap, Mile 28.5.

I will describe two hikes that begin here: *Marys Rock,* with outstanding views: round trip 3.7 miles; and Pass Mountain A. T. Hut: circuit 3.4 miles, a somewhat easier hike through the woods, with no views. See below.

History: The Panorama development is on the south side of Thornton Gap. The gap is named for Francis Thornton, who about 1740 bought land and built a mansion in the Piedmont nearby. Thornton owned most of the hollow to the east, as well as the "F.T. Valley" between Sperryville and Old Rag. His mansion, *Montpelier,* is still standing; you'll see it to the left of Highway 231 if you drive to Nethers to climb Old Rag. (Page 138.)Look back after you pass it to see the front of the building, which has columns much like those at Mount Vernon.

The road across the mountain here is very old. In 1746 the colony of Virginia was petitioned to build a road across the Massanutten (then called Buffalo Mountain), and through the gap to "Mr. Thornton's Mill." The road was built. Shortly before the revolution it was improved and operated as a turnpike by Frank Skinner (another early settler; he gave his name to Skinners Ridge, which descends from Buck Hollow Overlook, Mile 32.9.) After the revolution William Russel Barbee took over the toll road and surfaced it with gravel. Beside it he built Hawsberry Inn. (The historical marker beside the highway, U.S. 211, calls it Hawburg.) For many years Hawsberry served as an overnight stopping point for stagecoaches and wagons crossing the mountain. And it was the birthplace of Virginia's most famous sculptor, William Randolph Barbee (1818-1868).

Before the Park was established, food and lodging were available at the Panorama Tavern, which was beside the highway near the present entrance station. The tavern was replaced by the restaurant when the Skyline Drive-U.S. 211 interchange was built in the early 1960's.

Geology: Thornton Gap lies between Pass Mountain to the north and Marys Rock to the south. A geologic fault passes through the gap, separating the lava flows of the Catoctin formation from granodiorite of the Pedlar formation. Marys Rock, 1,200 feet above the gap, is granodiorite, and towers over the much younger lava flows on Pass Mountain. The mountains south of the fault were thrust high above those to the north.

HIKE: *Marys Rock.* Outstanding views. *Round trip* 3.7 miles; total *climb* about 1,210 feet; *time* required 3:40. A medium-difficult hike. Parts of the trail are somewhat rough and rocky; none of it is very steep.

Take the short connecting trail to the A.T., and turn left. You now have a long, steady, fairly gentle climb — at first through woods, and later through thickets of mountain laurel. Worth noting is a big oak tree beside the trail, about 1.1 miles from the start.   A mile and three quarters from Panorama, the A.T. turns 90 degrees to the left. Continue straight ahead here, and go another 0.1 mile to the viewpoint on Marys Rock. The two sketches show part of what you can see. To the left of Three Sisters (at the left edge of the first sketch) you have a view across the Valley to Newmarket Gap in the

Massanutten, with the town of Luray filling a good part of the Valley.

The high point on Marys Rock, elevation 3,515, is about 200 feet behind the viewpoint. It's less than 100 feet to a point from which you can see far to the left, to The Pinnacle and Stony Man. If you have non-slip shoes and a good sense of balance, go a hundred feet farther to the highest point. I can think of only four points in the Park that offer a 360-degree view. This is one of them.

How did Marys Rock get its name? Nobody knows.

Legend: Francis Thornton brought his beautiful young bride, the former Mary Savage, to the summit of this mountain to show her the vastness of his lands. He presented the lands to her, and they christened this summit

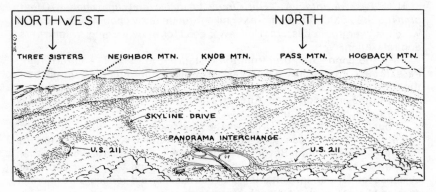

View from Marys Rock. (No. 1.)

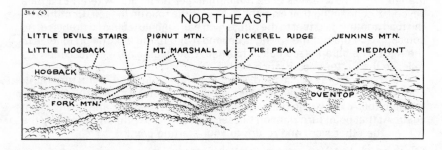

View from Marys Rock. (No. 2.)

Marys Rock. (In some accounts, the bride was the former Mary Taliferro, or Mary Taliafero; but in all versions she was young and beautiful. One historian says that Francis and Mary climbed to this viewpoint every year, on their wedding anniversary. Another says they spent their wedding night here.)

Fact: Francis Thornton married his cousin, Frances Gregory (whose mother was Mildred Washington, aunt of George Washington.) Their children were John, William, and Mary. That wipes out the beautiful-young-bride stories, but daughter Mary has legends of her own.

Legend: Francis Thornton brought his daughter Mary to this summit, to show her the land she would inherit. *Fact:* Mary inherited a great deal of land from her father, but none of it can be seen from here.

Legend: Mary Thornton, as a small child, climbed to this point alone, and returned with a bear cub under each arm.

Legend: A semi-beautiful mountain girl named Mary (not Thornton) lived in Thornton Gap. She fell in love with a handsome stranger, who lived with her for a while and then moved on, promising to return. Every day Mary climbed this rock, hoping to see her lover returning, until she finally gave up and jumped off. (This story has been told in many languages, in many different versions. My favorite is called "Madam Butterfly". You see, there was this Japanese girl, and . . . .)

HIKE: *Pass Mountain A. T. Hut. Circuit* 3.4 miles; total *climb* about 670 feet; *time* required 3:00. A medium-easy hike through fairly open woods, a part of which is overgrown pasture. No views; good for birdwatching, wildflowers, and relaxation.

Take the connecting trail from the restaurant to the A.T. and turn right. Pass through an overgrown clearing below the restaurant and, 0.2 mile from the start, cross U.S. 211. Go another 0.1 mile to Skyline Drive, cross the Drive and continue on the dirt road. After 100 feet, the A.T. turns off to the left; stay on the road; you will return via A.T.

About 0.6 mile from the Drive, as the road takes a sharp turn to the right, you'll see a large green tank down to your left; it stores water for the Panorama development. Beyond the turn the A.T. joins the road briefly, then goes off to the left again. Stay on the road. Beyond this point you'll see evidence of former inhabitants: old road traces, old fences, and pioneer species of trees, which suggest a former clearing.

About 0.7 mile after you leave the A.T., you'll pass a damp grassy area on the left, where there was once a mountaineer homesite. A tenth of a mile beyond, a connecting trail from the A.T. joins the road on the left. Continue on the road another 100 feet to the hut, which has a picnic table and fireplace. As you approach the hut the spring is beyond it and to the left; the pit toilet is to the right. The blue-blazed Pass Mountain trail begins here; it descends 2.2 miles to the Butterwood Branch trail.

Start back on the service road. A hundred feet from the A.T. hut turn right, onto the connecting trail, which goes gently uphill for 0.2 mile to the A.T. Bear left onto the A.T. It will join the service road briefly, leave it, and finally join it again. At that point turn right on the service road. Cross the Drive, pick up the A.T. on the other side, and return to your starting point.

MILE 32.2, MARYS ROCK TUNNEL, North Portal. (For a note on the tunnel itself, see below.) *Geology:* The rock cut at the tunnel entrance has exposed a Catoctin feeder dike, where lava surged upward through a fissure in the granodiorite. The fissure is filled with solidified lava. It's easy to see from your car; the dike is about six feet wide and inclined at an angle, so that it seems to lean against the tunnel entrance. Slow down for a look if there's nobody behind you, but don't stop here. For a closer look, park at Tunnel Parking Overlook, Mile 32.4, and walk back through the tunnel.

MILE 32.4, TUNNEL PARKING OVERLOOK. Elevation 2,510 feet. From here you look out into the hollow of Thornton River, with Oventop Mountain extending across the view directly in front. Skinner Ridge lies to the right of the hollow; between it and Oventop you have a V-shaped view of the Piedmont, with Sperryville at the apex. To the left of Oventop you can see more distant mountains in the North Section of the Park: on the horizon, the two close-together summits are Mt. Marshall; farther right is The Peak; a little to the left of Mt. Marshall, and lower, is Fork Mountain.

Geology: Near the crest of Oventop, a little to the left of center, are cliffs of Old Rag granite. The cliffs that rise on the west side of the Drive, across from the overlook, are granodiorite of the Pedlar formation. The rocks are strongly foliated — cracked into parallel layers so they appear to be stratified. The rocks exposed beside the Drive, from here to Milepost 39, are granodiorite.

About the tunnel: It was blasted through the ridge about 1932. It intercepted a number of water channels, so that water fell constantly from the rocks — in winter forming huge icicles, and piles of ice on the road. To solve this problem, the tunnel was lined with concrete in 1959.

Various publications give various figures for the length of the tunnel. I measured it and found the following: Total length (i.e. length of the centerline of the road with rock overhead) 610 feet. Length of the concrete liner 584 feet. Length of the rock cut, at road level, 690 feet.

If you'd like a closer look at the Catoctin feeder dike at the north portal, walk through the tunnel with care, hugging the wall. Drivers won't be expecting pedestrians in the tunnel, or at the north end of it. An alternative to walking through the tunnel is to climb over it. There was once a trail that went from the parking area across the ridge to the north portal. It has been abandoned for some years, but you may still .be able to follow it. The beginning, at the south end, has been blocked with brush. Once you get past that, it's a little easier.

MILE 32.9, BUCK HOLLOW OVERLOOK. This is only a wide place in the road; you may be tempted to pass it by, especially if you're going south. But stop; this overlook has a fine view. The elevation here is 2710 feet.

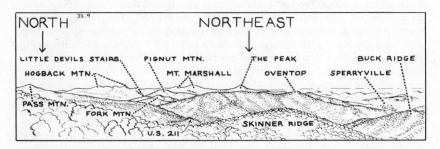

View from Buck Hollow Overlook.

Skinner Ridge descends straight out from the overlook, with Buck Hollow to the right of it. (A hike through Buck Hollow begins at Mile 33.5, page124.) To the right of Buck Hollow is Buck Ridge, which rises to eye level at your right, beyond the right edge of the sketch. Beyond the high part of Buck Ridge, and rising a little above it, is Hazel Mountain. On the sketch, the diagonal ravine under the high point on Mount Marshall is Big Devil Stairs.

Dendrology: Directly downhill in the gulch below the north end of the overlook, and less than 100 yards away, is a hemlock that may be the oldest and largest tree in the Park. You'll have to climb down to its base to really appreciate the size of it. Its age has been estimated at 700 years.

MILE 33.0, HAZEL MOUNTAIN OVERLOOK. Elevation 2,770 feet. Drinking fountain (turned off in winter.) Along the outer edge of the overlook are boulders of granodiorite that you can climb up on to see the view. You're looking straight out across the head of Buck Hollow to the high part of Buck Ridge, with the top of Hazel Mountain barely visible beyond it. To the right are two mountains: the nearer is Catlett Mountain; the other, more distant and more rugged in outline, is Old Rag. The high point around to the extreme right of your view is The Pinnacle.

The area around Buck Ridge, Hazel Mountain, and Catlett Mountain, is known as "Hazel Country." Hikes into the area begin at Mile 33.5 (see below.) As I've said before, there were good and bad neighborhoods in the mountains, just as there are in a city. Hazel Country may have been a bad one. Here are some quotes from the accounts I've read: "ignorant . . . uneducated . . . murders . . . squatters . . . drunken brawls . . . survival of the fittest . . . general disorder . . . mountaineer escapades . . . inhospitality . . . mysterious . . . forbidding . . . wild . . . lawless." Up to now, I've found no witness for the defense.

MILE 33.5, PARKING AREAS, both sides of Drive. Elevation 2,830 feet. *Hikes* to *Buck Hollow, Hazel Country, Meadow Spring* trail, *Byrds Nest Shelter* No. 3, and *Marys Rock.*

For Buck Hollow or Hazel Country, use the parking area on the east side of the Drive. The Buck Hollow trail begins at the north end of the parking area. The Hazel fire road, which was reclassified as a trail in 1976 but still looks like a road, begins at the south end.

HIKE: *Buck Hollow. One way* 3.1 miles; total *climb* about 45 feet; *time* required 2:40. This is a fairly easy, pleasant hike beside a stream, with no waterfalls, not much water, and no views. There are some very rough stretches in the last half. This is not a popular place; if you want to escape from the crowds, you can probably do so here.

Because this is a one-way hike, you'll have to leave a car at the bottom of the trail, or arrange for someone to meet you there. At Thornton Gap, Mile 31.5, take U.S. 211 east toward Washington. At the foot of the ridge, 2.6 miles from Panorama, the road makes a broad 180-degree turn to the right, around a picnic area. Read your odometer here. Continue 1.1 miles to a small parking area on the right, at the foot of the Buck Hollow Trail. The time required for the hike, 2:40, does not include driving time.

The trail descends steeply at the beginning, then much less so, passing through a young forest with scattered hemlocks and mountain laurels. You'll be seeing hemlocks, some of them quite large, along most of the route; there's a big grove of them to the right of the trail just 0.3 mile from the start. About 0.7 mile from the Drive the trail swings right and crosses a rocky stream bed, then descends along the ridge some distance from the stream. Later it swings left, descends to the stream, and turns sharp right. From here on, watch the blue blazes. After another quarter of a mile the trail turns left and crosses the stream; but the trail is so badly eroded that you will probably miss the turn unless you're watching the blazes.

(A double blaze means the trail is about to change direction. If you run out of trail, and can't find any blazes, cross to the left bank of the stream; you'll find the trail there, within a hundred feet of the water.)

For a considerable distance, the trail follows an old mountaineer road that once went to a sawmill farther up the hollow. From time to time traces of old logging roads join the trail, but there's no chance of getting lost; if in doubt, look for the blue blazes. Stretches of the road are badly eroded, rough and rocky. The trail crosses the stream again and after another quarter of a mile leaves the road trace, narrows, and becomes much smoother. It promptly crosses the Buck Hollow stream for the last time, then crosses the Thornton River. Both crossings are easy unless the water is abnormally high.

U.S. 211 is less than 200 yards away, through what was once a grassy clearing near an old homesite. The area is now overgrown with black locust, *Ailanthus,* and Japanese honeysuckle. In summer you may find pink phlox in bloom here, still surviving from an old flower garden.

HAZEL/NICHOLSON HIKES

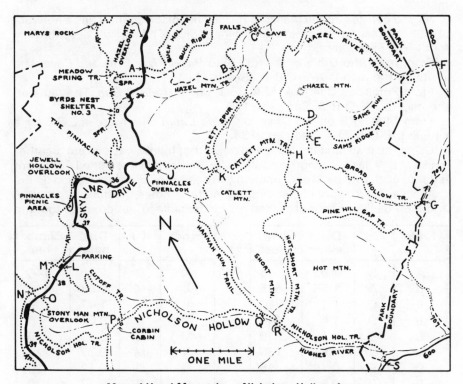

Map of Hazel Mountain — Nicholson Hollow Area

The area shown on the map above, from Hazel Mountain and Hazel River southwest to Nicholson Hollow, was well populated before the area became a Park. It included dozens of mountaineer homesites, and a network of roads and trails built by the mountain people. A portion of the old Hazel Mountain road was maintained by the Park as a fire road until 1976, when it was reclassified as a trail. Some of the roads and trails have been maintained as Blue-Blazed trails by volunteer members of the Potomac Appalachian Trail Club. Others have been abandoned and allowed to grow up and fade away, or to erode into gullies.

Nearly all the mountaineer cabins were torn down when the Park was created. Here in the Hazel/Nicholson country several cabins, for one reason or another, were left standing. Their shingled roofs have long ago caved in, and their walls are leaning and coming down. But there's enough left, in several places, to give you some feeling of how the mountain people lived. The best examples are in Nicholson Hollow, Hannah Run, Broad Hollow, and along the Hot-Short Mountain trail. The one that's easiest to get to from the Drive is on the Corbin Cabin Cutoff trail (See page 134.)

Throughout the area you'll find evidence of the former inhabitants if you're looking for it: old road traces, rock walls, rock piles that were accumulated in clearing space for gardens and cornfields, decaying split-rail fences, gate posts, a few strands of barbed wire, many abandoned orchards, and in some places rusting washtubs, buckets, and other scrap metal.

As you can see on the map, the Hazel/Nicholson country has a network of interconnecting trails that offer a wide choice of hikes. I will describe only four hikes in the area:

From here (the Drive at mile 33.5) to *Hazel River Falls and Cave.* The route on the map is A-B-C-B-A. (See below.)

From Pinnacles Overlook, Mile 35.1, down *Hannah Run.* The route on the map is J-K-Q-R-S. See page 130.

From Mile 37.9 on the Drive to *Corbin Cabin.* The route is L-P-L (or a circuit: L-P-O-N-M-L. See page 134.

Using the map, and the table and notes that follow, you can put together a hike of any desired length and difficulty. Because I've assigned a different letter to each trail head and junction you can lay out your route, add up the distances and amount of climbing, consult the notes that follow the table, and then decide if your proposed hike is feasible. (Caution: note that the

From	To	Dist. miles	Climb feet	From	To	Dist. miles	Climb feet
A	B	1.55	15	K	Q	2.45	140
B	A	1.55	625	L	M	0.04	0
B	C	1.1	60	L	P	1.47	30
B	D	1.6	445	M	L	0.04	5
C	B	1.1	370	M	N	0.77	245
D	B	1.6	130	N	M	0.77	225
D	E	0.18	15	N	O	0.17	20
D	H	0.5	50	O	N	0.17	20
E	D	0.18	0	O	P	1.81	25
E	F	2.32	20	P	L	1.47	1065
E	G	2.2	20	P	O	1.81	1070
F	E	2.32	1590	P	Q	2.06	30
G	E	2.2	1445	Q	K	2.45	1540
H	D	0.5	45	Q	P	2.06	800
H	I	0.55	10	Q	R	0.23	15
H	K	1.2	365	R	I	2.16	1390
I	H	0.55	0	R	Q	0.23	60
I	R	2.16	75	R	S	1.73	60
J	K	1.24	100	S	R	1.73	355
K	H	1.2	230	S	T	0.3	40
K	J	1.24	745	T	S	0.3	0

amount of climbing depends on which way you're going. Thus the total climb from *A to B* is 15 feet; while from *B to A* it's 625 feet.)

A to B and *B to C* are described below, as part of the hike to Hazel River Falls and Cave.

B to D. From falls road junction to Hazel School site. About 0.6 mile from the junction at "B" the trail crosses a branch of the Hazel River. Forty feet short of the crossing, the Catlett Spur trail comes in on the right. About 0.8 mile further on, the Hazel River trail joins on the left; it descends 2.8 miles to the Park boundary. After less than a quarter of a mile more, the trail curves rather sharply to the right. Here, in the overgrown clearing on your left, was the Hazel School.

D to E. From Hazel Mountain trail to junction of Sams Ridge and Broad Hollow trails. Blue-blazed. At the junction, the Sams Ridge trail goes left; the Broad Hollow trail goes right.

D to H. Hazel Mountain trail, from Hazel School site to Catlett Mountain trail. As you reach point *H,* the Catlet Mountain trail (*H to K*) comes in on the right, at a concrete marker post.

E to F. Sams Ridge trail, from Broad Hollow trail to Virginia secondary road 600. Blue-blazed. About 0.4 mile from the start is a mountaineer homesite on the right; the evidence includes a stone foundation, apple trees and rose bushes, and a spring. The trail leaves the Park after 1.4 miles. It continues down the ridge on private property, then swings left and reaches a road 2.0 miles from the start. The Hazel River is just beyond the road, and the Hazel River trail comes in from the left here. Turn right on the road, and go 0.3 mile to Virginia secondary road 600.

E to G. Broad Hollow trail, from Sams Ridge trail to Virginia secondary road 707. Blue-blazed. Along this route are at least five homesites with ruins of cabins still visible; three of them can be seen from the trail.

H to I. Hazel Mountain trail, from Catlett Mountain trail to Hot-Short Mountain trail. As you reach point *I,* the Hot-Short trail comes in on your right, at concrete marker post. Ahead, the Hazel Mountain trail continues for half a mile to the Pine Hill Gap trail.

H to K. Catlett Mountain trail. Blue-blazed. There are many signs of former habitation, such as overgrown clearings, a stone wall, old road traces, and an old orchard. About 0.1 mile before you reach point *K,* the Catlett Spur trail comes in on the right.

I to R. Hot-Short Mountain trail, from the Hazel Mountain trail to Nicholson Hollow trail. Blue-blazed. There were at least eight homesites along this route. Several chimneys and a ruined house are visible from the trail.

J to K. Hannah Run trail, from Pinnacles Overlook to Catlett Mountain trail. Blue-blazed. No view, no homesites.

K to Q. Hannah Run trail, from Catlett Mountain to Nicholson Hollow trail. Ruins of three mountaineer cabins and a chimney are visible from the trail.

L to M. From Skyline Drive at Mile 37.9, at the head of Corbin Cabin Cutoff trail, to the A.T. This short connecting trail begins diagonally opposite the head of the Cutoff trail, across the Drive and parking area.

L to P. Corbin Cabin Cutoff trail, from Skyline Drive at Mile 37.9, to Corbin Cabin. Blue-blazed. Ruins of two mountaineer cabins are visible from the trail.

M to N. Appalachian Trail, from side trail to Corbin Cabin Cutoff trail, to side trail to Nicholson Hollow trail. White-blazed. (Near point *N,* the A.T. crosses an old road trace. This is the Crusher Ridge trail.

N to O. Head of Nicholson Hollow trail (Mile 38.4) to A. T. Blue-Blazed. To reach the A.T. from the top of the Nicholson Hollow trail, turn left (south) and walk along the Drive a little less than 100 yards. Cross the Drive and continue on what appears to be an overgrown fire road, gently uphill. About 50 yards from the Drive, the blue-blazed Crusher Ridge trail comes in on the right. The connecting trail continues ahead, narrows, and descends to the A.T. (if you're going north on the A.T., you can use the Crusher Ridge trail as a shortcut; the A.T. crosses it less than 200 yards from its beginning.)

O to P. Nicholson Hollow trail, from the Drive at Mile 38.4 to Corbin Cabin. Blue-blazed. The blue-blazed Indian Run trail comes in on the right, about 150 yards before you reach Corbin Cabin.

P to Q. Nicholson Hollow trail, from Corbin Cabin to Hannah Run trail. Blue-blazed. There are a number of old mountaineer homesites along this trail.

Q to R. Nicholson Hollow trail, from Hannah Run trail to Hot-Short Mountain trail. Blue-blazed.

R to S. Nicholson Hollow trail, from Hot-Short Mountain trail to Weakley Hollow fire road. Blue-blazed. About 1.4 miles from the Hot-Short trail you cross the Park boundary, and then continue on private land. There are two streams to ford: first the Hughes River, and then its tributary Brokenback Run. Neither crossing is easy except in dry weather. When the path dead-ends in a well-defined private road, turn left and go less than 100 yards to the Weakley Hollow fire road. (To reach this point by car, see page 139.)

HIKE: Hazel Falls and *Cave. Round trip* 5.3 miles; total *climb* about 1,070 feet; *time* required 4:45. Mostly easy walking , but with a short rough stretch near the beginning, and about 200 yards of fairly steep trail near the end. See map, page 125; the route is A-B-C-B-A.

Take the Hazel Mountain trail (yellow-blazed) on the east side of the Drive, at the south end of the parking area. About 0.4 mile from the Drive, the Buck Ridge trail comes in on the left. Continue, mostly downhill, through medium-age woods with occasional good-sized trees, many young hemlocks, and a great deal of mountain laurel—some of it quite old. A mile from the Drive you pass a homesite on the left, and a seepage of water across the road. There are pear trees in the abandoned orchard here.

About 1.6 miles from the Drive, the trail forks, at point "B" on the map. Take the left fork (yellow-blazed) and continue through a former clearing, 0.8 miles to the junction near point "C" on the map. Here the Old Hazel trail branches off to the left. It descends through Beech Spring Hollow and, about 1.7 miles from here, reaches U.S. 211.

From the junction, take the narrow foot trail that goes to the right. It starts off easy, but soon becomes rough and steep. After 300 yards you reach a point a hundred feet short of the Hazel River. (To the left, the river goes about 2.5 miles before it reaches the Park boundary. This is beautiful, rugged country—fun to explore. There are dozens of faint trails that lead nowhere, made by bear and deer and other explorers, and there is a network of old road traces. This is for *experienced hikers* only.)

Turn right. About 150 yards upstream you come to a small natural amphitheater. Ahead is the falls—not very high, but pretty nevertheless—with a pool at its base. Between you and the falls, a large hemlock is success-fully holding onto the rocks. On your right rises a 40-foot cliff, and the rock overhangs to form a nearly horizontal ceiling eight or nine feet above the ground. At the downstream end of the overhang is the cave. A very modest cave. You can explore all of it by daylight or, at night, by the light of a single match. But this overhang and cave must surely provide the best natural shelter in the park. You can stay dry in a driving rain, or sleet-free in a blizzard.

Backcountry camping under the overhang is a marvelous experience, with one disadvantage: on summer weekends you'll find it crowded.

MILE 33.5, MEADOW SPRING PARKING, west side. This is a paved parking pulloff, about 100 feet south of the Hazel Road parking area, and on the other side of the Drive. Access to *Byrds Nest Shelter* No. 3. The easiest route to *Marys Rock* summit begins here.

HIKE: *Marys Rock Summit. Round trip* 2.9 miles; total *climb* about 830 feet; *time* required 2:55. Magnificent views. A medium-easy hike, with a few rough spots and a few short stretches that are moderately steep. (See map, page 125, you're just below point "A", near the upper left.)

About 25 yards from the start, the trail takes a sharp switchback to the left; watch the blue blazes here. The Meadow Spring is about 0.4 mile from the Drive, on your right, just before the trail makes a 90-degree turn to the right. (According to one of the Marys Rock legends, Francis Thornton and his bride Mary spent a night beside this spring, on their way to the summit.) Fifty feet beyond the turn you'll see the ruins of Meadow Spring Cabin at the left edge of the trail. (The original cabin was built by mountaineer Perry Sisk in 1930 for members of the Potomac Appalachian Trail Club, who used it as a base camp while laying out trails in this area. It was torn down in 1939, and a larger cabin was built by the Park Service. The new cabin burned down to the ground on Thanksgiving Day, 1946, under mysterious circumstances. The hikers who had rented the cabin claimed to have left it, with all fires out, just ten minutes before a column of smoke was spotted from the lookout tower on Hogback Mountain, nine miles to the north.)

Continue uphill to the junction with the A.T., 0.7 mile from the Drive. (From here, *Byrds Nest Shelter* No. 3 is 0.7 mile to the left.) Turn right, and follow the A.T. for a little more than 0.6 mile, to a junction where the A.T. turns 90 degrees to the right, and a side trail goes 0.1 mile to the left, to a viewpoint on Marys Rock. Turn left onto the side trail. (For notes on Marys Rock, and sketches of the view, see page 121.)

MILE 33.9, FIRE ROAD, west side. Elevation 2,850 feet. This is the service road for Byrds Nest Shelter No. 3. You can hike to the shelter from the Meadow Spring parking area, Mile 33.5. (See above.)

MILE 35.1, PINNACLES OVERLOOK. Elevation 3,320 feet. *Hikes.* The overlook has an impressive view down the hollow of Hannah Run and across the foot of Corbin Mountain to Old Rag. To the right, outside the sketch, you can see part of the profile of Stony Man.

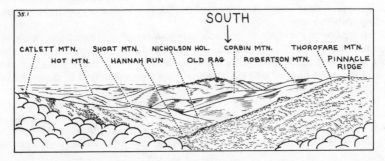

View from Pinnacles Overlook.

Hannah Run is of interest to anyone who wants to study the remaining evidence of the mountain people. Three ruined cabins and a free-standing chimney are visible from the trail. The Hannah Run trail connects with a network of other trails. (See map, page 125.) If you want to plot your own course through the network, read "Hazel/Nicholson Hikes", page 125. Here, I'll describe a one-way hike down Hannah Run, and outline a fairly strenuous circuit hike via Hannah Run and the Hot-Short and Catlett Mountain trails.

HIKE: *Hannah Run trail,* from Pinnacles Overlook to Weakley Hollow fire road. *One way* 5.7 miles; total *climb* about 315 feet; *time* required 4:25. Ruins of mountaineer cabins. A moderately difficult hike. Parts of the trail are rough, and about 250 yards of it are quite steep. See map, page 125; your route is J-K-Q-R-S. Since this is a one-way hike, you'll have to leave a car at the bottom, or have someone meet you there. For directions, see page 139.

The trail begins at an opening in the wall, near the north end of the overlook. It descends along the ridge crest with a few switchbacks, and is smoother than most of the blue-blazed trails. A little more than 0.4 mile from the Drive, at the right side of the trail, is a rather remarkable "deer" tree—a result of breakage many years ago in an ice storm. Note that a twin tree of the same size and age was undamaged in the storm. The trail continues downhill, with a couple of short easy climbs to skirt two knobs on the ridge crest.

About 1.1 miles from the Drive, at a concrete marker post, the Hannah Run trail turns 90 degrees to the right. (Ahead is the Catlett Mountain trail.) Up to now you've been following a fairly new trail that was cleared for Park visitors. Now you'll follow an old mountaineer trail to the first cabin, and then what used to be a road.

After you turn right at the junction, the trail is almost level for a while, then begins to descend, then descends steeply. The next 250 yards are steep and slippery—slow going. Descend to Hannah Run, which is only a trickle here; then climb the ridge on the other side. A hundred yards beyond the stream, note the split-rail fence on the right. Go forty yards more, and note the ruined structure on your right; it was probably a pigpen.

After another forty yards the trail makes a sharp left turn, at the corner of a ruined mountaineer cabin. This one was bigger than most—about 20 feet square, with a loft of the same size, and a ten- by twenty-foot leanto. There must have been a porch on the left, since the door there is three feet off the ground. When people lived here, the area was cleared for a third of a mile downstream (to the left as you sat on the porch), and the ridge straight ahead was cleared to the crest and beyond. So this was a porch with a view.

The next cabin is 0.2 mile farther, on the left. It's smaller and older than the first. There must have been a porch on the side farthest from the trail, with a view down the hollow. After another 150 yards you reach another ruin, also on the left. This is much the oldest of the three—well along in the process of fading into the land.

From here on it's obvious that you're following an old road. Split-rail fences come and go, or end at gate posts on either side of the road. Here and there you see chestnut stumps, only partly decayed, where trees were cut more than fifty years ago. At one point a chestnut tree three feet in diameter was chopped and sawed down, and the rotting trunk is still there.

A mile and a half from the last cabin, the Hannah Run trail dead-ends at the Nicholson Hollow trail, in a stand of young hemlocks. To the right, it's 2.1 miles to Corbin Cabin, and 3.9 miles to Skyline Drive at Mile 38.4. To the left it's 2.0 miles to your destination—the Weakley Hollow fire road. Turn left, cross a ditch, and later descend to cross Hannah Run on the rocks. (Both stream and ditch once had a bridge strong enough to support an automobile.) About a hundred yards beyond the stream, the Hot-Short mountain trail comes in on the left.

Continue ahead on the old road, which in places is rough and eroded. Hughes River, on your right, flows among large boulders, with an occasional good pool. It's 1.4 miles from the Hot-Short junction to the Park boundary. Go another quarter of a mile on private land, to a ford at Hughes River. Crossing on the rocks is difficult in dry weather, and impossible when the stream is high. (You may or may not find a one-log foot bridge, with a flimsy handrail, just upstream from the ford.)

After a few yards more, cross a second stream—Brokenback Run (sometimes mistakenly called Weakley Run)—easier than the Hughes River crossing, but still no cinch. Beyond the second stream, the trail dead-ends in a private road. Turn left and go 90 yards to the Weakley Hollow fire road. From here, the Old Rag parking area is 0.3 mile to your right. Your car, I hope, is waiting for you in a parking area to your left.

As we go to press the situation at the fire road junction is this: as you look up the private road toward the Nicholson Hollow trail, you'll see a sign on each side that says "No Parking Between Signs." Both signs have been shot full of holes. Near the right-hand sign is a mailbox that says "Tranquility Farm."

A few years ago I met a Mr. Dodson who owns, or owned, the land where I think your car is parked. Mr. Dodson told me that the owner of Tranquility Farm was a newcomer to the area, who bought land and moved in right after World War I. In this neighborhood the terms "newcomer" and "tranquility" are both relative.

HIKE: *Hannah Run,* Hot-Short and Catlett Mountain trails. *Circuit* 9.1 miles; total *climb* 2,755 feet; *time* required 8:50. This is a long, difficult, and tiring hike, which I offer as a possible alternative to the one-way trip described above. See map, page 134. Your route is J-K-Q-R-I-H-K-J.

As above, to the junction of the Nicholson Hollow and Hot-Short trails (point "R" on the map.) Turn left onto the Hot-Short trail. The trail follows an old mountain road up the hollow between Hot Mountain, on the right, and Short Mountain on the left. There were at least eight mountaineer homesites in the hollow; you can see the ruins of one of them from the trail.

When you reach the Hazel Mountain trail, turn left; walk a little more than half a mile to a marker post where the Catlett Mountain trail comes in, and turn left. The trail skirts the north slope of Catlett Mountain. There are many signs of former inhabitants: overgrown clearings, a stone wall, old road traces, and an old orchard. When you rejoin the Hannah Run trail at point "K" on the map, 1.2 miles from the Hazel Mountain trail, keep straight ahead and continue another mile and a quarter to your starting point.

MILE 35.6, ROAD TRACE, west side. This looks like the beginning of a trail, but it isn't. Fifty feet up the road trace, and then fifty feet to the right, you'll find water flowing from a pipe. (An unprotected water source; use purification tablets.) This is the surplus from a spring that supplies the Pinnacles picnic area and Pinnacles ranger quarters. Sometimes, during the summer season, there is no surplus. The road trace goes on for less than 0.2 mile, and ends at a rock outcropping. It was probably used to quarry rock for the guard wall beside the Drive.

MILE 36.4, JEWELL HOLLOW OVERLOOK. Elevation 3,320 feet. *A.T. access; hikes.* I will suggest two hikes that start here: A round trip to The

Pinnacle, and a one-way hike via Marys Rock to Panorama; both have outstanding views.

The overlook is divided into two parts, with a bulletin board in the north part and a drinking fountain (turned off in winter) in the south part. *A.T. access* is via a hundred-foot trail from either end of the overlook. Distances on the A.T.: South (to the left, from the south end of the overlook) it's 1.2 miles to the parking area beside the Drive at Mile 37.9. North (to the right, from the north end of the overlook) it's 4.9 miles to Panorama, at Mile 31.6 on the Drive.

The overlook has a view into the head of Tutweiler Hollow, which joins Shaver Hollow just this side of the lake and dam. Jewell Hollow is to the right of Leading Ridge, which forms the right-hand side of Tutweiler Hollow. In the distance, toward the right, is the sharp angle of Neighbor Mountain. A more distant peak, still farther right, is Knob Mountain.

Geography: Three counties meet at the south end of the overlook: Page County to the west; Rappahannock to the north and northeast, and Madison to the south and southeast.

Legend: Outlaws hid in this area because it was easy to evade a county sheriff, or even two of them, by stepping over a county line.

HIKE: *The Pinnacle. Round trip* 2.1 miles; total *climb* about 460 feet; *time* required 1:55. Views. A moderately easy hike, though part of the trail is rough and rocky.

Take the access trail at either end of the overlook, go about 100 feet to the A.T., and turn right. After you leave the overlook the trail climbs upward—not steeply but steadily—often between walls of mountain laurel. About a mile from the start the trail levels off, goes gently down for a few feet, then gently up to a second summit. Just as you start to descend for a second time, watch for a viewpoint on the left. This is your destination. Use some care here; the rock slopes downward to a sheer drop, and there is a point of no return.

The view looks across Jewell Hollow, with the sharp angle of Neighbor Mountain in the distance beyond it. The distant mountain with four humps, to the right of the Neighbor, is Hogback. To the right of Hogback, and much closer, is the rugged summit of Marys Rock.

HIKE: *Panorama via The Pinnacle* and *Marys Rock. One way* 5.3 miles; total *climb* about 805 feet; *time* required 4:30. A medium-difficult hike with good views; parts of the trail are rough and rocky, but the steepest parts are downhill. See map, page 134; Jewell Hollow Overlook is at left of center. Since this is a one-way hike you'll have to leave a car at Panorama, Mile 31.6, or have someone meet you there.

As above, to The Pinnacle. Continue in the same direction. About 0.2 mile beyond the summit, and after three switchbacks, watch for a side trail that goes back at a sharp angle on the left to a cleared viewpoint. If it's still clear when you get there you'll have an interesting view of Marys Rock, straight ahead, with more distant mountains in the North District on either side of it. Farther right is a view out into the Piedmont and, about 90 degrees to the right, of Hazel Mountain.

Return to the A.T. and continue downhill, by switchbacks, to a low point on the ridge at Byrds Nest Shelter No. 3. The shelter has pit toilets, several fireplaces, and a drinking fountain, which is turned off in winter. (About a hundred yards before you reached the shelter, you may have noticed water coming from a pipe on your left. That's surplus water from the spring that supplies the drinking fountain. You may find water here for a time after the fountain has been turned off in the fall.)

From the front of the shelter there's a good view, framed by trees, across the Valley to the Massanutten. Luray is a little to the left of center.

Beyond the shelter, the trail and service road coincide for a hundred yards. Then the road swings right and descends to the Drive at Mile 33.9; the trail goes a little to the left. Stay on the trail. About 0.6 mile beyond the shelter, the trail reaches a crest on the ridge and swings right. At this point look for rocks about 15 feet to the left, with a view over Jewell Hollow. To the left are The Pinnacle and Stony Man; to the right is Neighbor Mountain.

Less than 200 yards beyond this viewpoint, the Meadow Spring trail comes in on the right. (It descends for 0.7 mile to the Drive at Mile 33.5. The spring is a little less than halfway down.) About 0.4 mile beyond the Meadow Spring trail, look for two rocks on the left. The second has a good view. From left to right: Newmarket Gap in the Massanutten, Neighbor Mountain, the four humps of Hogback and then, farther right and much closer, Marys Rock.

After another quarter of a mile, the A.T. turns 90 degrees to the right; a side trail goes 90 degrees to the left, 0.1 mile to the viewpoint on Marys Rock. Go to the viewpoint, even if you're tired; it's well worth the extra effort. (For notes on Marys Rock, and sketches of the view, see page 121.)

Return from the viewpoint to the A.T. junction, and continue straight ahead. Descend steadily for 1.7 miles, to a side trail on the right, which goes about a hundred feet to the turnaround circle in front of the restaurant at Panorama.

MILE 36.7, PINNACLES PICNIC AREA. Elevation 3,350 feet. *A.T. access.* The road makes a loop around the picnic area; the A.T. parallels the west side of the loop, about 15 feet from the pavement. The comfort stations are to the right of the road near the beginning of the loop, with pit toilets for winter use behind them. Picnic tables, fireplaces, and several drinking fountains (turned off in winter) are scattered around the picnic area. Within the loop is a sheltered pavillion with tables and fireplaces, so you can have a picnic in the rain. There's a frost-free faucet, for winter use, about 50 yards north of the covered pavillion.

From the far end of the loop, at the second parking area, you can walk 120 yards south on the A.T. to a viewpoint. This is an easy walk on a smooth trail. The view duplicates that from Jewell Hollow Overlook, but you can see farther to the right. Toward the right, the highest thing on the horizon is Hogback, with four humps. Immediately in front of Hogback is Pass Mountain. Farther right, on the horizon, are the two peaks of Mount Marshall. You can just barely see the rocky summit of Marys Rock at the right end of the view.

MILE 37.3, SERVICE ROADS, both sides. Elevation 3,230 feet. The road on the east goes to the former Pinnacles dump, which is no longer used. Fifty yards to the South, the road on the west side goes a hundred yards to the Pinnacles ranger residence, and a scientific research facility, at the site of a former CCC Camp.

MILE 37.9, PARKING AREA, west side. Elevation 3,000 feet. *A.T. access.* See map, page 134. You are at point "L", near the lower left.

A.T. access is via a 50-yard trail which begins at the south end of the parking area. Distances on the A.T.: South (to the left), it's 1.2 miles to Stony Man Mountain Overlook, Mile 38.6. North (to the right) it's a mile and a quarter to the Jewell Hollow Overlook, Mile 36.4.

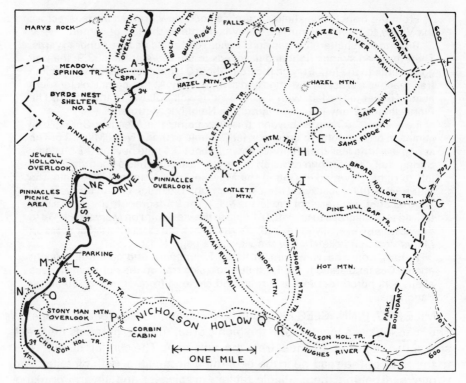

Map of Hazel Mountain — Nicholson Hollow area.

The *Corbin Cabin Cutoff* trail begins across the Drive from the north end of the parking area. This is the shortest route to Corbin Cabin and Nicholson Hollow, which is rich in ruined cabins and other evidence of the mountain people. At Corbin Cabin the Cutoff trail reaches the Nicholson Hollow trail, which in turn connects with a network of other trails. (See map.) I will suggest only two hikes that start here: Corbin Cabin via the Cutoff trail, round trip; and a circuit hike to the cabin, returning via the Nicholson Hollow trail and the A.T. If you'd like to devise other, longer hikes, see the discussion of "Hazel/Nicholson Hikes" beginning on page 125.

HIKE: *Corbin Cabin. Round trip* 2.9 miles; total *climb* about 1,095 feet; *time* required 3:10. See map above; your route is L-P-L. The upper half of the trail is somewhat rough and rather steep; the lower half is easy.

Except at the beginning, the trail follows a path built by the mountain people. At first it descends along a ridge crest through mountain laurels and young forest. Half a mile from the start, it swings left and descends the side of a ridge for about 200 yards, then turns right beside a dry stream bed. About 0.4 mile farther on, as the trail makes another turn to the right, look for a stone wall on the right, at a mountaineer homesite. The ruined cabin, 25 yards downhill on the left, was the home of John R. Nicholson.

The cabin had a single room about 12 by 18 feet, with a loft, a lean-to, and a covered patio. The chimney is still in good condition, and three walls are standing. The cabin was built of logs of various diameters, not very skillfully trimmed. The cracks were chinked with mud, and at least a part of the outside was covered with vertical clapboard. Inside, the mud was concealed in places by slats nailed to the logs. Some parts of the inside walls were covered with heavy asbestos paper; other parts still show evidence of whitewash, or peeling white paint. A round hole on the inside of the chimney shows that the cabin had a stove as well as a fireplace. On the outside, an inverted ,"V" of caulking on the chimney shows where the roof crest was. A small pool in the stream, fifty feet beyond the chimney, was a reliable water source.

When the hollow was inhabited by the Nicholson family this cabin was near one corner of a large clearing—nearly half a square mile in area—extending to Corbin Cabin and well beyond it, and from there nearly a mile downstream on both sides of the Hughes River, serving as garden space, cornfields, and pasture.

Continuing on the trail, it's another 0.3 mile to Corbin Cabin. This stretch is rich in evidence of the former inhabitants. There are ruins of several small farm buildings, a few strands of barbed wire, old grape vines, and piles and walls of rock: a byproduct of the struggle to create a workable garden plot—to expose enough soil in one place for a patch of corn. The trail descends to cross a small stream. About 250 yards beyond it is an old cemetery, a short distance to the right of the trail. It's not easy to find; the graves are marked only by uninscribed fieldstones.

Fifty yards before you reach a second stream, and fifty yards to the right of the trail, is another ruined cabin. This one was relatively fancy, with tongue-and-groove flooring, a stairway rather than a ladder to the loft, and a metal roof. This was the home of John T. Nicholson.

After you cross the second stream, Hughes River, walk a hundred feet to the junction with the Nicholson Hollow trail, at point "P" on the map. To your left, it's 4.0 miles downhill to the Weakley Hollow fire road; to your right it's 1.8 miles uphill to Skyline Drive at Mile 38.4. Directly ahead is the locked Corbin Cabin. If it's occupied, please keep your distance. If you'd like to rent it for your own use, write to the Potomac Appalachian Trail Club, 1718 N St., N.W., Washington, D.C. 20006.

Corbin Cabin was built by George Corbin, an inlaw of the Nicholsons, in 1909 when he was 21. According to Mr. Corbin's own account he borrowed $500 to remodel the cabin and put on a tin roof, shortly before it was condemned in 1936 and taken over by the Park. George Corbin received $500 for the whole property—land, cabin, and new tin roof. Members of P.A.T.C. repaired and enlarged the cabin in 1953-54, and have since been responsible for its maintenance.

About twenty families, most of them Nicholsons, lived in Nicholson Hollow between Corbin Cabin and the present Park boundary. All the land that was reasonably flat was cleared for gardens, cornfields, potato patches, pastures, and orchards. There was a school about two miles downstream from Corbin Cabin, near the mouth of Hannah Run. In early days the school also served as a church, and a preacher came from Sperryville once a month. Later the Hughes River Church was built near the schoolhouse and Warren Corbin, a brother of George, served as preacher. A doctor came to the hollow from Criglersville when he was needed.

George Freeman Pollock, founder and owner of the Skyland resort before it became part of the Park, has unkind things to say about the Nicholson family in his book *Skyland*. According to Pollock the Nicholsons called this valley "Freestate Hollow", and considered it independent of the state of Virginia and not subject to its laws or taxes. Aaron Nicholson, patriarch of the family, was the king of Freestate Hollow, Aaron claimed to own all the land as far as the eye could see, because he had walked around it. The Nicholsons were in fact squatters, who owned nothing. So says Pollock.

Aaron Nicholson, the "king", lived in a two-story house about 0.2 mile downstream from Corbin Cabin. In winter, when the leaves are down, you can see the ruined house from the trail. In summer you have to leave the trail, cross the stream, and look for it.

HIKE: *Corbin Cabin. Circuit* 4.3 miles; total *climb* about 1,350 feet; *time* required 4:20. A medium-difficult hike; part of the trail is rough. See map, page 134; your route is L-P-O-N-M-L.

As above, to Corbin Cabin. At the trail junction, as you face the cabin, turn right onto the blue-blazed Nicholson Hollow trail. From here to the Drive, the trail follows an old mountain road. The lower half of it is badly eroded, and in places you have to scramble over rocks that vary in size from a quart to a bushel. About 250 yards from the cabin, the blue-blazed Indian Run trail swings off to the left. (This too was once a road. It climbs to the saddle of Thorofare Mountain, joins the Corbin Mountain trail, and continues to the Old Rag fire road. Fun for experienced hikers with lots of time.)

Continue on the Nicholson Hollow trail. Less than a quarter of a mile from Corbin Cabin, the trail crosses Indian Run (no relation to the Indian Run in the North Section of the Park). About 1.1 miles beyond the stream crossing, the walled-in Dale Spring is at the left edge of the trail; it's unreliable in dry weather. The trail swings gently right around the head of Nicholson Hollow, then turns sharp left for a final nearly-straight stretch through scrub oaks and mountain laurels.

When you reach the Drive go left (south) for nearly a hundred yards. Cross the Drive and continue on the blue-blazed trail, beyond the yellow posts and chain, to where the blue-blazed Crusher Ridge trail comes in on the right. You can, if you wish, continue straight ahead to the A.T. at point "N" on the map, then turn right. But I suggest that you take a shortcut by turning right onto the Crusher Ridge trail. Go about 150 yards, turn right onto the A.T., and go about 0.6 mile to a trail junction with a marker post. The parking area at your starting point is 130 feet to the right.

MILE 38.4, NICHOLSON HOLLOW TRAIL. Elevation 3,100 feet. The trail goes east from the marker post. But don't park here. Use the grassy area on the east side of the Drive, a hundred yards farther south. Or park at Stony Man Mountain Overlook, Mile 38.6.

MILE 38.5, GRASSY PARKING AREA, east side. *Hikes.* Park here to use the *Nicholson Hollow trail.* Look out for a rock in the grass, about ten feet from the pavement, near the north end of the area. The rock is badly scratched on top, showing that cars have run into it. The head of the Nicholson Hollow trail (point "O" on the map, page 134) is on the east side of the Drive, less than a tenth of a mile to the north. As you can see on the map, this trail connects with a number of other trails, which I have described earlier under "Hazel/Nicholson Hikes", page 125. Here I will only outline a one-way hike to the mouth of the hollow.

HIKE: *Nicholson Hollow trail* to Weakley Hollow fire road. *One way* 5.8 miles; total *climb* about 130 feet; *time* required 4:20. Mountaineer cabins (ruins); stream, cascades, pools. Your route on the map is O-P-Q-R-S. Even though it's nearly all downhill, I've classified this hike as moderately difficult because parts of the trail are rough and rocky. This is a one-way hike, so you'll have to leave a car at point "S" on the map, or arrange for someone to meet you there. (Directions for reaching point "S" by car are on page 139.)

From its beginning the trail descends for 1.8 miles, following an old mountain road, to Corbin Cabin. (For notes on Corbin Cabin, Nicholson Hollow, and the Nicholson family, see the Corbin Cabin Hikes, above.)

Continue in the same direction beyond Corbin Cabin and the Cutoff trail, for 2.1 miles to point "Q" on the map, where the Hannah Run trail comes in on the left. Cross a ditch, and then descend to cross Hannah Run on the rocks. A hundred yards beyond, the Hot- Short Mountain trail comes in on the left. Go another 1.4 miles, with the Hughes River on your right, to the Park boundary; then another quarter of a mile on private property. Cross the Hughes River, and then Brokenback Run. (Both crossings may be difficult unless the water is unusually low.) The trail dead-ends in a private road. Turn left here, and go less than a hundred yards to the Weakley Hollow fire road, at point "S" on the map.

MILE 38.6, STONY MAN MOUNTAIN OVERLOOK. Hughes River Gap. Elevation 3,100 feet. *Water, toilets, A.T. access.* (As you approach the overlook *from the south,* the high point ahead is The Pinnacle. As you enter the overlook *at its north end,* you look directly ahead to the profile of Stony Man.) The view here is straight out to the town of Luray, in the Page Valley. Beyond it, the low notch in the Massanutten on the far side of the valley is Newmarket Gap. Because of the lights of Luray and other towns in the Valley, this overlook is well worth a stop after dark.

This is a long overlook, in two parts, with a bulletin board near the middle. The drinking fountain (turned off in winter) is on the wall at the south end. A short trail goes from the south end of the overlook to the toilets, and continues to the A.T. Distances on the A.T.: South (to the left) it's 2.0 miles to the dining hall at Skyland. North (to the right) it's 1.2 miles to the parking area at Mile 37.9 on the Drive.

Trivia: This is the second-longest overlook in the Park. Hogback Overlook, Mile 20.8 to 21.0, is 75 feet longer.

MILE 39.1, PARKING AREA, west side. A.T. *access; hikes.* The A.T. is less than fifty yards uphill from the parking area. Several hikes can be started here, but I will recommend only one: Little Stony Man. (Hikes to Stony Man summit and hikes on the Passamaquoddy trail are best started from Mile 41.7.)

Geology: The hidden contact between the Pedlar and Catoctin formations crosses the ridge a hundred feet north of the parking area. From this point south, for about 25 miles, nearly all the rocks exposed beside the Drive are greenstone—ancient lavas of the Catoctin formation. I'll mention some of the exceptions when we get to them.

HIKE: *Little Stony Man. Round trip* 0.9 mile; total *climb* about 270 feet; *time* required 1:00. Sheer cliffs, with good views. An easy hike, though part of the trail is rather rough.

Go to the A.T. and turn left. The trail climbs steadily for a third of a mile, then swings right and climbs to the ridge crest. There, at a concrete marker post, a side trail on the left goes first to the upper cliff of Little Stony Man, and then to Stony Man summit. Continue straight ahead, to the viewpoint on the lower cliff of Little Stony Man.

Looking to the left from the viewpoint, you can see the higher cliffs of Stony Man. With a little imagination you can make out the eye notch, nose, mustache, and beard. The town of Luray is straight out in the Valley. To the right you can see two stretches of Skyline Drive, with Stony Man Mountain Overlook on the left of the more distant one. In the distance, a little to the right of the overlook, is the sharp peak of Marys Rock; farther right, and a little closer, is the Pinnacle.

Little Stony Man is a good place to watch the sunset, especially if you've brought a flashlight, so you can stay a while after the sun is gone.

Geology: You're standing on top of the second Catoctin lava flow. The cliffs that rise above you are lava of the third flow. When enough time elapsed between eruptions, soil and sediments collected on top of the older lava. That's what happened here. As the molten lava of the third eruption advanced it churned up soil, sand, and mud. The rock that rises beside the trail here is worth close study. The greenstone contains red-brown lumps of ancient mud and soil, grains of sand, and some silvery schist that may have been formed from a layer of volcanic ash that fell before the lava flow. (The rocks are also dotted with white, green, and gray lichens.)

MILE 39.7, HEMLOCK SPRINGS OVERLOOK. Elevation 3,380 feet. *Drinking fountain* (turned off in winter.) The overlook has a view into the head of Nicholson Hollow, which bends to the right at the foot of the ridge. The nearby ridge to your right is a typical site for hemlocks, which grow in cool, damp parts of the Park. The high point a little to the left of center is The Pinnacle, with a "V" shaped view of the Piedmont to the right of it. Still farther right is the rounded dome of Hazel Mountain, and then the broader dome of Catlett Mountain.

There's a concrete reservoir below this overlook. Hemlock Spring was developed here to supply water for the drinking fountain and toilets at Stony Man Mountain Overlook, Mile 38.6.

MILE 40.5, THOROFARE MOUNTAIN OVERLOOK. Elevation 3,595 feet. The sketch identifies the principal features of the left-hand part of the view. Farther right is Robertson Mountain—sharply cone-shaped as seen from here—and beyond it the rocky face of Old Rag.

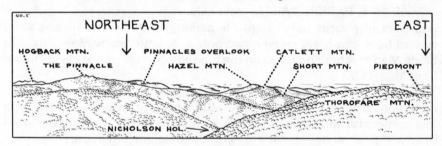

View from Thorofare Mountain Overlook.

A hike to Old Rag Summit takes a full day; but it's a rewarding experience if you have the time. Although the peak is only 3,291 feet high, climbing it requires a great deal of effort. Old Rag stands alone. Hikes begin at the bottom, rather than on Skyline Drive. For want of a better idea, I will describe the Old Rag Hikes here. I will recommend two of them: a circuit hike starting at the Weakley Hollow fire road; and a less strenuous trip starting on the Berry Hollow fire road.

HIKE: *Old Rag* summit. *Circuit* 7.2 miles; total *climb* about 2,380 feet; *time* required 7:30. Outstanding views. This is a difficult hike because of its length and amount of climbing. Parts of the trail are quite rough; parts are steep; much of the hike is a scramble over bare rocks. See map, page 139. The hike starts at the Park boundary, on the Weakley Hollow fire road, at the point labeled "Parking" near right center of the map. *Caution:* On weekends in good weather, Old Rag is crowded; the nearest parking space will be 0.8 mile from the beginning of the trail.

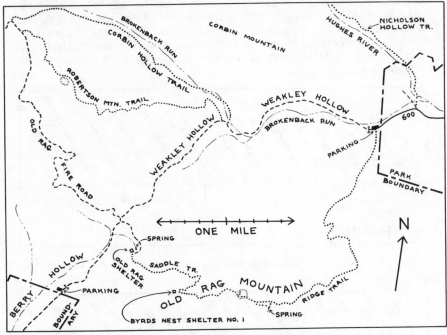

Map of Old Rag Hikes.

To reach *Weakley Hollow fire road* by car: Leave the Drive at Thornton Gap, Mile 31.5. Turn left on U.S. 211, and go through Sperryville to the junction with U.S. 522 at the far end of town, a little more than seven miles from the Drive. Turn right on 522; go a block, and follow 522 to the left. Go 0.6 mile and turn right onto Virginia 231. Go about 7.8 miles to a junction, with signs that say 602, Peola Mills, and Nethers. Turn right onto Virginia secondary road 602; go about 0.4 mile, cross the Hughes River on a bridge, and turn right on Va. 601. From here on, stay on what appears to be the main road, although its number will change from 601 to 707 and then to 600. A little less than 3.5 miles from the bridge, the road makes a sharp turn to the left; a private road continues more or less straight ahead, and there's a small, privately owned parking area on the right. (Park here, if possible, if you're leaving a car for a one-way hike on the *Hannah Run* or *Nicholson Hollow trails.* This is point "S" on the map used for those hikes.)

For the Old Rag circuit hike follow the road to the left, another 0.3 mile to the parking area at the beginning of the trail. On pleasant weekends, the lot will be full. Turn around and go back to the nearest parking space. *Do not block the road or access to private property;* if you do, your car will be towed away.

Take another look at the map. You will climb Old Rag via the ridge trail, continue across the summit and descend on the saddle trail, then return to your starting point via the Weakley Hollow fire road. The trail begins across the road from the parking area. It climbs easily but steadily for about three quarters of a mile, then becomes much steeper as you climb the ridge. After another half a mile, more or less, you reach the top of the ridge and come out on the rocks. This is where the rock scramble begins. You'll climb over granite boulders, or around them. At many points you'll have a wide view of the Piedmont to the left, or across Weakley Hollow to the Blue Ridge on the right.

The trail is blue-blazed; if you're in doubt where it goes, follow the blazes. At one point it passes between sheer walls of granite, less than three feet apart, where the rock underfoot forms a rough natural stairway. This is a dike, where molten lava once poured through a fissure in the granite. The lava has been completely eroded from the top of Old Rag, except in the dikes. The rocks that form the natural stairway between the granite walls are vestiges of the ancient lava.

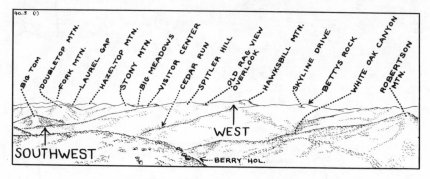

View from Old Rag. (No. 1.)

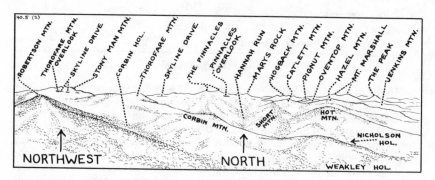

View from Old Rag. (No. 2.)

The ridge trail has several "false summits"; you'll climb what appears to be the summit, only to see another, higher crest farther on. The real summit has a concrete marker post. Walk twenty yards beyond the marker, turn right, and go past the boulders to the view. From the top of the highest boulder you have a view of 360 degrees. The two sketches identify the principal mountains that you see from here. Part of the view to the left is cut off by a second, slightly lower summit of Old Rag. When you're ready, return to the trail and turn right; go about 200 yards, and take the side trail on the right to Old Rag's second summit. From there you can look back to the first summit and, from another point, across the Old Rag saddle toward the mountains to the west and southwest.

Before you leave the second summit, look for a number of large holes, usually filled with water, in the surface of the granite rocks. Locally, these potholes are called "buzzard baths". How did they get there? *Conjecture:* Maybe pockets of softer material, once enclosed by the granite, have eroded away. Or perhaps this was once a river bed, and holes were eroded by sand and rocks in the swift current.

Now return to the trail. You can shorten the return trip by going back the way you came on the ridge trail—2.8 miles. But you'll have to scramble over all those rocks again. If you turn right, you can go back by the Old Rag saddle trail and fire road. This route is longer—4.4 miles—and somewhat rough; but it's downhill all the way, and there's nothing to climb over.

To return via the *Saddle Trail:* turn right, and descend along the ridge crest for 0.4 mile to a marker post in the Old Rag saddle, with Byrds Nest Shelter No. 1 in sight ahead. Turn right; descend for 1.1 miles to the Old Rag Shelter and spring. Continue on the fire road. (In spring, look for showy orchis and a large patch of periwinkles beside the road, both on the right.) About 0.4 mile from the shelter you'll reach a double junction. Here the Berry Hollow road goes to the left. The Old Rag fire road continues straight ahead, and reaches the Drive at Mile 43.0. Turn right onto the Weakley Hollow fire road, which goes 2.6 miles to your starting point.

History: The former village of Old Rag was near here, and the Old Rag Post Office was at the road junction. (The roads have been relocated, but by only a few feet at this point.) Originally, the Park intended to preserve some or all of the mountaineer homes in this area. But maintenance proved too difficult, and the houses were torn down shortly after the end of World War II. I have a photograph, taken from Old Rag summit in 1934, which shows a number of houses in Weakley Hollow. Cornfields extended more than halfway up the steep slope of Robertson Mountain, on the west side of the Hollow.

Wildflower note: Along the Weakley Hollow road I've found several species that are not common in the Park, including pennywort, *Obolaria virginica;* water carpet, *Chrysosplenium americanum;* and sweet pinesap, *Monotropsis odorata.* About a mile from the junction, in the second half of May, look for showy orchis in bloom on both sides of the road.

A mile and a quarter from the fire road junction you reach the mouth of Corbin Hollow, where the Robertson Mountain trail, and then the Corbin Hollow trail, come in on the left. (Both go to the Old Rag fire road.)

The mountain people who lived in Corbin Hollow were not nearly as well off as those in Nicholson and Weakley Hollows. The fault lies in the hollow itself: it's narrow and rocky, not suitable for farming. Brokenback Run flows from Corbin Hollow, and the road crosses it on a bridge. You'll cross it once more, with no help from a bridge, a tenth of a mile before you reach your starting point at the foot of the ridge trail.

HIKE: *Old Rag Summit* from Berry Hollow. *Round trip* 5.4 miles; total *climb* about 1,760 feet; *time* required 5:20. This is a fairly difficult hike, via fire road and the Old Rag saddle trail. The saddle trail is rough and rocky, and sometimes steep. Nevertheless, this is the easiest route to Old Rag summit. The hike starts from the parking area at the Park boundary in Berry Hollow (which was named for its early settlers, the Berry family; not for berries.) To reach the starting point by car:

Berry Hollow Parking Area. From Thornton Gap, Mile 31.5, follow the directions for *Weakley Hollow* fire road, page 139, until you reach the sign that says 602, Peola Mills, Nethers. *Do not* turn here. Continue ahead another 2.2 miles to Etlan, and turn right onto Virginia 643. Drive 4.5 winding miles to a road junction where 643 turns sharply to the left. Turn right here, onto 600, and follow it for about 4.7 miles to the parking area at the Park boundary.

The hike begins at the parking area (near the lower left corner of the map, page 139.) Take the fire road uphill, beyond the chain, and continue about 0.9 mile to the junction with the Old Rag fire road. Turn right, and go 0.4 mile to the end of the road; the Old Rag Shelter is in view ahead on the right, and there's a spring still farther right in the gully. Turn left onto the Old Rag Saddle trail and climb steadily. Near the top of the ridge there's a ledge, on the right side of the trail, with a view across the hollow to Robertson Mountain.

On the ridge top, a mile from the Old Rag Shelter, is a concrete marker post. Byrds Nest Shelter No. 1 is in view on your right. Turn left and climb a little less than half a mile to Old Rag summit, which is also marked with a concrete post. Twenty yards before you reach the post, turn left; go around the boulders to find the view. For notes on the Old Rag summit, and sketches of the view, see page 140. Return via the same route to your starting point.

MILE 41.0, ROAD TRACE, west side. About 100 feet south of the milepost, an old road goes uphill on the west side of the drive. This is the entrance to an abandoned quarry, which was used during the construction of Skyline Drive.

MILE 41.7, SKYLAND, NORTH ENTRANCE. Elevation 3.680 feet (highest point on Skyline Drive.) Food, lodging, gifts, bar, *hikes.* See map, page 143; you're near the middle of the map. The hikes begin at the Nature Trail Parking area, which is on your right after you turn in on the entrance road. To reach the office and dining hall (which I've labeled "Skyland Lodge" on the map) follow the signs: after you pass the parking area on the right, turn first to the left, then to the right.

There are evening campfire programs and conducted walks at Skyland during the summer. For information on time and place, see the folder on Visitor Activities (posted on bulletin boards.)

The Skyland resort is much older than the Park. It was founded by George Freeman Pollock, a self-made legend in his own time. The interpretive sign in front of the recreation hall tells his story. If you'd like to know more about him and the good old days at Skyland, read Pollock's own book, *Skyland.* It's available wherever books are sold in the Park. But remember that this is a legend writing about a legend, so take it with a grain of skepticism.

The recreation hall is on a paved loop that surrounds a grassy area. (See map on the facing page.) A short distance uphill from the left (south) end of the loop, you come to Massanutten Lodge, on your right. It was built by Addie Narin Hunter in 1911, the summer before she married George Freeman Pollock. Now, during the summer season, it's open as a Visitor Information Station on weekends, and intermittently during the week.

I will suggest two hikes, both beginning at the Nature Trail parking area: the Stony Man Nature Trail, and a circuit using the Passamaquoddy trail and the Stony Man ridge trail. (I will describe a hike to Millers Head from the south entrance to Skyland.)

HIKE: *Stony Man Nature Trail. Round trip* 1.6 miles; total *climb* about 340 feet; *time* required 1:40. An easy, gradual climb to the cliffs of Stony Man summit; part of the trail is rather rough. The hike is self-guiding, using numbered posts and a pamphlet. The pamphlet dispenser is beside the trail at its beginning, in the corner of the parking area nearest the Drive. See map, page 143.

About 0.4 mile from the start, the nature trail crosses the Stony Man ridge trail. Continue straight ahead for less than 150 yards, to a junction where the trail rejoins itself after making a loop around the summit. Keep right. In less than 0.3 mile, reach a broad clearing with a horse hitching rail. (You have passed the inconspicuous summit of Stony Man—elevation 4,010 feet, the second-highest point in the Park—on your left.) Straight ahead is a 100-yard path to a viewpoint on the cliffs. The horse trail comes in from the left. The trail that goes sharp left is your return route along the Nature Trail.

Go straight ahead, to the viewpoint on the rocks. By moving around a little, you can piece together a view of more than 180 degrees. Ahead is a broad view of the Page Valley, with the Massanutten Mountain beyond it. The town of Luray is a little to the left. To the far left, the highest point in sight is Hawksbill. Farther right you can look down on Skyland, and beyond it the rounded summit of Bushytop. The ridge that descends to the right from Bushtop abruptly changes slope at the observation point on Millers Head.

Looking down the ridge to your right, you can see the two-tiered cliffs of Little Stony Man. Beyond them are two short stretches of the Drive, with Stony Man Mountain Overlook to the left of the second one. In line with the second stretch of Drive, but five miles away, is the grassy area at Thornton Gap. The sharp peak to the right of the gap is Marys Rock; still farther right, closer, and not so sharp, is The Pinnacle.

Note: Near the Stony Man summit, in late summer and early fall, you may see small trees with bright red berries that, on close look, resemble tiny tomatoes. This is mountain ash.

History: There was once a small copper mine near the summit of Stony Man. Some ore was mined in the early 1800's, but operations were stopped before 1850. In 1881 the Richards Mining Co. bought the copper-mining rights on 340 acres for $1500, and began to work a quartz vein that was only an inch thick at the surface, though it widened to four inches farther down. The vein assayed 12.5% copper (mostly as green copper carbonate.) In 1882, nine men were employed in drilling and blasting, and a sample assayed at 47% copper and ½% silver. In 1883 the shaft reached a depth of 100 feet, and

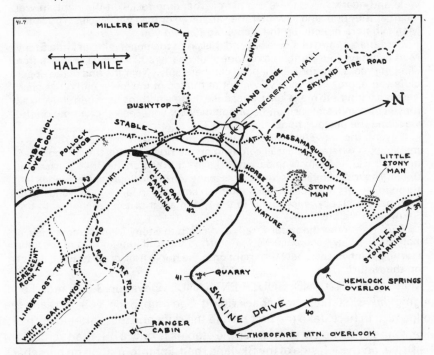

Map of Skyland — Stony Man — Limberlost area.

was then abandoned. The value of the ore in the narrow vein was less than the expense of extracting it.

HIKE: *Passamaquoddy Trail. Circuit* 3.5 miles; total *climb* about 770 feet; *time* required 3:10. An interesting, not very difficult walk, with outstanding views from Stony Man Summit and Little Stony Man. (See map, page 143.)

From the Nature Trail parking area, follow the sidewalk west (away from the Drive), and go 50 feet beyond the parking area to the horse trail. Turn left, go to the paved road, and turn right. Walk beside the road, keeping to the right where it forks. The A.T. crosses the road about 0.2 mile from the parking area. Turn right on the A.T. Pass through a grove of hemlocks, go about .15 mile to a dirt road, and turn right. Pass an abandoned side road that goes uphill on the right, and continue to a fork in the road. The right branch goes 50 yards to a pumphouse. The left branch, with a yellow chain, is the old Skyland-to-Luray road which provided access to Skyland before the Drive was built. The A.T. resumes on the far side of the road, at a concrete marker post.

Fifty yards from the marker, the enclosed pumphouse at Furnace Spring is set into the hillside on the right. Excess water, if any, runs under the trail. This spring once supplied water to a copper smelter; hence its name. It now supplies water to the Skyland development, as it has since the earliest days of Skyland.

Trivia: The 0.8-mile section of A.T. between Furnace Spring and Little Stony Man is the Passamaquoddy trail. In 1932 Pollock, then still proprietor of Skyland, had a trail built between these points. The present A.T. follows almost the same route; in several places you can see a trace of the old trail just a few feet up the bank. Pollock called this the Passamaquoddy Trail because, he said, *Passamaquoddy* is a Maine Indian word meaning "abounding in pollock" (a kind of fish.)

Continue, with some ups and downs, along the steep slope below the Stony Man cliffs. Less than half a mile beyond the spring, where the trail is wide and nearly level, there are big overhanging rocks on the right. In wet weather they drip, and in winter they are often draped with icicles. The Stony Man cliffs are directly up the slope, high above you.

Less than a third of a mile beyond this point the upper cliffs of Little Stony Man begin on your right, and continue for nearly 200 yards. (These are fine climbing rocks, but for experienced climbers only.) Near the end of the upper cliffs you approach a wide viewpoint at the top of the lower cliffs. The view here is exciting—to me at least—because there's nothing between you and all those cubic miles of air that begin just beyond your toes. (For a note on the view and the geology here, see page 137.)

Beyond the viewpoint the trail swings right, and in 200 yards reaches a marker post where a side trail comes in on the right. Ahead, the A.T. goes 0.4 mile to the Little Stony Man parking area at Mile 39.1 on the Drive. Turn right, uphill. The trail climbs by switchbacks to the top of the upper cliffs, swings left through laurels and scrub oaks, and then emerges in fairly open woods. You now have a steady, easy climb to the trail marker at the junction with the Stony Man Nature Trail.

Turn right onto the nature trail, and climb to Stony Man Summit. (For a note on the view, see page 143.) Return to the trail junction. To reach your starting point you can now turn right onto the horse trail, or go straight ahead on the Nature Trail.

MILE 42.5, SKYLAND, SOUTH ENTRANCE. Elevation 3,515 feet. Food, lodging; *hikes;* stables, horseback riding. See map, page 143. To reach the Lodge turn in here, take the first turn to the right and then, after a tenth of a mile, to the left. The parking lot for the stables is only a hundred yards from the Drive, on the left side of the Skyland road. For information on horseback rides, ask at the stables.

HIKE: *Millers Head. Round trip* 1.6 miles; total *climb* about 450 feet; *time* required 1:35. A fairly easy hike on a good, graded trail, down a rocky ridge to an observation platform with a fine, nearly 360-degree view.

Turn in toward Skyland, and pass the stables on your left. Where the road forks, keep to the left (see map, page 143.) Watch for a gravel road on your left; turn in there, and park in the grass. (The A.T. passes this point.)

Note: In winter, the Skyland area may be closed to cars. To hike to Millers Head in winter, park in the White Oak Canyon parking area (Mile 42.6) and walk along the Skyland entrance road to the Millers Head parking spot. The round trip to Millers Head from the White Oak parking area is 2.3 miles, with a total climb of about 600 feet.

From the Millers Head parking spot, walk 80 yards up the paved road to a sign that marks the Millers Head trail. Turn left onto the trail, which enters the woods at the downhill edge of a locust grove. (If you can't find the trail, take the gravel road instead. It joins the trail in 0.2 mile, near the summit of Bushytop; when you get there, turn left.) On the Bushytop summit the shack with a microwave antenna on the roof is part of the telephone system: it's cheaper to connect the Skyland telephones to the valley by radio than by wires. If you hear a humming sound inside the shack it's the power transformer—not bees.

A hundred feet beyond the Bushytop summit the trail switches back sharply to the left; a side trail goes 30 feet straight ahead to a viewpoint (sometimes clear, sometimes overgrown) that overlooks Kettle Canyon. (On October 14, 1951, Swami Premananda scattered the ashes of George Freeman Pollock into the head of Kettle Canyon.)

The main trail descends steadily, by switchbacks, to a low point with a concrete trail marker. About 250 yards beyond the marker is a view to the left, across Buracker Hollow. The rock at your feet here is covered with rock spikemoss (*Selaginella rupestris*), which is rather rare in the Park; it's not really moss, but a somewhat higher plant.

A little farther on, the trail comes out on the ridge crest, with Buracker Hollow on the left and Kettle Canyon on the right. Beyond, the trail drops down to the right side of the ridge by a double switchback. There, where you see a hemlock on the right, note the rock face on your left: a miniature rock garden with several species of moss and several of ferns, especially polypody. Continue another 200 yards to the observation platform on Millers Head, elevation about 3,465 feet.

The view from the left wall (i.e. to the left of the steps as you mount the platform), from left to right: Pollock Knob, Timber Hollow Overlook, Bettys Rock, and Hawksbill Gap. The high point is Hawksbill, with Nakedtop a little lower and to its right. From there the ridge descends to the community of Ida, at the mouth of Buracker Hollow. (The clear area a short distance below the observation platform is a hang-glide launching site. For permission to launch, call Park Headquarters, 999-2243.)

From the front wall you look across the Page Valley to the Massanutten, with the town of Luray a little to the right of center.

From the right-hand wall you see Bushytop at the far right; to the left of it are some of the buildings at Skyland. The high point is Stony Man; to the left of that is The Pinnacle. Still farther left, and more distant, are the sharp peak of Marys Rock and the grassy clearing at Thornton Gap. To the left of The Pinnacle, and closer, is Stony Man Mountain Overlook.

Now back to the left front corner of the platform: relax, look, and listen. On a typical summer day, if the wind is not too strong, you may hear all of these sounds within a few minutes: trucks and cars, cows, a train, a sawmill, hammering, a gunshot or two, a radio in Ida with commercials louder than the music, and the nearby humming of flies and bees and the chirping of a cricket.

MILE 42.6, WHITEOAK CANYON PARKING, east side. Elevation 3,510 feet. This is a long, paved parking area that begins a few feet south of the south entrance to Skyland. The *Whiteoak Canyon trail* begins near the north end of the parking area.

Whiteoak Canyon has been called the "scenic gem" of Shenandoah, which is an understatement. It's a place of wild beauty—a shady place of great boulders under tall hemlocks, of cascades and pools and sheer rock walls, and a steep gorge with six waterfalls. The trail, from the Drive to the first (and highest) waterfall, is in good condition, and the walking is easy. But farther down it gets steeper, and parts of it are rough and rocky.

As you might expect, this has always been one of the most popular places in the Park. Long before there was a Park, Whiteoak Canyon was the principal playground for the guests at Skyland. At that time the first falls could be reached by road. At the top of the falls were a bridge, a dam, a swimming pool, and bath houses. This spot was the scene of picnics and barbeques throughout the summer. Now the top of the falls has partially returned to its original wild state. But its popularity continues. The parking area holds 40 cars; on summer weekends you'll find the parking area full, and the canyon disappointingly crowded.

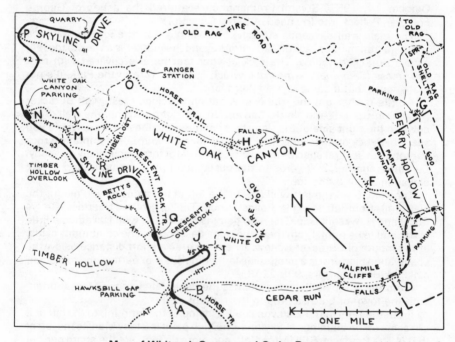

Map of Whiteoak Canyon and Cedar Run area.

The map above shows the principal trails in the Whiteoak Canyon area. The parking lot, at Mile 42.6 on the Drive, is at point "N", near the left-hand edge of the map. (Point "P", at the upper left corner of the map, is at the north entrance to Skyland.) I will describe several hikes in the area represented by the map:

From Mile 42.6, *Whiteoak Canyon* to the first falls. (N-K-L-H, and return by the same route.)

From Mile 43.0, a circuit through the *Limberlost* (M-R-L-M).

From Crescent Rock Overlook, a hike to *Bettys Rock;* another to *Limberlost* via the *Crescent Rock* trail (Q-R-L-M-R-Q); and a circuit hike using the A.T. and returning via the Crescent Rock trail (Q-N-K-L-R-Q).

From Hawksbill Gap, Mile 45.6, a circuit that includes all the waterfalls in *Cedar Run* and *Whiteoak Canyon* (A-B-C-D-F-H-I-B-A).

With the help of the map, and the notes and table that follow, you can put together a number of other hikes.

From	To	Dist. miles	Climb feet	From	To	Dist. miles	Climb feet
A	B	0.05	0	H	O	1.25	705
A	J	0.6	60	I	B	0.66	85
B	A	0.05	10	I	H	1.74	20
B	C	1.72	40	I	J	0.16	60
B	I	0.66	80	J	A	0.6	20
C	B	1.72	1475	J	I	0.16	0
C	D	0.82	80	K	L	0.25	0
D	C	0.82	695	K	M	0.16	15
D	E	0.6	20	K	N	0.59	205
D	F	0.9	120	K	O	0.82	150
E	D	0.6	240	L	H	1.5	60
E	F	0.75	275	L	K	0.25	60
E	G	1.1	450	L	M	0.78	100
F	D	0.9	140	M	K	0.16	0
F	E	0.75	75	M	L	0.78	25
F	H	1.9	1395	N	K	0.59	10
G	E	1.1	0	O	H	1.25	0
H	F	1.9	70	O	K	0.82	150
H	I	1.74	760	O	P	1.35	440
H	L	1.5	705	P	O	1.35	70

Table of Distances, Whiteoak - Cedar Run area. See map, page 146.

By using the Old Rag fire road, which goes along the top of the map, you can climb Old Rag from here if you have enough time and energy. Old Rag Shelter, which appears at the upper right corner of the map, is in the lower left part of the map on page 139.

If you follow the Whiteoak Canyon trail all the way to the bottom, you reach a parking area in BERRY HOLLOW, at point "E" on the map. To reach point "E" by car: Leave the Drive at Thornton Gap, Mile 31.5. Turn left onto U.S. 211, and go through Sperryville to the junction with U.S. 522 at the far end of town, a little more than seven miles from the Drive. Turn right on 522; go a block, and follow 522 to the left. Go 0.6 mile and turn right onto Virginia 231. Go about ten miles to Etlan, and turn right onto Virginia 643. Drive 4.5 miles to a junction where 643 turns sharply to the left. Turn right here, onto 600. Go about 3.6 miles, and cross the stream on a concrete-paved ford. Immediately turn left onto an unpaved road, to a small parking area. Continue, crossing a small bridge, to the parking area at point "E".

HIKE: *Whiteoak Canyon* to first falls. *Round trip* 4.6 miles; total *climb* about 1,040 feet; *time* required 4:15. See map, page 146. The trail starts gently downhill, swinging first right and then left around a swampy area. (In early spring those vigorous green shoots in the swamp are False Helibore, *Veratrum viride.*) Cross a small stream and, 0.6 mile from the start, cross the Old Rag fire road. After another quarter of a mile you reach the Limberlost trail in a grove of giant hemlocks. The biggest are from 350 to 400 years old. You will be among big hemlocks all the way down to the falls.

Go straight ahead past the junction. (*Geology:* note the disintegrating basalt boulder on your left—a good example of columnar jointing.) After a couple of hundred yards a small stream, a mere trickle, comes in from the right and flows beside the trail. One of the pleasures of the Whiteoak Canyon hike consists in watching this trickle grow, and join other trickles and grow some more, until it plunges over the falls in—what shall I say? In a dry August, a somewhat larger trickle. In spring, an awesome torrent. During a spring thaw, especially after a rain, Whiteoak Canyon is saturated. Water streams from every pore in the soil, and gushes from every crack in the cliffs. There's running water wherever you look, including the trail under your feet.)

Continue, downward. Pass cascades and pools and more tall trees (including an occasional white oak.) Pass cliffs and ledges and surrealistic boulders. Hemlocks grow on the boulders, and grip their sides with descending roots as with downturned fingers.

Then, a mile and a third from the Limberlost trail, you come to another trail junction with a concrete marker post. The trail turns left here, crosses the stream on a bridge, and then continues downstream on the left bank. (Straight ahead from the junction, a trail goes about 200 feet and dead-ends at the horse trail, which goes uphill to the right, and fords the stream on the left.) One way or another, get to the trail on the left bank of the stream, opposite the ford. Here the trail widens, and there's a hitching rail for horses. The top of the falls is ahead on your right, but there's no point in going there; you can't see the falls from the top.

Thirty yards farther, the horse trail comes in on the left. Continue straight ahead another 400 feet, to another widening in the trail. Diagonally ahead to the right are two rocky ledges. From the downstream ledge you have a fine view of the falls, which has a total drop of 86 feet. The stream, by the way, is Whiteoak Run. It was originally called Island Run, because of the island near point "E" on the map. It's the principal source of the Robinson River.

This is the first, and highest of six waterfalls on Whiteoak Run. Their heights are (numbered from top to bottom):

No. 1: 86 feet.
No. 2: 62 feet.
No. 3: 35 feet.
No. 4: 41 feet.
No. 5: 49 feet.
No. 6: 60 feet.

Below the first falls the canyon is narrow, and the trail is steep and rough. If you continue down the canyon to the sixth falls, and then return, you will add 2.7 miles and 1,110 feet of climbing to your hike. If you want to see all the falls, an alternative possibility is the Cedar Run-Whiteoak circuit hike from Hawksbill Gap (page 154.)

MILE 43.0, OLD RAG FIRE ROAD, *Limberlost trail.* Turn into the gravel fire road on the east side of the Drive, about 50 feet south of the milepost, and drive 0.1 mile to a small parking area on the left. I recommend that you use this parking area for only one purpose: the circuit hike on the Limberlost trail.

HIKE: *Limberlost trail. Circuit* 1.2 miles; total *climb* about 130 feet; *time* required 0.55. An easy hike, cool and shady, through an old orchard and a grove of giant hemlocks. See map, page 146. You're at point "M", near left center. Your route is M-R-L-K-M.

The trail begins across the road from the parking area, at its upper (south) end. At sixty yards, notice the dense carpets of soft haircap moss. Less than 0.2 mile from the start you enter a semi-open area—an old apple orchard. The trees produce pink flowers in early spring, and a lot of small, wormy apples in the fall. Near the far end of the orchard, on the left, are several crabapple trees; they're smaller than apple trees, with grayish bark and sharp twigs that resemble thorns.

About 150 yards after you leave the orchard, the path suddenly becomes shadier. Fifty yards farther, a swampy area begins on the left and parallels the trail, about 25 yards away. In spring, look for new green shoots of false helibore in the swamp, and yellow flowers of marsh marigold. When the trail reaches a marker post, it makes a sharp turn to the left.

(Straight ahead, the Crescent Rock trail goes 1.1 mile, climbing about 325 feet, to Crescent Rock Overlook, Mile 44.4. A hundred yards up this trail, on the right, is a junk heap abandoned by the CCC when they left the Park in 1942. If you're interested in recent "archeology", go on up and explore. I've found old car parts, stove parts, license plates, signs, a washing machine roller, a two-quart canteen. Just look, don't collect.)

Ahead, on the Limberlost trail, the first young hemlocks appear. As you continue they increase in number and size; and the undergrowth becomes progressively thinner, for several reasons. Hemlocks produce a shade too dense for many plants; and their fallen needles eventually make a thick, acid mulch in which the seeds of most plants can not germinate. Toward the beginning of the hemlock grove you'll see mountain laurels on both sides of the trail. Mountain laurel can stand a good deal of shade, and it likes acid soil.

About 0.6 miles from the start, the trail makes a sharp left turn in front of a hemlock more than three feet in diameter. You are now entering an area of big hemlocks, from 350 to 400 years old, called the Limberlost. The name was given by George Freeman Pollock, the founder of Skyland, who took it from the novel *Girl of the Limberlost* by Gene Stratton Porter. In the summer, Limberlost is one of the best places in the Park to find mushrooms, Indian pipes, mosses, pine drops, and other plants that thrive in deep shade.

Legend: or maybe *history:* It's only because of Pollock that these big trees are here. They were scheduled to be cut down. Pollock paid the lumbermen $10 per tree to leave them standing.

Continue, crossing a small stream on the rocks. This is a principal source of Whiteoak Run which, after growing considerably, forms the six beautiful waterfalls of Whiteoak Canyon. Beyond the crossing, note the tall red maple on the left; in early October it's a mass of brilliant color.

About 150 yards beyond the stream crossing is the junction with the Whiteoak trail, where you will turn left toward the Whiteoak parking area. Ahead, the Limberlost trail continues 0.1 mile to the Old Rag fire road. To the right, the Whiteoak Canyon trail goes 1.6 miles to the first falls in the canyon. As you approach the trail junction, notice the boulder ahead on the right. It's worth a closer look, because it shows a fine example of columnar jointing. After you turn left at the junction, and go another 100 feet, notice the fallen giant hemlock on the left; it was brought down by wind some years ago. This log will provide a home for small plants and animals for many years. Eventually mosses, fungi, and insects will reduce it to humus; and it will enrich the soil so that other trees may grow. Sixty yards farther on, notice the stand of ground cedar on the right. It's not a cedar but a clubmoss—one of the lower plants, which have neither seeds nor flowers. This plant was rather rare when the Park was created, because mountaineers used to sell it for Christmas decorations.

Continue less than 0.2 mile to the Old Rag fire road, and turn left. (The Whiteoak trail goes on ahead 0.6 mile to the parking area at Mile 42.6.) Walk less than 0.2 mile on the fire road to reach your starting point.

MILE 43.1 to 43.2. The Drive passes along the edge of an old orchard. Many apple trees are visible from the Drive; they bloom in late April and early May.

MILE 43.3, TIMBER HOLLOW OVERLOOK. Elevation 3,360 feet. *A.T. access.* Timber Hollow is the upper end of Buracker Hollow, which you can see down below, with a house and clearing. (Most members of the Buracker family pronounce the name BURR-uh-k'r, with the "uh" so soft that it's almost inaudible.)

To the far left, looking straight down the Drive, you see a high rocky ledge near the viewpoint on Bettys Rock. Farther right and more distant, the highest peak is Hawksbill, with Nakedtop to the right of it. A ridge descends from Nakedtop to the settlement of Ida—one of the seven resettlement locations to which families of mountain people were removed when the Park was established. The nearby crest on your right is Pollock Knob, elevation 3,580 feet, named for George Freeman Pollock, the founder of Skyland. It was dedicated on October 14, 1951, by Senator Harry F. Byrd, Sr.

History: Almost directly across the Drive from the overlook was CCC camp No. 1—the first CCC camp in the Park, and one of the first in the United States.

A.T. access. From an opening in the wall, a trail descends a flight of stone steps and continues another hundred feet or so to the A.T. Distances on the A.T.: South (to the left) it's 1.3 miles to Hawksbill Gap, Mile 45.6. North (to the right) it's 1.8 miles to the Dining Hall at Skyland.

Geology: Here, and for about a mile to the north and a quarter of a mile to the south, the exposed rocks are granodiorite of the Pedlar formation. Going from the overlook to the A.T. you pass a ledge of granodiorite on the right; in it are several veins of light-green epidote—probably the result of mineralization by the lava flow that once covered this area. Beyond Ida, at the mouth of the hollow, is Hershberger Ridge, consisting of sedimentary rocks of the Erwin formation. Beyond the ridge is the limestone of the Shenandoah Valley. Thus successively younger rocks are to be found at successively lower elevations as you go west—a result of the deep folding of the earth's crust that took place here.

MILE 44.4, CRESCENT ROCK OVERLOOK. Elevation 3,550 feet. *A.T. access. Hikes.* The overlook provides a narrow view out through Buracker Hollow to the settlement of Ida. Beyond and to the left of Ida is Hershberger Ridge. The high point on your left is Hawksbill, with exposed basalt cliffs and talus slopes. Lower than Hawksbill, and a little to the right of it, is Nakedtop.

From the south end of the wall, a graded trail goes a hundred yards to Crescent Rock, where the view is somewhat wider. On the nearby summit to the right, the cliff a little way down the left-hand slope is Bettys Rock. Farther left and more distant, the high point is Bushytop, from which a ridge descends to the abrupt angle at Millers Head, and then to the mouth of the hollow near Ida.

Legend: Crescent Rock was formerly called Sow Rock. Two mountaineers, chasing a sow, inadvertently chased her over this cliff.

Legend: Crescent Rock was formerly called Sours Rock, because a Miss Sours ended her life by falling or jumping from it.

Conjecture: One of these legends is an illegitimate offspring of the other.

Report: Before the Park was established, guests from Skyland had frequent picnics here at Crescent Rock. The rock was often the scene of religious revivals, as well as Easter sunrise services. When the Drive was built, extra parking space was provided here so that these activities could continue.

A.T. access. The *Bettys Rock* trail begins at the north end of the wall at the overlook. A few feet from the beginning, a side trail on the left descends to the A.T. Distances on the A.T.: South (to the left) it's 0.5 mile to Hawksbill Gap, Mile 45.6. North (to the right) it's 0.8 mile to Timber Hollow Overlook, Mile 43.3

I will suggest three hikes from Crescent Rock Overlook: Bettys Rock; Limberlost via the Crescent Rock trail; and Limberlost via the A.T. and return via the Crescent Rock trail.

> HIKE: *Bettys Rock. Round trip* 0.7 mile; total *climb* about 150 feet; *time* required 0:45. An easy walk to a ledge with a wide view. See map, page 146; you're at point "Q", a little below and left of center.
>
> The trail begins at the north end of the sidewalk in front of the wall, and climbs steadily and easily. There are a few rocks in the trail, so sturdy shoes would be helpful. The two sketches identify the principal features of the view, and require no comment.

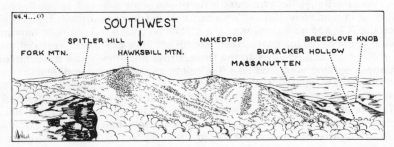

View from Bettys Rock. (No. 1.)

Wildflower note: Near Bettys Rock, in early spring, look for pink moss phlox, *Phlox subulata.* Later, a small white flower with leaves that are toothed at the end is three-toothed cinquefoil, *Potentilla tridentata.* Mountain laurel blooms here in June.

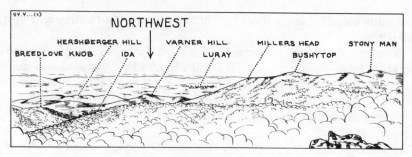

View from Bettys Rock. (No. 2).

Report: The rock is named for Betty (Mrs. James A.) Allis, whose husband built the trail to it many years ago.

HIKE: *Limberlost* via Crescent Rock trail. *Semi-circuit* 3.3 miles; total *climb* about 495 feet; *time* required 2:40. A medium-easy hike to a grove of tall hemlocks. The trail is not steep, and most of it is smooth; there's a rough, eroded stretch about 50 yards long. See map, page 146. You're a point "Q", below and to left of center. Your route is Q-R-L-K-M-R-Q.

The trail begins at a marker post across the Drive from the overlook, 25 yards south of the north entrance. It climbs a few feet, passes through a patch of mountain laurel, and then descends steadily. Along the trail you may find scattered junk: oil drums, paint cans, bottles, broken glass, scrap iron, and the remains of an old car. About a mile from the start, and 120 yards before you reach the Limberlost trail, you pass an abandoned dump on the left. For most of its length the trail follows an abandoned road. The road was built by the mountain people who once lived here. But junk and dump are the work of the CCC, which had a camp near Timber Hollow Overlook.

You join the Limberlost trail at a concrete marker post, at point "R" on the map. Turn sharp right here, follow the circuit trail around the Limberlost, come back to this junction, and then return uphill to your starting point. I have described the Limberlost circuit, beginning at "M", on page 149.

HIKE: *Limberlost* via A.T.; return via Crescent Rock trail. *Circuit* 4.6 miles; total *climb* about 780 feet; *time* required 3:45. A not too difficult hike to the Limberlost, a grove of giant hemlocks. Because I have described most of this hike elsewhere, I will only outline the route here. (See Limberlost via Crescent Rock trail, above; and Limberlost circuit, page 149.) On the map, page 146, you are at point "Q", and your route is Q-N-K-L-R-Q.

Take the Bettys Rock trail, at the north end of the sidewalk beside the wall. Almost immediately, turn left on a side trail and descend to the A.T. Turn right on the A.T. and go 2.0 miles to the stable, on your left. Turn right here and walk to the paved road, which is the north entrance of Skyland. Turn right and go about a hundred yards to the Drive. Cross the Drive, enter the Whiteoak Canyon parking area, and take the trail at its north (left-hand) end.

About 0.6 mile from the Drive, cross the Old Rag fire road; continue another quarter of a mile to the Limberlost trail, in a grove of giant hemlocks. Turn right. After you cross the stream watch for a sharp right turn, where there's a hemlock three feet in diameter at the left edge of the trail. Continue about a quarter of a mile to the trail junction at point "R". Turn sharp left, and go 1.1 miles uphill to your starting point.

MILE 45.0, WHITEOAK FIRE ROAD, east side, 50 yards south of the milepost. There's room to park two cars without blocking the fire road. On the map, page 146, you're at point "J", below the middle. From here, the walk to the first falls in Whiteoak Canyon is somewhat shorter and easier than from the Whiteoak parking area, Mile 42.6. The round trip from here is 3.8 miles, compared to 4.6 from the parking area; and the total climb is about 840 feet, compared to 1,040. But this is just a dirt road through the woods—not at all scenic.

MILE 45.6, HAWKSBILL GAP. Elevation 3,365 feet. *Hikes* to *Hawksbill* summit from the paved parking area. *Hikes* to *Cedar Run* and *Whiteoak Canyon,* starting across the Drive from the paved area. *Byrds Nest Shelter No. 2. A.T. access. Spring.*

There's a very small cemetery here in the gap. To find it, cross the Drive from the paved parking area and turn left. Walk 160 yards north beside the Drive, to a bitternut hickory tree on the right. Under the limbs of this tree, on the south side of the trunk and 40 feet from the Drive, are at least five graves: four close together, in line, and another about eight feet away. There may be other graves whose markers have been lost. The four in-line markers, reading outward toward the Drive: Allen R. Taylor, 1933-1933; Carol R. Taylor, 1936-1937; (illegible); Robert G. Taylor, 1939-1940.

A.T. access. Take the connecting trail from the north end of the paved parking area; it starts out nearly parallel to the Drive and then swings left, reaching the A.T. less than 100 yards from the start. Distances on the A.T.: South (to the left) it's 1.9 miles to Spitler Knoll Overlook, Mile 48.1. North (to the right) it's 1.3 miles to Timber Hollow Overlook, Mile 43.3.

Spring. Walk to the A.T. (see above), and continue on an unmarked trail that follows an old road trace downhill. Go a hundred yards, to a junction where the old road trace swings left, and a very faint trail goes straight ahead. The spring is on the faint trail, 67 feet ahead; the water comes out of a pipe that ends in a clump of yellow birches. The spring is unprotected; boil the water before drinking.

I will suggest four hikes that begin in Hawksbill Gap. A round trip to *Cedar Run* falls; a circuit to *Cedar Run* and *Whiteoak Canyon;* a short, steep route to *Hawksbill summit;* a longer but easier route to *Hawksbill summit.*

Cedar Run Canyon is a narrow, rocky gorge with a modest waterfall. No mountaineers lived in the canyon, because it has no place smooth enough and level enough for a pasture or garden. Compared to Whiteoak Canyon or Dark Hollow, this is not a popular place. The trail is narrow, rough, and steep, and its surface consists mostly of loose rocks. In Cedar Run the rewards are meager compared with the exertion required, unless solitude and exertion are rewards.

HIKE: *Cedar Run Falls. Round trip* 3.5 miles; total *climb* about 1,555 feet; *time* required 4:00. A moderately difficult hike on a rough, steep trail to a medium-sized waterfall. *Caution:* This trail has a history of frequent accidents. See map, page 146. You're at point "A", left of bottom center. Your route is A-B-C-B-A.

Start at the marker post across the Drive from the paved parking area. About 80 yards from the Drive, at point "B" on the map, cross the yellow-blazed Skyland-to-Big Meadows horse trail. Continue on the blue-blazed Cedar Run trail.

The trail soon begins to get worse, descending rather steeply on small, loose rocks. About a mile and a half from the start, the trail crosses Cedar Run, with a pool and miniature waterfall to your right. The trail climbs slightly, moving away from the stream and then turning back toward it; 250 yards beyond the ford you can look ahead to an impressive cliff on the other side of Cedar Run. The trail descends steeply and roughly, by switchbacks, to the stream. The falls are a little way upstream, to your left. There is no trail to the falls, and no view of the falls from the trail. Make your way upstream to a deep pool at the base of the falls. The total drop, from the top of the falls to the pool, is about 34 feet.

HIKE: *Cedar Run* and *Whiteoak Canyon. Circuit* 7.3 miles; total *climb* about 2,495 feet; *time* required 7:30. A difficult hike through two steep, wild gorges with nine waterfalls. This is for hikers accustomed to prolonged strenuous exercise. See map, page 146. Your route is A-B-C-D-F-H-I-B-A.

As above, to Cedar Run falls. Return to the trail and continue downstream a little less than half a mile, to the Park boundary, which is marked by red blazes on the trees on both sides of the trail. From here, take a short side trail down to the water. Look upstream, between two large boulders, to see a small but beautiful waterfall.

If you wish, you can cross the stream here; a trail of sorts continues downstream on the left bank. (At some future time this may become *the* trail, because the present trail crosses private property.)

On the present trail (on the right bank of the stream) continue downstream a little less than 0.2 mile to a concrete marker post. Turn left here, toward the water. (Avoid the abandoned trail that goes straight ahead on private property.) The trail swings right and parallels the stream. Less than 200 feet from the marker post, where the trail seems to disappear, you're supposed to turn left, ford the stream, and find the trail on the other side. (The red blazes on the left of the stream mark the Park boundary, not a trail.) After crossing the stream, join the trail that comes down the left bank. Then pass a side trail, on the right, that goes to the parking area in Berry Hollow.

Continue around the foot of the ridge and into the bottom of Whiteoak Canyon. Cross Whiteoak Run and reach the Whiteoak Canyon trail at point "F" on the map (page 146.) Turn left. About 0.7 mile from the junction, cross a stream that comes down from the right. This is the largest tributary of Whiteoak Run. It's also a source of some embarrassment, since its original name was Nigger Run. It was later changed to Negro Run, which didn't quite solve the problem. On the latest maps it has no name. A short distance upstream on Nameless Run are a good-sized waterfall and a pool deep enough to swim in.

Continue uphill through a narrow canyon on a steep, rough trail, past all six waterfalls of Whiteoak Run. Near the top of the upper falls, at point "H" on the map, the horse trail comes in from the right. After another 30 yards, the horse trail turns left and crosses the stream. Ford the steam here and stay on the horse trail, straight ahead and uphill. (If the water is too high, continue on the Whiteoak Canyon trail, cross the steam on a foot bridge, turn left, return to the horse trail, then turn right.)

Less than a tenth of a mile from the stream, the horse trail joins the Whiteoak fire road. Continue uphill on the fire road to point "I", where the road swings sharply to the right while the horse trail goes straight ahead. Take the horse trail to point "B", then turn right to reach your starting point. (Or, if you're very tired, continue on the fire road about 0.1 mile to the Drive, turn left, and return to Hawksbill Gap walking in the grass beside the Drive. That's a little shorter than the horse trail, and a great deal smoother.)

HAWKSBILL MOUNTAIN HIKES. Hawksbill Mountain, with an elevation
of 4,050 feet, is the highest point in the Park. An observation platform on
the summit offers a fine, wide view. Also on the summit is *Byrds Nest
Shelter* No. 2, with a picnic table and pit toilets. There's no water up there.
Camping is not permitted on or near the Hawksbill summit. There are three
ways to reach the summit:

A *short trail,* fairly rough and steep.

A leisurely *circuit via the A.T.,* returning by the short trail. Longer, not so
steep, not so rough; much more interesting.

A third route starts from Upper Hawksbill Parking, Mile 46.7. This
involves less climbing than either of the other routes, and is intermediate in
distance.

HIKE: *Hawksbill summit* via *short trail. Round trip* 1.7 miles; total *climb*
about 690 feet; *time* required 2:00. The trail is rough, rocky, and steep. It
starts near the middle of the paved parking area and goes straight into the
woods. See map, page 157. Hawksbill Gap is at the lower right.

Less than 50 yards from the start, look for a big white oak on the right;
tumerous growths have weakened it so that the center has rotted out, and you
can see all the way through it. A quarter of a mile from the start, a concrete
post marks a side trail on the left; it goes 25 yards to a reliable but unprotected
spring. (Boil the water before you drink.)

Climb steadily for another half mile, to a trail junction at the top of the ridge.
Turn right; continue past the shelter to the observation platform, less than 0.1
mile from the junction. For a note on the shelter and the view from the
platform, see page 156.

HIKE: *Hawksbill Summit* via *A.T. Circuit* 2.9 miles; total *climb* about 860
feet; *time* required 2:50. Parts of this route are moderately rough. The
steepest parts are downhill. See map, page 157.

Take the trail at the north end of the paved parking area. It starts out nearly
parallel to the Drive, then curves left and joins the A.T. less than 100 yards
from the start. Turn left on the A.T. and climb steadily. A little more than 0.4
mile from the start, the trail crosses the first of three talus slopes—slanting
rock piles formed by rocks rolling down from the disintegrating cliffs above.
But there's no reason to feel nervous about crossing a talus slope; there has
been relatively little movement of the rocks since the end of the last ice age.

Beyond the first talus slope, the next half mile is a rock-garden hike. The
mountainside to your left consists of tiers of wild rock gardens, one above
another, with a rich assortment of ferns, mosses, and lichens. The plants with
broad lily-like leaves are yellow beadlily, *Clintonia borealis,* which blooms in
late May and early June. (The flowers are yellow; the plant is sometimes
called blue beadlily because its fruits resemble blue beads.) Smaller plants
with thick fleshy leaves, growing where a small amount of soil has collected
on the rocks, are Allegheny stonecrop, *Sedum telephioides.* It blooms steadily
from mid-July to mid-September, with flowers that vary from deep salmon-
pink to nearly white.

Sixty yards beyond the first talus slope is a second, with a view to the right
across Timber Hollow, The highest point in sight, with rocky cliffs on its left
face, is Stony Man. Nearer, and a little to the left, is the rounded summit of
Bushytop, from which a ridge descends toward the left to the abrupt angle at
Millers Head.

After another 200 yards cross the third talus slope, with an overgrown view. Worth noting in late summer are several mountain ash trees, with compound leaves and masses of bright red berries. (The mountain ash is not an ash, but a member of the rose family.)

About half a mile beyond the third talus slope, the main trail splits at a narrow angle. Take the left-hand fork, which climbs 0.9 mile to the summit. The climb is steady, but not difficult. As you near the top you will pass several ledges on the left. All of them offer interesting views, but of course none can compare with the view from the summit. At two or more points a side trail branches off toward the right; keep left at all such junctions, until you come out in front of the shelter. This is *Byrds Nest* No. 2, the second of four open shelters for which materials were donated by the late Senator Harry F. Byrd Sr. Camping is not permitted on or near Hawksbill summit.

Continue 75 yards beyond the shelter to the observation platform, elevation 4,050 feet, the highest point in Shenandoah National Park. There's a broad view here. At the far left is the town of Stanley; just to the right of it, and much closer, is the rounded crest of Nakedtop, with cliffs on its right-hand slope. To the right of Nakedtop is Buracker Hollow, with the town of Ida at its mouth. From Ida a ridge rises toward the right to the angle at Millers Head, then to the rounded summit of Bushytop. The high point, with rocky cliffs on its left face, is Stony Man. Farther right and closer, down below you, is Crescent Rock. Still farther right, in the distance, is the rocky summit of Old Rag.

As you return, take the trail that goes to the left of the shelter, past the pit toilets, and another 60 yards to a junction. Turn left; from here the trail descends steeply for 0.7 mile to the parking area at your starting point. Two-thirds of the way down is a concrete marker post, from which a side trail on the right descends 25 yards to a spring. (This is an unprotected water supply; boil the water before drinking it.)

MILE 46.5, OLD RAG VIEW OVERLOOK, elevation 3,585. The profile of Old Rag is diagonally left. There's no other view here. For hikes to Old Rag summit, see page 138. Across the Drive from the north end of the overlook is a single yucca, which may be the only one in the Park. It sends up a flower stalk every four or five years.

MILE 46.7, UPPER HAWKSBILL PARKING. Elevation 3,635 feet. This is a large paved parking area on the west side, with a bulletin board and a drinking fountain (turned off in winter). *Hikes:* Hawksbill summit; and a circuit hike to Hawksbill summit via Rose River falls.

HIKE: *Hawksbill Summit. Round trip* 2.1 miles; total *climb* about 520 feet; *time* required 2:00. A fairly easy hike on a graded trail and a fire road. Good views from the summit. See map, page 157. You're near bottom center.

The trail goes into the woods from the drinking fountain. After a short steep stretch you have a steady, easy climb through young oak forest. Two-thirds of a mile from the start, the trail dead-ends in a dirt road. Turn right. (To the left, the road goes about half a mile to the Drive at Mile 47.1.) After another quarter of a mile, a trail crosses the road at a sharp angle. To the left it goes about 0.8 mile to the A.T.; to the right, 0.8 mile to Hawksbill Gap, Mile 45.6. Continue on the road to the pit toilets and shelter, then go another 75 yards to the observation platform. For notes on the shelter and the view, see above.

HIKE: *Rose River Falls* and *Hawksbill Summit. Circuit* 9.7 miles; total *climb* about 2,465 feet; *time* required 8:45. This hike is difficult, tiring, and fun. It

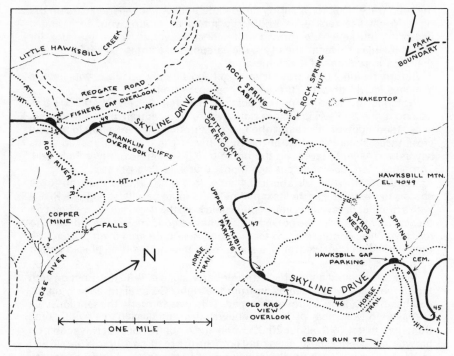

Map of Hawksbill — Fishers Gap area.

includes a view from the highest point in the Park; one of our prettiest waterfalls; a mountaineer homesite, and a touch of history. See map above. Upper Hawksbill parking is near bottom center.

Cross the Drive from the south end of the parking area. Turn right and walk in the grass beside the Drive, less than a hundred yards, to a large wooden sign. Turn left, and enter the woods on an abandoned road. Less than 400 feet from the Drive, the horse trail comes in from the left and joins the old road. *Note:* you will walk three miles on the horse trail; *horses have the right of way.*

About half a mile from the Drive, watch for a concrete post on the left, that says "Mile 6.5 Horse Trail." (That's the distance back to the stable at Skyland.) Beyond, the trail begins to swing to the right. About 0.3 mile beyond the marker, look for two wooden signs: the first says "Horse Trail to Skyland", and the second "Horse Trail to Big Meadows." Beyond the second sign, the trail narrows abruptly. Between signs, 30 feet from the first one, the old road trace leaves the horse trail and goes 30 degrees to the left. It resembles a game trail, overgrown with bushes; it goes less than 0.2 mile to a mountaineer homesite. If you want to explore, you might note the direction of the sun as you leave the trail, so that you can return by keeping the sun in the opposite direction. Here's how to reach the homesite:

About a hundred feet from the trail, the road trace passes six feet to the left of an oak tree with a double trunk. Thirty yards farther, look for a big sharp rock sticking up in the middle of the road. Continue a hundred feet more. Then, with another double-trunk oak 40 feet ahead, and the remains of a rotting rail fence on your left, leave the road trace and go 30 degrees to the right. (As an alternative, if the road trace seems easy to follow, stay with it; it swings to the left, then makes a sharp switchback to the right and heads directly for the homesite.)

After leaving the road trace and going 30 degrees to the right, continue in a straight line, joining a rotting rail fence on your right. About 120 yards from the road trace, look for a spring on the left, and two abandoned cars on the right. You'll see rock piles and scrap metal all around you, including a bedspring, buckets, and tubs. (Don't collect souvenirs; leave the junk for others to enjoy.) In sight ahead are the gateposts of a former picket fence, and the filled-in remains of a chimney.

Return to the horse trail. If in doubt, go directly uphill. If you have a compass, go northwest, Turn left on the horse trail.

Watch for the Mile 7.5 marker post on the horse trail; less than 300 yards beyond it, the trail swings to the right, where an older trail, now abandoned, goes steeply downhill straight ahead. Pass through a grove of hemlocks, and cross three small branches of the Rose River. Then, a few hundred yards beyond the Mile 9 marker on the horse trail, join the Rose River Falls trail. Turn sharp left, downhill, passing a post that says "No Horses."

Continue downhill for about 0.4 mile, to a point where the trail turns sharply to the right. For the next half mile the route parallels the Rose River, with a number of cascades and pools visible from the trail. From a low point on the trail, 0.7 mile from the horse trail, you have a good view of the falls, on the left. If you like, continue a few feet more to where the trail swings up to the right; ahead on the side trail are some rocks that offer sitting places with a view of the falls.

Now turn around and go back three-quarters of a mile, to the junction with the horse trail, which comes in from the right. Go straight ahead, uphill, another half mile to a gravel fire road. This was formerly the Gordonsville Turnpike. In November of 1862 Stonewall Jackson passed this point, going from right to left, with about 20,000 men and a number of supply wagons, on his way to Fredericksburg. Turn right onto the fire road, go 40 yards uphill, and cross the Drive. Continue about a hundred yards on the fire road (not the paved road into Fishers Gap Overlook) to the Appalachian Trail, and turn right.

The A.T. passes several ledges with views to the left and, a third of a mile from the fire road, goes along a ledge below Franklin Cliffs. Continue 0.9 mile to a side trail on the right that goes to Spitler Knoll Overlook; then another 0.6 mile to a side trail on the left that goes to Rock Spring Cabin. Less than 0.3 mile beyond the Rock Spring Cabin trail, watch carefully for a side trail that doubles back sharply to the right. Turn right onto this trail; it climbs steadily for 0.9 mile to Hawksbill summit. Where side trails branch off toward the right, keep left, until you come out in front of the shelter on the summit. The observation platform is 75 yards beyond the shelter. For a note on the shelter, and on the view from the platform, see page 156.

Return past the shelter and take the service road that starts near the far rear corner. Follow the road downhill about a third of a mile, to a trail that comes in from the left at a marker post. Turn left onto the trail, and walk two-thirds of a mile to your starting point.

MILE 47.1, FIRE ROAD, west side. This is the service road for Byrds Nest Shelter No. 2, on Hawksbill summit.

MILE 47.25, GEOLOGY. *Rock lovers only.* If you're going south, park in the grass on the right, just before the beginning of the curve. Look out for a ditch and culvert, marked with a white pipe. Going north: park in the grass on your right, at about the middle of the curve. Near the south end of the curve, on the east side, look for basalt with veins of sedimentary rock one to four inches thick, and five to ten feet above road level. The veins show a variety of colors, from yellowish to pale dull purple. The sedimentary material was picked up by the cooling base of the lava flow as it advanced over the sediments of an ancient stream.

MILE 47.8, FIRE ROAD, west side. This is the service road for Rock Spring Cabin. There's a parking area for people using the cabin; it's at Mile 48.1, at the north end of Spitler Knoll Overlook.

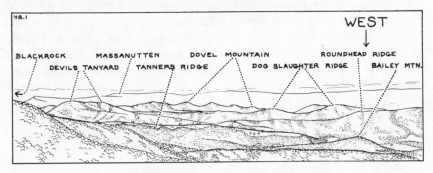

48.1

BLACKROCK   MASSANUTTEN   DOVEL MOUNTAIN   ROUNDHEAD RIDGE

DEVILS TANYARD / TANNERS RIDGE   DOG SLAUGHTER RIDGE   BAILEY MTN.

WEST

View from Spitler Knoll Overlook.

MILE 48.1, SPITLER KNOLL OVERLOOK. Elevation 3,285 feet. *A.T. access.* Parking for *Rock Spring Cabin* is at the north end of the overlook. The ridge behind the overlook is the former site of Spitler ranch.

This is a very long, curving overlook. From the middle: the high mountain to your left, about 1.5 miles away, is Blackrock—the site of Big Meadows Lodge and campground. The sketch shows only a small part of the view, to left of center. Straight out from the middle of the overlook is the town of Stanley, at the foot of Roundhead Ridge. To the right of center, on this side of the valley, is Hershberger Ridge. At the far right, the relatively nearby rounded summit is Nakedtop.

A.T. access is via a short trail from the north end of the overlook. Distances on the A.T.: South (to the left) it's 1.3 miles to Fishers Gap, Mile 49.4. North (to the right) it's 1.9 miles to Hawksbill Gap, Mile 45.6.

Geology: Here, and for a quarter of a mile in each direction along the Drive, the exposed rocks are granodiorite of the Pedlar formation.

MILE 49.0, FRANKLIN CLIFFS OVERLOOK. Elevation 3,140 feet. The overlook has a narrow view down the hollow to the Shenandoah Valley, and to the Massanutten Mountain on the far side. The town of Stanley, a little to left of center, is at the foot of Roundhead Ridge. Farther right, and more distant, is the larger town of Luray. To your left, the high summit is Blackrock; a little way down from its high point, and a little to the left, is Big Meadows Campground. Still farther left you can see Fishers Gap Overlook, with a short stretch of the Redgate Road below it.

The A.T. passes along a ledge at the foot of the cliff, but it's not readily accessible from the overlook. I've read that the cliffs were named for General William B. Franklin, a Union officer in the Civil War.

MILE 49.4, FISHERS GAP and FISHERS GAP OVERLOOK. Elevation 3,070 feet. *Hikes,* fire road crossing, *A.T. access.* The overlook is hidden from the Drive by a large wooded island; its north entrance is just south of the fire road. On the fire road, 100 feet west of the Drive, there is parking space for two or three cars. A few yards farther down the road is the A.T. For hikes beginning at Fishers Gap, I suggest that you park in the overlook. The view from the overlook is limited: a narrow V-shaped view down Fox Hollow (not the same as the Fox Hollow near Dickey Ridge), and across the Valley to the Massanutten. But a stop here is worth while for other reasons.

A.T. access is via a 55-yard trail which begins at a large rock where the parking area narrows at the south end of the overlook. Distances on the A.T.: South (to the left) it's 1.5 miles to the Big Meadows Amphitheater. North (to the right) it's 1.4 miles to Spitler Knoll Overlook. The A.T. crosses the fire road just to the north, which makes possible a very short "leg-stretcher" hike, as follows:

> HIKE: *A.T. below the overlook. Circuit* 0.3 mile; total *climb* about 30 feet; *time* required 0:20. Take the short access trail at the south end of the overlook. Turn right on the A.T., then right on the fire road. When you reach the Drive, turn sharp right into the north entrance to the overlook, and return to your starting point.

Wildflower note: The purple clematis, *Clematis verticillaris,* is an uncommon wildflower, but it blooms beside the A.T. below the overlook, usually in late April. It's a vine, producing large showy flowers with four long, limp, pale-purple sepals. In early April look for the pale violet flowers of hepatica, which is usually the first spring flower to bloom.

The fire road that crosses the ridge just north of the overlook is the old Gordonsville Turnpike. On the east side it descends through the Rose River valley, leaves the Park, and becomes Virginia secondary road No. 670. Three miles outside the boundary it passes the semi-famous Graves Mountain Lodge, near Syria. On the west it's called the Redgate Road. It descends 4.3 miles to the Park boundary, where it becomes Virginia secondary road No. 611, and continues to Stanley.

History: In November of 1862 Stonewall Jackson used this road to lead his army of 15,000 (or 20,000 or 25,000) men across the mountain on the way to Fredericksburg, where he was instrumental in defeating the Union Army under General Burnside.

Uncertain history: According to one writer, this road was built in the 1790's. Another says it was built during the Civil War as a military road. Claude Yowell, historian of Madison County, Va., says it was first called the Blue Ridge Turnpike, and was built in 1849-50.

Legend: This is called the Redgate Road because there was a red toll gate across it here in Fishers Gap. *More likely:* on the south side of the road was a large fenced meadow, with a farm road passing through it. The farm road reached the Gordonsville Turnpike through a red gate in the fence.

On the east side of the ridge, the road descends into Dark Hollow. Various writers, apparently influenced by the word "dark", have written that the mountaineers who lived there were moonshiners and criminals, who waged bitter mountain feuds. Other reports say that the people of Dark Hollow were decent and law-abiding.

I will recommend four hikes that begin at Fishers Gap Overlook:

Rose River Falls: round trip 2.7 miles
Rose River Falls and Hogcamp Branch: circuit 4.0 miles.
Davids Spring: round trip 1.8 miles.
Davids Spring and return by horse trail: circuit 3.2 miles.

HIKE: *Rose River Falls. Round trip* 2.7 miles; total *climb* about 720 feet; *time* required 2:35. A not-too-difficult hike to a rather small but very pretty waterfall. See map, page 166; Fishers Gap Overlook is near right center.

Park in the overlook, and walk out the north entrance road. Cross the Drive, walk a hundred feet down the fire road, and turn left onto a graded trail. (At first, this is a foot trail and horse trail combined; horses have the right of way.) About 0.6 mile from the start, the horse trail turns off to the left; go straight ahead here. A mile from the start the trail turns abruptly to the right.

The next part of the trail is invitingly cool and shady, with more and more evergreens. There's a rough stretch, but it's short. A hundred yards beyond the abrupt right turn, in a grove of hemlocks, the Rose River comes down on the left and parallels the trail. As you walk, look for small cascades and pools and miniature waterfalls. After another quarter of a mile you're at the top of the falls, which consist of several separate cascades. A hundred feet farther is a low point on the trail, with the highst falls in view to your left. If you wish, go on a few feet more, to where the trail swings up to the right. Straight ahead on the side trail are some rocks where you can sit and watch the falls.

Trivia: Rose River was named for early settlers, not for flowers. On an old map (1795) it's called Rows River.

HIKE: *Rose River Falls* and return via *Hogcamp Branch. Circuit* 4.0 miles; total *climb* about 910 feet; *time* required 3:45. A slightly difficult hike, with one stream crossing. A few parts of the trail are rough, a few steep, and a few are sometimes damp and slippery. But, besides the falls, you'll see dozens of pools and cascades and miniature falls. See map, page 166. Your route is down the Rose River trail, past the falls and copper mine, up Hogcamp Branch to the bridge, and then up the fire road.

As above, to Rose River Falls. Continue another third of a mile; the trail leaves the stream there and swings to the right, with a grove of young hemlocks on your left. Beyond the hemlocks is a triangle of nearly level land bounded by the trail, Rose River, and Hogcamp Branch. This is a favorite back-country camping site. There was once a mountaineer homesite here. And before that it was a favorite campsite of the Indians. Many arrowheads have been found here.

After the trail swings right for a second time it parallels a stream, the Hogcamp Branch, on the left. Two hundred yards farther, a "trail" of pale blue-gray rock chips goes steeply uphill on the right, to the filled-in shaft of an old copper mine. To the left is a weathered concrete monolith; it supported an air compressor that supplied the pneumatic drills.

History: The copper mine was worked from 1845 to 1850, then abandoned. In 1902 the Blue Ridge Copper Co. was formed to resume operations here. Three shafts were opened (all of them now filled.) The ore was in narrow veins through the basalt, consisting of blue and green carbonates of copper, a little cuprite, some chalcopyrite, and some native copper. The ore was rich, but getting it out of the basalt was not economically feasible.

Less than a tenth of a mile beyond the copper mine, cross the Hogcamp Branch and turn right. (Straight ahead, a side trail climbs 0.3 mile to the fire road.) The trail ascends through lower Dark Hollow, with the Hogcamp Branch on your right, and reaches the fire road after 0.9 mile of climbing. Of all the trails in the Park, this is my favorite. The stream is rarely out of sight, and it has an endless variety of cascades and pools. There are wildflowers in summer, from Indian pipes to three-leaved *Sedum* (just before you get to the fire road.) The moss that grows on rotting logs here is too green to believe. It's a long climb; when you want to rest, go down to the stream, find a rock to sit on, and watch the water.

When you reach the fire road, turn right and cross the bridge, pausing to look to your left at a long, narrow waterfall. Thirty yards beyond the bridge, the Dark Hollow Falls trail goes uphill on the left. (If you make a side trip to the base of the falls you will add 0.3 mile and 145 feet of climbing to your hike.) About 0.6 mile from the bridge there's a big, much-branched sugar maple — evidence of a former mountain homesite. Other clues are grape vines, artificially leveled areas, and spots where lawn-type grass still grows. The Cave family cemetery is near here, on the left side of the road. Continue steadily uphill to the Drive in Fishers Gap, about 1.1 mile from the bridge.

HIKE: *Davids Spring. Round trip* 1.8 miles; total *climb* about 470 feet; *time* required 1:40. An easy hike along the A.T., past a hemlock grove and a mountaineer homesite. See map, page 166. Fishers Gap Overlook is at right center.

Take the access trail at the south end of the overlook, go to the A.T., and turn left. The trail descends for a few feet, then begins a long, steady, easy climb. About 250 yards from the start, notice a tremendous basalt rock on the left, in the process of splitting and breaking up. A quarter of a mile farther, the hemlocks begin; and after another 400 yards you're deep in a grove of large hemlocks, where you will notice several things: it's dark and cool and quiet; there is little or no undergrowth, and the ground is carpeted with fallen needles. If you stop and listen, in summer, you'll hear insects and birds, and an occasional car sound in the distance, and sometimes the shout of children in the Big Meadows Campground, half a mile away. If there's a gentle wind in the treetops you'll hear a steady rain of tiny hemlock needles.

From the trail, near the middle of the hemlock grove, you can look downhill to a concrete watering trough about 25 yards away. A little farther down the hill, and a hundred yards to the left, is further evidence of an old homesite, which you may find worth exploring. (If you get lost down there, go straight uphill to return to the trail.)

Two hundred yards after you emerge from the hemlock grove, you cross a small stream that flows from right to left. This is Little Hawksbill Creek, just 300 yards from its source at Davids Spring. Cross the stream, leave the trail, and follow the stream uphill to the spring. In April, look for the yellow flowers of marsh marigold, *Caltha palustris,* one of the first flowers to show color in the spring. The broad green lily-like leaves in and near the water are false helibore, *Veratrum viride.* In late summer, near the spring, look for the pink-white flowers of white turtlehead, *Chelone glabra.*

Davids Spring flows prettily out from the roots of a tree. Don't drink; the spring drains the campground. Looking upstream from a point 20 or 30 feet below the spring, you'll find one or more trails on the left, going about 50 feet uphill to the A.T. To return, go to the A.T. and turn left. Note, on the map, that Davids Spring is only a few feet from a trail junction. To return to Fishers Gap be sure you're on the A.T. (white blazes) and going *downhill.*

HIKE: *Davids Spring* and return via horse trail. *Circuit* 3.2 miles; total *climb* about 590 feet; *time* required 2:45. This is a hike for people who like to take a chance. It makes use of an abandoned trail—the former Swamp Nature Trail. I can't predict what condition it will be in when you read this. See map, page 166. Your route is: A.T. to Davids Spring, left on the abandoned trail, left on the present Nature Trail, then left again onto the horse trail.

As above, to Davids Spring. Where the A.T. makes a 90-degree turn to the right, turn left onto the unblazed abandoned trail. If you're able to follow it, you'll reach a small grassy area about 0.8 mile from Davids Spring. Here a small stream emerges from Big Meadows Swamp. In summer and fall it's usually dry. Flowers bloom here throughout the spring and summer, including blue-flag iris, thinleaf sunflower, American burnett and, in August, the brilliant red cardinal flower.

After another fifty yards you'll reach a trail junction; turn left here. Walk another fifty yards to the horse trail, turn left, and cross the stream. The rest of your hike is mostly downhill, and mostly on the bed of an old mountaineer road. (Remember that you're on a horse trail, and that horses have the right of way.) When you reach the Drive, turn left and walk in the grass on the left side of the road. Bear left into the south entrance of Fishers Gap Overlook, and return to your starting point.

MILE 50.7, DARK HOLLOW FALLS PARKING. Elevation 3,425 feet. It has been said that of all the waterfalls in the Park, Dark Hollow Falls is closest to the Drive and easiest to get to. (But see Mile 1.4 on page 82.) This parking area is also the closest access to Big Meadows Swamp. I will recommend two *hikes,* one to the falls and one to the swamp.

Trivia: Mile 50 to Mile 51 is the shortest mile on the Drive: just eight-tenths of a mile long. When the mileposts were put in, the Drive did not go through the deep cut in the hillside to the south of here, as it does now. Instead it made a loop to the east, starting near the south end of the parking area.

HIKE: *Dark Hollow Falls. Round trip* 1.4 miles; total *climb* about 440 feet; *time* required 1:25. Take the trail at the north end of the parking area. It crosses the stream and then goes downhill along its left bank. This is Hogcamp Branch, which drains Big Meadows Swamp and becomes the principal tributary of Rose River. You may find it dry at the beginning, but it will gradually acquire enough water to make a satisfactory waterfall.

The trail descends easily for 0.6 mile to the head of the falls. I suggest that you stay on the trail here. There's no view from the top of the falls, and the rocks there are slippery and dangerous. The trail swings away from the stream and goes uphill for a few feet before swinging right and descending to the base of the falls. On the trail between top and bottom of the falls you'll pass a tremendous rock that looms on your left, just where the trail swings sharply to the right. Except in dry summer months, water constantly trickles and drips down the face of this rock, promoting the growth of mosses, ferns, and liverworts. On cold winter days there's an enchanting display of stalactites and stalagmites of ice.

There's a fine view of the falls from the bottom. The water drops 70 feet, in a series of cascades, over the crumbling greenstone of an ancient lava flow. Thomas Jefferson once stood here and admired the falls. (Jefferson spent a great deal of time exploring these mountains, and studying their plants and animals. He was so fond of the Blue Ridge that at Monticello he put the outbuildings below ground, so as not to interfere with his view of the mountains.)

(Below the falls, the trail descends another 145 feet in about 300 yards to the Rose River fire road, passing a number of small waterfalls and cascades.)

HIKE; *Big Meadows Swamp. Round trip* 0.5 mile; total *climb* about 90 feet; *time* required 0:30. If you like wildflowers, and if it's blooming time, then I strongly recommend this hike. It's short and easy.

Go to the north (downhill) end of the parking area and cross the Drive to the concrete marker post at the beginning of the trail. In early April, look for *Hepatica* in bloom beside the trail near the Drive. Continue, with the stream down to your left, past a side trail on the left that comes down from the Big

Meadows Visitor Center. A little less than 0.2 mile from the start, the stream flows under the trail. Go another 40 yards, cross the horse trail, and continue to another junction. Turn right, and go fifty yards to a small grassy area where a stream emerges from Big Meadows Swamp.

There you'll find a great variety of plant life. Blooming starts in April, with violets and winter cress, cinquefoil and pussytoes. It builds to a climax in early July, with dozens of species in bloom, then tapers off to a few asters and stiff gentians that persist into October. Things to look for at various seasons include wild yam, blue-eyed grass, yellow star grass, marsh marigold, early and tall meadow rue, blue-flag iris, New York ironweed, cutleaf coneflower, swamp rose, boneset, thorowort, cowbane, burnett, thinleaf sunflower, and the deep blue flowers of closed gentian. But the one special plant of the swamp, which you won't find elsewhere in the Park, is the cardinal flower. It's a species of *Lobelia,* with flowers of a deep, saturated red. It starts to bloom, in most years, about the tenth of August, and goes on for two or three weeks. Look for it in the stream bed, both above and below the point where you cross the stream.

This area is not a part of the swamp, but only the place where the stream emerges from the swamp. In summer and fall, you're likely to find the stream bed dry. But the water, when there is any, deserves special attention. In March you may see toads or frogs (and, if you come at night with a flashlight, salamanders.) A little later there are egg masses; small eggs in more or less spherical masses of clear jelly: frogs. Eggs in strings of jelly: toads. Large, tan-colored eggs in loose masses, or small eggs in whitish jelly: salamanders. Starting in April: tiny tadpoles that grow larger in size and fewer in number as time passes. Few if any will become adults before the swamp pools dry up, as they do each summer. In late spring look for caddisfly larvae in the water; and on the surface, whirlygig beetles and water striders.

MILE 51.0, BIG MEADOWS, NORTH ENTRANCE. To reach the Visitor Center or to walk in the meadow, turn right here, then left into the parking area. (For gas, food, lodging, picnicking, and camping, use the south entrance at Mile 51.2)

Harry F. Bryd Sr. Visitor Center. Information, publications, exhibits, and a movie about the history of the area. The Visitor Center was opened to the public in April, 1966. Visitors sometimes ask about the materials it's made of. Here are some answers: The wood paneling is butternut. The floor of the lobby is crab-orchard sandstone from Tennessee. The exterior stonework is of sandstone from the Massanutten Mountain. Exhibits in the Visitor Center summarize and illustrate the human history of the Park. The movie is shown frequently, on a regular schedule. Slide programs may be shown from time to time. Ask at the information desk.

The Visitor Center is worth a stop even when it's closed. Go around to the balcony at left rear and look out over the meadow, which has been a meadow for centuries. It was probably created by fire, set by lightning or by Indians. Indian fires, with some help from elk and bison, kept it open. Blueberries and strawberries grow in the meadow. And because deer like to browse around its edges, the meadow made hunting easier. After the Indians, white mountaineers grazed their cattle here.

The metal plaque on the rail shows how the meadow looked on July 3, 1936, when the Park dedication ceremony took place there. Thousands of people were seated on chairs, on chestnut logs, and on the ground. Bands played from bandstands beside the speakers platform. Amplifiers and loudspeakers carried the sound to everyone, and the program was broadcast from coast to coast by NBC and CBS radio. After speeches by Harold Ickes (Secretary of the Interior) and George Peery (Governor of Virginia), President Franklin D. Roosevelt dedicated the Park in a short speech that ended with

"We seek to pass on to our children a richer land and a stronger nation. And so my friends, I now take great pleasure in dedicating Shenandoah National Park — in dedicating it to this and to succeeding generations of Americans for the recreation and for the re-creation which we find here."

As the plaque shows, the meadow was much larger then than it is now. It extended, with a few islands of trees, to the ridge in front of you, and down the other side. Behind you it reached the present site of Big Meadows Campground. It stretched from Fishers Gap, Mile 49.4, to beyond Milam Gap, Mile 52.8. Estimates of its present size vary from 144 to 160 acres. The Park, by mowing and burning, is trying to keep what remains of the meadow. This is the only environment of its kind in the Park. It produces wildflowers that don't grow in the woods.

There was once a "ghost forest" of dead chestnut trees here at Big Meadows, where the Visitor Center and parking area are now. You can see one of the ghost trees at the extreme left in the dedication photo on the metal plaque. Also at the left edge of the photo is a CCC Camp — Camp Fechner, named for the Director of the CCC.

Several mountains can be seen from the balcony. A little to the right of center is Fork Mountain, just outside the Park. The antenna tower on its summit belongs to the State Police. (*Legend:* During the Civil War a heliograph on Fork Mountain was used to send messages, by flashes of reflected sunlight, to Washington, D.C.). Diagonally right (behind a tree if you're standing on the balcony) is Hazeltop. Cat Knob is between Hazeltop and Fork Mountain. Old Rag is in the distance at the far left, with pale gray granite cliffs on its left face.

I recommend a walk in the meadow. *Distance,* as far as you want. *Time,* whatever you can spare. This is primarily a wildflower walk; but there are birds to be watched, and a good chance of seeing deer at twilight. Traces of the CCC camp are still visible. A great many arrowheads have been found here, but they're now getting rare.

MILE 51.2, BIG MEADOWS, SOUTH ENTRANCE. Elevation 3,510 feet. Turn in here for food and lodging, gasoline, camping and picnicking, etc. The gas station is in sight at the junction. To reach the *Wayside* pass the two entrances to the gas station, then turn right and immediately right again, into the parking area. (What's a Wayside? It's a snack shop, a campstore with groceries and camping supplies, and a gift shop.) The restrooms are reached from outside the building, at the end nearest the gas station. For other features of Big Meadows see the map on page 166, and the following list.

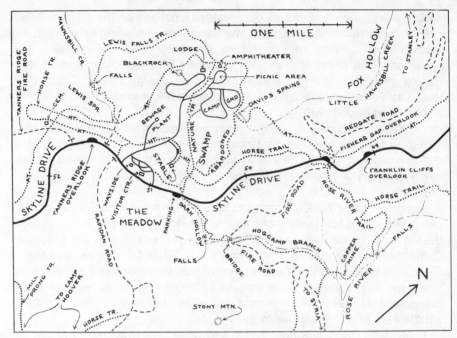

Map of Fishers Gap — Big Meadows area.

Stables, wagon rides. Turn right at the junction about 0.4 mile from the Drive. Park in the first paved parking area on the left and follow the trail, which begins at the far end of the lot, to the stables.

Trailer sewage disposal. Continue past the stables parking area to the disposal area, on your left.

Campground. At the junction 0.7 mile from the Drive and partway up the hill, bear right. Keep right where the road forks, just before you reach the campground entrance station.

Laundry, showers, firewood, ice. Use the parking area on your left, just after you pass the campground entrance station. These facilities are available only when there's a ranger on duty at the entrance station.

Picnic area. Take the left fork just before you reach the campground entrance station, then keep to the right and follow the one-way loop around the picnic area. There are three parking areas on the loop. Park in the second one for the *Amphitheater* (Sunday morning church services and nightly campfire programs during the summer.) Use the same parking area for hikes on the *Lewis Falls Trail.* (See below.)

Big Meadows Lodge. Go directly away from the Drive at Mile 51.2, keeping straight ahead at all intersections until you reach the small traffic circle in front of the Dining Hall, 0.9 mile from the Drive. Ask here about reservations for motel-type units or rustic cabins. Meals are available at the dining hall except in winter. There's a taproom downstairs, and a gift shop near the entrance.

HIKE: *Blackrock summit.* A very easy hike to a high point with a good view. The trail, marked by a sign, starts at the far end of the parking area beyond the Dining Hall. *Round trip* from the Dining Hall, 0.4 mile; from the end of the parking area, less than 0.2 mile. Total *climb* about 60 feet. *Time* required (from the Dining Hall) 0:25.

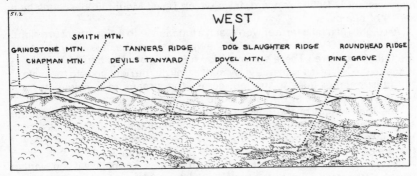

View from Blackrock.

Just before you reach the summit you may see a small shack to the left, with a microwave antenna on top. This is part of the Big Meadows telephone system. On the far side of the shack are underground tanks that store water for the Big Meadows development. Continue to the rocky viewpoint, elevation 3,721 feet. *Caution:* the rock is rather slippery, even when dry.

The sketch shows the left-hand part of the view. At the foot of Roundhead Ridge is the town of Stanley; Luray is diagonally right. After dark, the lights of the two towns make a beautiful display. On a very clear day you can look far up the Valley to your right, to a peak at the north end of the Massanutten near Front Royal. Farther right you can see several peaks in the North District of the Park. At the extreme right, and fairly near, the highest point you see is the rounded summit of Hawksbill. The second highest, farther left and more distant, is Stony Man.

HIKE: *Story-of-the-Forest Nature Trail. Circuit* 1.8 miles; total *climb* about 290 feet; *time* required 1:30. An easy, self-guiding hike, with interpretive posts beside the trail for about two-thirds of its length. The trail starts at the Byrd Visitor Center and passes through a forest in various stages of succession. It ends at the Big Meadows Wayside, near the Visitor Center parking area.

HIKE: *Lewis Falls* (also called Lewis Spring Falls). *Circuit* 3.3 miles; total *climb* about 990 feet; *time* required 3:10. A pleasant walk to a high, pretty waterfall, on a mostly good trail with a few stretches that are rough, rocky, and steep. *Note:* if it's a sunny day and your schedule is flexible, take this hike in mid-afternoon. Then you'll have the sun behind you as you view the falls, and there's a chance you'll see a rainbow in the mist.

Start from the amphitheater parking area (the second parking area on the loop around the picnic grounds.) See map, page 166. Walk down through the amphitheater to the A.T. Turn left, go about 200 feet to a trail junction, and bear right, downhill. (As the map shows, you can also start the hike from the Lodge. Start out clockwise around the traffic circle; bear left onto the paved trail, turn left at the junction a few yards down the hill; go a little more than 0.1 mile to the A.T. and continue diagonally left, downhill, on the falls trail.)

A quarter of a mile from the junction there's a view to the right, into the Page Valley. The town you see is Stanley, at the foot of Roundhead Ridge. Two-thirds of a mile from the start, the trail passes along the base of a cliff that rises steeply on your left. After another hundred yards you'll make a switchback first to the right and then to the left. The trail is steep at both switchbacks, and in wet weather it's slippery. A little more than 0.4 mile beyond the switchbacks, the trail passes briefly over bare rock with a view to the right of the main Blue Ridge, and Tanners Ridge (with clearings and houses) descending from it toward the right. Beyond Tanners Ridge, a little to the right of straight out from the trail, is Chapman Mountain; farther right and more distant is Devils Tanyard, from which Dovel Mountain descends by a series of bumps.

An eighth of a mile farther, you reach a junction with a side trail. Turn right, and go about 50 yards to a wide flat viewpoint above the falls. (You can't see the falls from here.) There's a view down Pine Grove Hollow, with Tanners Ridge to the left of it. From this viewpoint a trail on the right goes to the base of the falls; another goes to the left, across the stream, to a viewpoint from which you look back at the falls. Go to the viewpoint first.

The total height of the falls is 81 feet. It starts its drop in two separate streams (one of which disappears in dry weather), then strikes a mossy rock halfway down, and divides further. In mid-afternoon or later on a sunny day, if there's enough water to make mist, you'll see a rainbow.

Now return to the viewpoint at the top of the falls, and decide if you want to take the other trail down to the bottom. It's about 250 yards of tough going — rough, rocky, and steep. But I find it worth the effort. Return once more to the viewpoint at the top of the falls. Go left to the main trail and then turn right — rather steeply uphill.

The trail climbs steadily, passing through a dark grove of hemlocks. The trail is rich in plant species. I'm especially fond of two that occur in fall. One is grass-leaved blazing star, *Liatris graminifolia,* with leaves that look like large blades of grass, and a spike of small, thistle-like purplish flowers. The other is a velvety-red puffball, *Calostoma sp.,* that grows out of a blob of jelly.

About 0.6 mile above the falls, the trail passes the site of the Lewis Spring Shelter (which was demolished in 1976), then swings left and dead-ends in a dirt road. To the left, the road goes 0.1 mile to the old sewage treatment plant. Straight ahead is a door in the side of the hill, and behind it is a pump that sends most of the output of Lewis Spring up to the underground storage tanks on Blackrock.

Turn right on the dirt road. Thirty yards from the junction, a side trail on the right goes 100 feet to Lewis Spring. It's completely enclosed; you'll hear gushing water behind the padlocked door. This spring is not only the principal source of water for the Big Meadows development; it's also the source of Hawksbill Creek, which forms Lewis Falls and then, much later, flows through the town of Luray before joining the Shenandoah River.

Back on the road: continue uphill another 25 yards to the A.T. crossing. Turn left, and continue a steady, easy climb on the A.T. About 0.6 mile from the dirt road, pass a narrow side trail on the right; it goes 0.2 mile to the summit of Blackrock. About a hundred feet beyond this junction look for two side trails to viewpoints on the left. The second one is better. The view is much the same as that from Blackrock, though not as wide. See sketch, page 167.

Continue for less than 0.4 mile to the falls trail crossing. If you're going to the Lodge, turn right here, and turn right at every opportunity until you find yourself in front of the dining hall. If you're returning to the Amphitheater parking area go straight ahead another 200 feet, watching for the side trail that goes up to the right through the amphitheater.

MILE 51.3, RAPIDAN ROAD, east side. The road goes 6.3 miles to Camp Hoover and, eventually, to Criglersville. Camp Hoover is easier to walk to from Milam Gap, Mile 52.8.

MILE 51.4, SERVICE ROAD, west side. This road provides the easiest access to Lewis Falls. I'll outline the route, though I recommend the slightly longer circuit hike from the amphitheater (see above.)

HIKE: *Lewis Falls. Round trip* 2.5 miles; total *climb* about 795 feet; *time* required 2:25. Park in the grass beside the road. Follow the road downhill, crossing the horse trail twice and the A.T. once. Pass a short side trail on the left, that goes to the enclosed Lewis Spring. Continue 30 yards to a locked door in the hillside on your right. (Behind it is a pump for the Big Meadows water supply.) Turn left here, onto the falls trail. Descend for 0.6 mile to a trail junction; take the side trail to the left, and go 50 yards to a viewpoint at the top of the falls. For a note on the falls, see page 168.

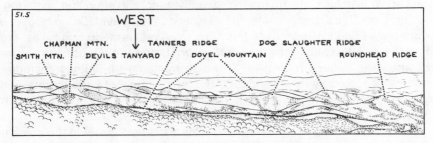

51.5   **WEST**

CHAPMAN MTN.   ↓   TANNERS RIDGE   DOG SLAUGHTER RIDGE
SMITH MTN.   DEVILS TANYARD   DOYEL MOUNTAIN   ROUNDHEAD RIDGE

View from Tanners Ridge Overlook

MILE 51.5, TANNERS RIDGE OVERLOOK. Elevation 3,465 feet. The sketch identifies most of what you see from here. To the right of Roundhead Ridge is the town of Stanley. The name of Dog Slaughter Ridge fascinates me; I can't determine its origin, though several people have offered unpremeditated conjectures. *Fact:* Slaughter was the name of a mountain family in this area.

If you're here in the third week of July, take a minute to climb the bank across the Drive and look for the wood lily, *Lilium philadelphicum,* with fairly short stems, whorled leaves, and red-orange flowers marked with black. The lilies are getting scarcer, and there may be none when you read this. I hope this brief mention does nothing to hasten their extinction.

MILE 51.6, TANNERS RIDGE FIRE ROAD, west side. Elevation 3,465 feet. *A.T. access; cemetery.* The area is worth exploring if you have time. The A.T. crosses the fire road 0.3 mile from the Drive. Distances on the A.T.: North (to the right) it's 1.5 miles to the Big Meadows amphitheater. South (to the left) it's 1.1 miles to the Drive crossing in Milam Gap, Mile 52.8. The cemetery is on the right side of the road, beside the A.T. There are a few old markers here, but most of the graves are relatively new. This is an active cemetery; burials still take place from time to time.

The A.T. toward the south is interesting. About 0.2 mile from the fire road, where water flows under the trail through a pipe, there's a spring 25 yards to the left. (It's hidden by vegetation in summer.) Ahead, an old road trace comes from Tanners Ridge and joins the trail. In the woods to the left is ample evidence of a mountaineer homesite: the spring, piles of rock, pieces of scrap metal, and the stone foundation of a small structure.

Mile 52.8, MILAM GAP, elevation 3,230 feet. *A.T. crossing; Camp Hoover Hikes.* There's a large parking area on the west side. Distances on the A.T.: North (on the west side of the Drive) it's 1.1 miles to the Tanners Ridge fire road, and 2.6 miles to the Big Meadows amphitheater. South (on the east side) it's 2.8 miles to Bootens Gap, Mile 55.1.

Trivia: There are a great many apple trees in and around Milam Gap; most are Milam apples—the variety most often grown by the mountain people. I don't know which name came first. I have an unconfirmed report of a mountain family named Milam.

Camp Hoover Hikes. During his presidential administration, Herbert Hoover came to his camp on the Rapidan River for relaxation and "working" holidays, much as later presidents have used Camp David. Camp Hoover is a not-too-difficult hike from Milam Gap. I will recommend two hikes: one directly down the Mill Prong trail, and return by the same route; the second a somewhat longer circuit hike. Three of the camp's buildings, including the one occupied by the President, are still standing and still maintained. An interpretive sign and map at the camp tell the story. You're free to explore the whole area *unless the camp is occupied.*

President Hoover, at the end of his administration, donated the camp to the government for use by future presidents or other high government officials. When the Park was created, Camp Hoover became a part of it. But the camp is still used from time to time by members of Congress, cabinet officers, and other VIPs. Therefore, if you see that the camp is occupied, please don't go any closer.

HIKE: *Camp Hoover* via Mill Prong trail. *Round trip* 4.1 miles; total *climb* about 870 feet; *time* required 3:50. Moderately rough in spots; not steep; three stream crossings, two of them very easy. See map below. Milam Gap is below and to the left of center.

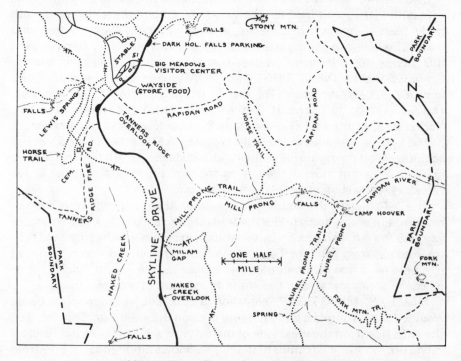

Map of Milam Gap — Camp Hoover area.

Take the A.T. on the east side of the Drive, walk about 50 yards to the trail junction, and turn left onto the Mill Prong trail. For a third of a mile the trail descends gradually through overgrown fields and orchards, then enters older woods. Cross two small branches of the Mill Prong at 0.7 and 1.1 miles from the start. Thirty yards beyond the second crossing, the horse trail from Big Meadows comes in on the left. *Note:* for the next 0.8 mile you'll be on the horse trail; horses have the right of way.

Less than half a mile beyond the trail junction, watch for a small waterfall on the right, where a cascade of water flows down over a sloping rock that spans the full width of the stream. Fifty yards beyond the falls, the trail turns right and crosses the stream. Use a little caution here; the rocks are slippery. Pieces of pipe that you may see on the far side of the stream were part of the original water supply system for Camp Hoover.

After another 0.3 mile, the trail ends and joins a road. Turn right, and follow the road to a small parking area. From here, the Laurel Prong trail goes to the right. (See the circuit hike, below.) Turn left to explore Camp Hoover (unless, as I said, it's occupied.) The three original cabins that are still standing are *The President,* in the middle; *The Prime Minister* (which was used by Ramsey MacDonald, prime minister of Great Britain), on the right; and *The Creel* (which was occupied by two presidential assistants), on the left.

Go on around to the porch on the far side of *The President.* It's a little unusual in that it was built around the trees that were standing there; the Hoovers tried to disturb the area as little as possible. A short distance down below the porch, the Mill Prong, coming from the left, and the Laurel Prong, coming from the right, meet to form the Rapidan River. (The very small stream that flows through the camp was man-made; it's called Hemlock Run.)

The President's cabin is open to the public one weekend a year—usually on the Saturday and Sunday nearest to Hoover's birthday, August 10. On that day, free buses carry visitors to Camp Hoover from the Byrd Visitor Center, Mile 51.0. (If you'd like more information about Camp Hoover, see "Herbert Hoover's Hideaway" by Darwin Lambert. It's available at the Visitor Center.)

Return to Milam Gap the way you came. Looking at the map, you might be tempted to return by the Rapidan fire road to make a circuit hike. I don't recommend it. From Camp Hoover it's 6.3 miles via fire road to the Drive at Mile 51.3, though it seems a great deal longer when you're walking it.

HIKE: *Camp Hoover* via Mill Prong trail; return via Laurel Prong and A.T. *Circuit* 7.4 miles; total *climb* about 1,520 feet; *time* required 6:30. This is a moderately difficult hike because of its length and the amount of climbing; but no part of it is very rough or very steep. There are several stream crossings, all of them rather easy. (See map, page 170; the Laurel Prong trail joins the A.T. below the bottom of the map.)

As above to *The President.* Return past the small parking area on your right and keep straight ahead on the Laurel Prong trail. The trail follows an old road trace, which at first is a service road leading to the camp water source. The first half-mile is yellow-blazed. Half a mile from Camp Hoover, after you emerge from a grove of hemlocks, watch for a junction where the road trace swings left and becomes the yellow-blazed Fork Mountain trail. The Laurel Prong trail, which is blue-blazed beyond this point, continues straight ahead.

Wildflower notes: In late summer look for closed gentians here at the trail junction. In other seasons you may find a short side trip on the Fork Mountain trail worthwhile. The Laurel Prong is less than 200 yards from the main trail. Before you reach it you'll enter a rich stand of the great rhododendron, *Rhododendron maximum,* which extends a quarter of a mile downstream and more than half a mile upstream. As far as I know, this species grows nowhere else in the Park, though *Rhododendron catawbiense* occurs at several places in the South Section. Because the Hoovers planted a number of flower species near the camp, it's tempting to think they planted the rhododendrons here. But I find a description of them that was written in the early 1920's—years before Hoover selected this area for his camp. The flowers are beautiful: pink in bud, then white when fully opened, then fringed with pink as they grow older. They're usually at the height of bloom about the middle of July.

Continuing on the Laurel Prong trail: there will be several stream crossings; not much water, but rocky or muddy. Traces of human habitation: a rock pile, a rock wall, and a decaying rail fence. If the rhododendrons are in bloom, you'll see them on your left from several points along the trail. At 0.6 mile from the Fork Mountain trail you'll cross the Laurel Prong and start to climb. After three-quarters of a mile of easy climbing, you reach a trail junction on the ridge crest in Laurel Gap. To the left is the Cat Knob trail. Stay on the Laurel Prong trail, which turns 90 degrees to the right.

From Laurel Gap, follow the trail along the south slope of Hazeltop, with the Conway River basin to your left, for exactly one mile to its junction with the A.T. Turn right. Less than half a mile from the junction, the A.T. crosses the crest of Hazeltop, elevation 3,816 feet—the third highest point in the Park (after Hawksbill and Stony Man) and the highest point on the A.T. within the Park. Continue, mostly downhill, another two miles to your starting point in Milam Gap.

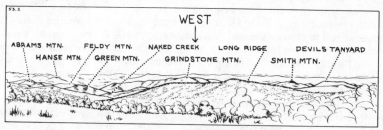

View from Naked Creek Overlook.

MILE 53.2, NAKED CREEK OVERLOOK. Elevation 3,250 feet. The overlook provides a view down the valley formed by the east branch of Naked Creek (See sketch.) The town in the Valley, out beyond the mouth of the hollow, is Elkton. The house over on Long Ridge is outside the Park. Out of sight on the far side of Smith Mountain is Steam Hollow which, I've heard, got its name from the steam produced by the moonshine stills that used to operate there.

Naked Creek Falls is down in the hollow, less than a mile from the overlook. (See map, page 170; you're in the lower left part of it. I had to cheat a little to get the falls on the map; actually, they should be just below the bottom edge.) The falls are worth seeing if you like exploring and have enough experience to do so safely. There is no trail; this is a cross-country hike through the woods. And as with any bushwhacking enterprise, you can expect to find some rocks and brambles. I suggest you start at the south end of the overlook, go downhill to the stream, then downstream to the falls. To return, with no chance of getting lost: go uphill from the falls to the Drive, then turn left and walk along the Drive to the overlook.

MILE 53.6 to 54.6, *Wildflower note:* Scattered along both sides of the Drive in this area are plants that look like giant Queen Anne's lace, with flat-topped umbels of white flowers that bloom in June. Because the plants often grow eight or ten feet high they look like they belong in the tropics, or maybe on Venus. This is cow parsnip, *Heracleum maximum.*

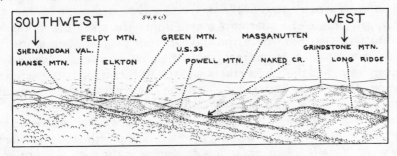

View from Hazeltop Ridge Overlook. (No. 1.)

MILE 54.4, HAZELTOP RIDGE OVERLOOK. Elevation 3,265 feet. The two sketches identify most of what you can see from here. On a clear day you can look to the left of Hanse Mountain and straight up Beldore Hollow to distant peaks in the South Section of the Park. The distant rounded summit at the extreme left, with clearings, is Flattop.

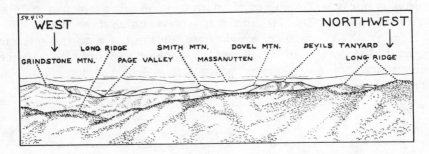

View from Hazeltop Ridge Overlook. (No. 2.)

MILE 55.1, BOOTENS GAP. Elevation 3,235 feet. *Fire road,* east side. *A.T. access, hikes, history, geology.*

Turn onto the fire road if you want to stop here. There's a parking area on the left, about 25 yards from the Drive. The A.T. crosses the fire road a few feet beyond the parking area. Distances on the A.T.: North (to the left) it's 2.9 miles to the Drive crossing in Milam Gap, Mile 52.8. South (to the right) it's 2.4 miles to the Slaughter fire road, near Mile 56.8 on the Drive.

Although Camp Hoover is easier to reach from Milam Gap, Mile 52.8, a hike from here would not be difficult. The round-trip distance is 6.7 miles. Go left on the A.T. for a little less than half a mile; turn right onto the Laurel Prong Trail and go one mile to a low point on the ridge, in Laurel Gap. Turn left and go 1.9 miles to Camp Hoover. (For a note on Camp Hoover, see page 170.)

The fire road descends a little more than a mile to the Park boundary, where it enters a Virginia Wildlife Area. There's a large wild area there, along the Conway River and its tributaries, which deserves exploring if you have the proper equipment and experience.

History: The *Fairfax Line,* which marked the southwest boundary of the huge land grant owned by Lord Fairfax, was surveyed from the source of the Conway River, about a quarter of a mile from here, and crossed the ridge near Bootens Gap. From here, the surveyors laid out a line across the Page Valley and the Massanutten, the Shenandoah Valley beyond the Massanutten, and then a few ranges of the Alleghenies, to the estimated location of the source of the Potomac River. They reached the Potomac at a point several miles downstream, surveyed their way upstream to the source, calculated the direction of the true boundary, then surveyed their way back to Bootens Gap, marking the Fairfax line with stone markers as they went. (One of these markers is on display in the Byrd Visitor Center, Mile 51.0.)

On reaching Bootens Gap, the surveyors found that they had missed their starting point by only a hundred yards. This is a remarkable performance. The line was 76.5 miles long; the country was a lot rougher then than now, and surveying instruments were less sophisticated. The surveying party started from Bootens Gap on September 10, 1746, and returned on February 24, 1747. Its leaders were Thomas Lewis (whose journal is our principal source of information on this subject), and Peter Jefferson (father of Thomas Jefferson, who was then three years old.)

Geology: Walk a tenth of a mile north on the Drive, to the rock cut opposite Milepost 55. The basalt rock face shows thick lenses of pale green epidote, and thin veins of epidote and quartz, making a photogenic display of muted colors.

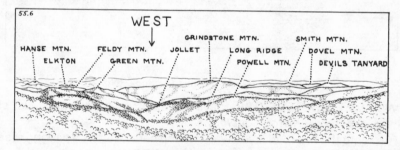

View from The Point Overlook.

MILE 55.6, THE POINT OVERLOOK. Elevation 3,235 feet. The sketch shows the left part of the view. To the left of Hanse Mountain (at the left edge of the sketch) you can see, on a very clear day, distant peaks in the South Section of the Park. Devils Tanyard, at the right on the sketch, is a little to right of center of the overall view. Farther right, with houses on it, is the upper end of Long Ridge. The high point at the extreme right is Hazeltop.

The clump of trees below the overlook hides the middle of the view. To see it all, I suggest that you walk a hundred yards to a viewpoint. From an opening in the wall, stone steps descend to a narrow trail (which may be somewhat overgown in late summer.) The trail swings left and goes around the grove of trees to a viewpoint ledge. The view here is more exciting than that from the overlook because of the sheer drop from the ledge, and because the Drive and cars are out of sight.

Geology: The rocks exposed in the road cut across from the overlook are Catoctin basalt with layers of volcanic tuff. The tuff, which is compressed volcanic ash, is best seen opposite the south end of the overlook where it is separating into thin shale-like flakes and falling down the bank. Many of the flakes are soft enough to crumble between your fingers, while the basalt is considerably harder.

MILE 56.4, BEARFENCE MOUNTAIN PARKING, west side. *Hikes, A.T. access.* In summer, conducted hikes to Bearfence summit begin here at the parking area. (For day and time see the Activities Schedule, posted on bulletin boards and available free at the Visitor Center, Mile 51.0.)

Bearfence Mountain, elevation 3,620 feet, reportedly got its name from the palisade-like rocks, resembling a fence, that surround its summit. From the summit you have a 360-degree view; this is one of only four or five places in the whole Park from which you can see all around you. The hike to the summit is fairly easy in that it's short, with less than 300 feet of climbing. It's difficult in that part of it is pure rock scramble for which you'll use both hands and perhaps from time to time the seat of your pants. But the climb is not dangerous if you observe a few simple precautions.

PRECAUTIONS: Don't take dogs, or children that have to be carried. Wear hiking boots with non-skid soles. Don't try this climb when the rocks are wet, or covered with ice or snow. Be prepared for sudden strong gusts of wind that might make you lose your balance. Look carefully before reaching for handholds on the rocks; as in any very rocky place on the mountain, rattlesnakes sometimes occur.

The trail begins across the Drive from the parking area, and goes uphill from the edge of the grassy bank. (The trail that goes downhill into the woods from the parking area leads nowhere, and soon disappears.)

I will recommend two hikes: to the summit and back; and a circuit that continues beyond the summit and returns by A.T.

HIKE: *Bearfence Summit. Round trip* 0.8 mile; total *climb* about 275 feet; *time* required 1:10. Take the trail that goes uphill, across the Drive from the parking area. About 60 yards from the Drive, note a low, flat boulder on each side of the trail. Both are sandstone of the Swift Run formation. Bearfence Mountain is surrounded by Swift Run sandstone, though its summit is capped with Catoctin basalt.

About 200 yards from the Drive, the trail crosses the A.T. Distances on the A.T.: North (to the left) it's 1.3 miles to Bootens Gap, Mile 55.1. South (to the right) it's 1.0 mile to the Slaughter fire road near the Drive at Mile 56.8.

Continue straight ahead on the blue-blazed trail. It goes partly along the ridge crest and, in places, drops down on the left side to go around several false summits. Don't settle for any of those, thinking you've reached the top. When you get to the actual summit you'll have a clean, unobstructed 360-degree view. The two sketches on page 176 identify its principal features.

Geology: About halfway between the A.T. and the summit, you cross the contact between the Swift Run and Catoctin formations. On the blazed trail, they are separated by a very thin layer of quartz pebbles. The rocks, especially the basalt near the summit, are weathered and lichen-covered, which makes them hard to identify. But at several places you can see where the advancing lava picked up pebbles, sand, and mud. Elsewhere you can see veins of quartz and epidote in the basalt.

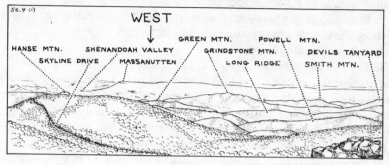

View from Bearfence Mountain. (No. 1.)

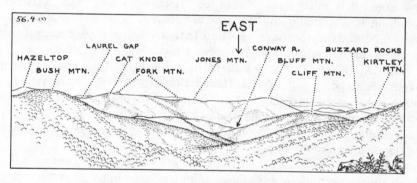

View from Bearfence Mountain. (No. 2.)

Return by the same route or, if you wish, continue on the circuit hike described below. This is longer, but requires less rock scrambling than going back the way you came.

HIKE: *Bearfence Summit. Circuit* 1.2 miles; total *climb* about 380 feet; *time* required 1:45 (about 35 minutes longer than the round trip.)

As above, to Bearfence summit. Continue in the same direction, descending, following the blue blazes. The rock scramble is a bit difficult, but it's short. A hundred yards from the summit, a short side trail on the right goes 55 yards to the A.T. Keep straight ahead, climbing a low knob, and 110 yards from the junction reach a side trail on the right that goes 20 feet to a ledge with an overgrown view. A second ledge, about 50 feet to the left of the first and 10 feet down, has a wide, clear view — more or less the same as in the No. 1 sketch, above.

Return to the trail and turn right; cross the summit of the small knob, and descend to the A.T. Turn *left* onto the A.T. for a 90-yard walk to another ledge, on the left, with a view. The low, rounded, nearby summit toward the left is Cliff Mountain. Beyond it, much higher and sharper, is Bluff Mountain. From the ledge you look straight down to the mouth of Devils Ditch, which joins the Conway River at the foot of the hollow. The high point beyond the hollow is Buzzard Rocks.

Geology: The ledge you're standing on is sandstone of the Swift Run formation. All the rocks you'll see on your way back are of the same material, except for a few basalt boulders that have rolled down from the summit.

Return to the A.T. and go right, back the way you came. Pass two side trails (the two ends of the "Bearfence loop") that join from the right. Continue a quarter of a mile beyond the second side trail, to where the main Bearfence trail crosses the A.T. Turn left here, and return to your starting point.

MILE 56.4 to 56.8. *Wildflower note:* Mountain laurels, scattered along the bank on the east side of the Drive, bloom in June.

MILE 56.8, FIRE ROADS, both sides. *A.T. access; Bearfence A.T. Hut; explorer hikes.* On the west side of the Drive the Meadows School fire road descends for 1.4 miles to the Park boundary. The Meadows School and two mountaineer homes were beside the road, just inside the boundary.

On the east side, the Slaughter fire road crosses the A.T. about a hundred yards from the Drive, near a small parking area. Distances on the A.T.: North (to the left) it's 2.4 miles to Bootens Gap, Mile 55.1. South (to the right) it's 1.0 mile to Lewis Mountain Campground. Beyond the A.T. the fire road forks. The right branch goes to the Bearfence A.T. Hut. The left branch is the fire road; it descends to the Park boundary at the Conway River, 3.3 miles from the Drive. If you turn left there you'll enter a Virginia Wildlife Area, then continue upstream beside the river, near the boundary between the Wildlife Area and the Park. This is wild and beautiful country, and I recommend it for exploration by *experienced hikers.*

MILE 57.25. *Wildflower note:* Trumpet honeysuckle, *Lonicera sempervirens,* grows on the rocks here, on the west side of the Drive. It's fairly common along the Drive, but this is one of the easiest places to see it from a moving car. It starts blooming in the second half of May, and the flowers look like strings of bright red firecrackers.

MILE 57.5, LEWIS MOUNTAIN FACILITIES. Elevation at entrance, 3,390 feet. Picnic area, cabins, conducted walks and campfire talks, campstore, telephone, campground, showers, *A.T. access.* Open about mid-April through October. (The Lewis Mountain development was opened in 1940 "for negroes". Segregation ended in 1950.) For schedules of walks and talks see the folder "Visitor Activities", posted on the bulletin boards.

After you turn in on the entrance road, the second side road on your left is the beginning of a one-way loop around the picnic area. The amphitheater is a short distance to the right of the loop, near its beginning. Beyond the entrance to the picnic area you come to the campstore (with telephone) on the right, and a row of furnished cottages on the left. Each cottage has a bathroom, lights, heat, towels, linen, and a covered cooking area with a fireplace, grill, and picnic table. You can buy supplies and rent cooking utensils at the campstore. To reserve a cottage write ARA Virginia Skyline Co., Inc., P.O. Box 727, Luray, Va., 22835, telephone (703) 743-5108.

Beyond the campstore begin the one-way clockwise loops around the campground. The A.T. passes around the picnic area and the campground, and can be reached from several places. For example: as you enter the campground, keeping to the far left, there's a short access trail on your left, opposite the first campsite. Celandine, *Chelidonium majus,* blooms along the access trail in May and June. It's yellow, with four petals.

MILE 57.5 to 60.2. *Wildflower note.* Two flowers that might attract your attention are scattered along the Drive in this area. Both bloom in May. Star-of-Bethlehem, *Ornithogalum umbellatum,* is a small white lily with grass-like leaves. Spiderwort, *Tradescantia virginiana,* has rather large, dark blue-violet three-petaled flowers, and slender blade-like leaves about a foot long.

MILE 58.6 to 58.8. This is, unofficially, the "Green Tunnel." Branches meet above the road to form a green tunnel in summer, and sometimes an ice tunnel in winter.

MILE 59.1, THE OAKS OVERLOOK. Elevation 3,125 feet. The view is overgrown. You can look above the treetops and across the Page Valley to the Massanutten. The town a little to left of center, between the overlook and the south end of the Massanutten, is Elkton.

MILE 59.5, POCOSIN FIRE ROAD, east side. Elevation 3,125 feet. *A.T. access, hikes, Pocosin Cabin.* There's a small parking area at the left of the fire road, 60 yards from the Drive. The A.T. crosses the road about 0.1 mile from the Drive. Distances on the A.T.: North (to the left) it's 1.8 miles to Lewis Mountain Campground. South (to the right) it's 3.4 miles to the South River Falls trail near South River Picnic Area.

I will recommend two hikes that start here: a round trip to the ruins of Upper Pocosin Mission, and a rather long circuit hike that includes the mission ruins, a mountaineer cemetery, and South River Falls.

Conjecture: Pocosin is of Indian origin, possibly from the Algonquin *pakwesen* meaning damp or wet land.

Less than 0.1 mile beyond the A.T. crossing, a broad trail leaves the fire road on the right and goes 200 feet to the locked *Pocosin Cabin.* Feel free to go look it over *unless* it's occupied. If you'd like to rent the cabin for your own use, write Potomac Appalachian Trail Club, 1718 N St., N.W., Washington, D.C. 20036.

HIKE: *Upper Pocosin Mission. Round trip* 1.9 miles; total *climb* about 425 feet; *time* required 1:55. An easy hike, via fire road, to the site of a former church and mountaineer settlement. See map, page 181. You're at the right-hand edge, above center. Your route is N-M-L-M-N.

Follow the fire road, past the chain and the A.T. crossing, and past the side trail to the cabin. About a mile from the parking area the road levels out and swings left. Look for a concrete marker post on the right, near the start of the yellow-blazed Pocosin trail. As you turn onto the trail, the first ruin is about 100 feet diagonally left. It was part of the Episcopal Mission here—not a mountaineer cabin. Explore if you wish, remembering that snakes like to take cover under old lumber piles.

Twenty yards from the ruined house are the steps of the church. The church is gone, and its foundation is crumbling. As I write this, two walls of a small side room are standing, one with a wooden door frame. There are various graffiti on the frame, including: "E. B. Samuels born here 1915, visited here July 21, 1974." "This church has gone up and down in my life-time, W. E. Samuels."

Twenty-five yards beyond the church steps are the ruins of a wooden structure, now unidentifiable, under a large chestnut oak. The vines on the upper limbs of the oak are loaded with grapes in autumn—but way up out of reach. On the other side of the Pocosin trail, which once was a road, and beyond the remains of a fence, is an abandoned cemetery with fieldstone markers, and the site of at least two houses. Explore if you wish, then return to your car the way you came.

HIKE: *Pocosin Mission* and *South River Falls. Circuit* 8.5 miles; total *climb* about 1,830 feet; *time* required 7:30. A long and tiring hike which includes ruins, a cemetery, and the falls. See map, page 181. Your route is N-M-L-K-J-D-C-B-F-M-N.

As above to Pocosin Mission, and continue on the abandoned road, which is now the Pocosin trail. Descend to the small stream, then climb easily uphill for a while. Some parts of this trail may be overgrown in summer, but you should have no trouble following the old roadbed. Rattlesnakes have been reported here; carry a stick if the grass is high, and use it to part the grass in front of you as you walk.

About 1.2 miles from the mission, the trail flattens out in an overgrown grassy area and enters an old orchard, which still produces quantities of edible fruit. Watch for a marker post where the trail turns sharply to the right. The less-used trail goes about 150 yards diagonally left to the South River Cemetery—which is fenced, carpeted with periwinkle, and rather attractive as cemeteries go. Although inside the Park, and though overgrown with black locust and other pioneer trees, the cemetery is still active. None of the graves with inscribed markers is very old.

Return to the main trail and turn left. Go about 200 yards to the South River fire road, with an old stone wall on your left for a part of this distance. Turn right on the fire road, which runs along the Park boundary (marked by red or orange blazes.) After 250 yards the boundary turns 90 degrees to the right, and you enter a Virginia Wildlife Area. You re-enter the Park where a chain blocks the road. Less than half a mile beyond the chain, a less-used road comes in at a sharp angle from the left. Turn left onto this road, which soon narrows to a trail and, less than half a mile from the junction, reaches a marker post where a trail comes in from the right. (Ahead, it's three-quarters of a mile to the bottom of South River Falls.) Turn right and go about 250 yards to a viewpoint, on your left, with a fine view of South River Falls.

The falls has a total drop of 83 feet. Halfway down, the stream divides, so that the falls has the form of an inverted "Y". From the observation point return to the trail and turn left, passing along the edge of a steep gorge, to the head of the falls. (Keep going; there's no view from the top of the falls.) Continue uphill, with a couple of switchbacks, to the A.T. crossing 1.2 miles from the falls observation point. (Ahead, uphill, it's a tenth of a mile to the South River Picnic Area, which has water and toilets.)

Turn right on the A.T. Cross the South River fire road after half a mile, and continue another 2.9 miles to the Pocosin fire road. Turn left and go less than 0.1 mile to your starting point.

MILE 61.3, BALDFACE MOUNTAIN OVERLOOK. Elevation 3,345 feet.
The view here is especially attractive because of the rocky ledge beyond the wall and the oak tree that spreads over it. The sketch names some of the things you can see.

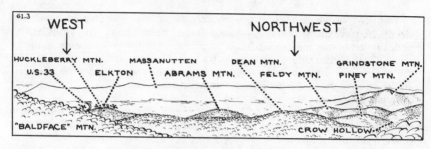

View from Baldface Mountain Overlook.

Trivia: I can't find "Baldface Mountain" on any map. The nearby summit to your left is nameless on the maps. In the 1930's there was a CCC camp half a mile south of here; its mail was addressed to "Baldface, Va.," but was delivered through the Elkton Post Office.

MILE 61.8, SERVICE ROAD, west side; ABANDONED ROAD, east side. A.T. access. See map, page 181; you're a little left of upper center. There's parking space in the grass on the east side, just north of the abandoned road.

The service road on the west side was once used by the Park's maintenance division for earth storage. It goes about a thousand feet, then ends. The area is fairly level, and still relatively open.

Along the east side of the Drive here, on both sides of the abandoned road, there was a CCC camp during the 1930's. The abandoned road goes an eighth of a mile to the A.T., then continues for 75 yards to a sort of amphitheater in front of the quarry face. There is little evidence of the CCC occupation except a few bricks, a few lumps of coal, a little scrap metal, and some piles of decaying chestnut boards near the quarry.

MILE 62.7, SOUTH RIVER OVERLOOK, elevation 2,950 feet. The overlook has a V-shaped view down the valley of South River and out to the Piedmont. The high point diagonally right is Saddleback. A few feet north of the overlook, a fire road leaves the Drive on each side.

On the west, the Dry Run fire road goes about 2.0 miles to the Park boundary. The Dry Run falls are off the road, but worth a trip by *experienced explorers.* About 1.8 miles from the Drive, the fire road makes a sharp turn to the right. After you complete the turn the falls will be diagonally ahead and left, straight downhill, about an eighth of a mile away. If there's a good flow of water, you should be able to hear the falls from the road. As I said, *experienced hikers only.*

On the east, the South River fire road (point "G" on the map, page 181) crosses the A.T. about a quarter of a mile from the Drive (at point "F.") The road is an alternate route to the South River falls; but I recommend starting from the picnic area, a tenth of a mile to the south.

MILE 62.8, SOUTH RIVER PICNIC AREA. *A.T. access; hikes to South River Falls* and *South River Trail Maintenance Building.* Open all year; drive in. The head of the South River Falls trail is on your right as you drive into the third parking area. It crosses the A.T. about 150 yards from the road. Distances on the A.T.: North (to the left) it's 3.4 miles to the Pocosin fire road near Mile 59.5 on the Drive. South (to the right) it's 3.0 miles to the Drive crossing in Swift Run Gap, Mile 65.5.

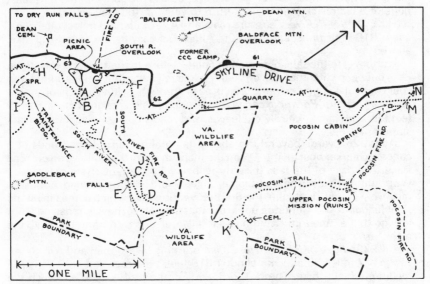

Map of Pocosin — South River area.

South River Falls is at the head of a deep and precipitous rocky gorge. It's the third-highest falls in the Park, with a drop of 83 feet in two stages: first, a single stream falls to a pool about halfway down the cliff, where it divides and falls the rest of the way in two separate streams. The falls are best seen from an observation point a little way downstream, on the left bank of the gorge. I will suggest three different hikes to the falls, listed here in order of increasing difficulty. See map above.

1. Falls observation point and return. Route: A-B-C-B-A.

2. Falls observation point; return by fire road and A.T. Route: A-B-C-D-J-F-B-A.

3. Base of the falls and return by fire road. Route: A-B-C-D-E-D-J-F-B-A.

HIKE: (1): *South River Falls. Round trip* 2.6 miles, total *climb* about 850 feet; *time* required 2:25. A moderately easy hike; the return trip is a steady climb.

Follow the trail past the drinking fountain and continue downhill, crossing the A.T. in less than 0.1 mile. Continue downhill on a long straight stretch through an overgrown clearing; the stone walls to the left are evidence that this was once a cornfield or pasture. *(Wildflower note:* the flowering spurge, *Euphorbia corolata,* is common along this trail; its small white flowers bloom in mid-summer.) The trail swings left, descends by switchbacks, then straightens out again as the stream joins it on the right.

Cross a tributary stream (often invisible under the rocks, but clearly audible.) Looking ahead you can see what appears to be sky at the base of the trees—a clear indication that the bottom of the hollow drops away suddenly, and the stream plunges over a waterfall. After another hundred yards you'll come to a concrete trail marker on the left, and maybe a pile of brush at the right (to discourage people from going to the top of the falls. Reason: you can't see the falls from the top, but you can risk your life there.)

Continue another 0.1 mile to a second trail marker. The observation point is 30 feet to the right—a ledge on which the Park has built a guard wall. From there you have a fine view of the falls and, across the gorge, of the northeast ridge of Saddleback Mountain. Return to your car the way you came.

HIKE (2): *South River Falls,* fire road, and A.T. *Circuit* 3.3 miles; total *climb* about 910 feet; *time* required 3:05. Almost as easy as the round-trip hike, above.

As above, to the falls observation point. Return to the trail and turn right. Pass between cliffs that rise on your left and fall away (but not alarmingly) on your right. (*Wildflower note:* you'll pass through a long patch of small-flowered leafcup, *Polymnia canadensis*—a composite that grows from 6 to 10 feet tall, with large, weirdly-cut leaves, and yellow flowers that bloom in late summer.)

About 250 yards beyond the observation point the trail dead-ends at a concrete marker post (point "D" on the map), in a trail that follows an old road trace. The base of the falls (hike three, below) is three-quarters of a mile to your right. Turn left. The trail soon becomes more obviously a road. About 0.4 mile from point "D" it joins the South River fire road, which comes in on the right (at point "J"). Continue uphill another 0.8 mile to the A.T. crossing. Turn left; go half a mile to the South River Falls trail and turn right, uphill, to the picnic area.

HIKE (3): *Base of South River Falls,* returning by fire road and A.T. *Semi-circuit* 4.7 miles; total *climb* about 1,315 feet; *time* required 5:00. This is a medium-difficult hike. The last 275 yards of the trail, as you approach the base of the falls, are rocky and steep.

As above, past the falls observation point to the trail junction at point "D" on the map. Turn right. This trail was once a mountaineer road that went out to the Piedmont. It curves gradually around to the left, into a cove formed by a small tributary of South River, then makes a sharp switchback to the right. (At this point you're outside the Park, but will return shortly.)

The road trace continues to curve right at the mouth of the cove, and suddenly widens as it reaches the bank of the stream. (This was a turnaround when the road trace was used as a Park fire road. The old mountaineer road crossed the stream here, turned left, and continued downstream on the right bank.) From here on, the trail climbs on a narrow, somewhat graded, sometimes steep trail over the rocks in the bottom of the gorge. It's 275 yards, with a climb of 105 feet, to the gravelly "beach" at the base of the falls. The trail passes directly under the falls observation point, which is 115 feet above the stream.

Go back the way you came, as far as the junction at point "D" on the map. Continue straight ahead. After 0.4 mile, the South River fire road comes in from the right. Continue another 0.8 mile to the A.T. crossing and turn left. Go 0.5 mile to the falls trail, turn right, and return to your starting point.

HIKE: *South River Trail Maintenance Building. Round trip* 1.7 miles; total *climb* about 225 feet; *time* required 1:30. An easy, pleasant walk on the A.T. and a service road. In spring and summer there are wildflowers in abundance along the way. See map, page 181. Your route is A-B-H-I and return.

Start down the South River falls trail (which begins at the third parking area on the loop around the South River picnic area, Mile 62.8.) Reach the A.T. in less than 0.1 mile, and turn right. A third of a mile from the junction the A.T. joins the service road, which comes in on the right (Skyline Drive, at Mile 63.1, is less than 200 yards to the right.) Continue ahead on the service road. After 300 yards the road swings left while the A.T. goes ahead. Stay on the road, and follow it another quarter of a mile to its end. The PATC Trail Maintenance Building is 50 yards ahead. Fifty feet before you reach the end of the road, a side trail on the left goes a hundred feet downhill to a spring. Beyond the Trail Maintenance Building is the beginning of the blue-blazed Saddleback Mountain trail, which goes about 1.1 miles around the summit of

Saddleback Mountain and joins the A.T. about 0.9 mile to the left of point "H" on the map.

The immediate area of the spring and maintenance building may deserve exploration. There was a mountaineer homesite here. You can find a few apple trees, and there are rose and lilac bushes nearby.

MILE 63.1, SERVICE ROAD, east side. This is the service road for South River Trail Maintenance Building; it joins the A.T. less than 200 yards from the Drive. I don't consider this an A.T. access because there's no safe parking here. To reach either the A.T. or the South River Trail Maintenance Building, start at the South River Picnic area. (See the Hike to the South River Trail Maintenance Building, above.)

MILE 63.2, DIRT ROAD, west side. This is the entrance to the *Dean Cemetery*, which is less than 200 yards from the Drive. There's a turnaround at the end of the road. If you're deeply interested in the history of the mountain people, this cemetery deserves a visit. There are more than 100 graves here. The oldest I could find is that of James Dean — born January 15, 1797; died May 22, 1862. But many graves are marked by uninscribed fieldstone, and some of these may be older.

MILE 64.4, HENSLEY HOLLOW OVERLOOK. Elevation 2,560 feet. The sketch names the principal features of the view. The cleared strip that goes over Lick Ridge is not a road, but a power line. The town of Elkton is shown on the sketch. The town of Shenandoah is on the far side of the Valley, and just to the left of Huckleberry Mountain. The relatively nearby ridge this side of Grindstone Mountain has no name on the maps.

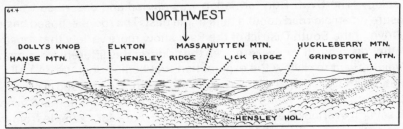

View from Hensley Hollow Overlook.

History: The town of Elkton, at the junction of routes 33 and 340, began on the bank of the Shenandoah River at the mouth of Elk Run. It was named for Elk Run in 1881. Before that it was called Conrad's Store.

Geology: The rock exposed in the road cut across the Drive is of the Swift Run formation. It's mostly phyllite—a slaty rock with lustrous surface in a fresh break, due to thin scales of mica. This is hard to see on the weathered, lichen-covered rock. But it's easily seen where the rock is disintegrating, and you can pick up a freshly broken piece from the bottom of the rock face.

MILE 64.5, *Wildflower note:* The feathery flowers that grow on the bank on the east side of the Drive, blooming in late May and early June, are Allegheny goatsbeard, *Aruncus dioicus,* a member of the rose family.

MILE 64.9, PARKING PULLOUT, west side. This parking area is not an overlook but the site of the former Swift Run entrance station. There's a view of sorts from the north end. To the left you can see some of the ridges in the South Section of the Park. Hanse Mountain, a little to the left of center, is mostly hidden by the trees. The town of Elkton is a little to the right of center.

Wildflower note: There are dogwood trees on both sides of the Drive in this area. They bloom in early May. In some years they put on a spectacular show; in others the bloom is skimpy. It all depends on the weather.

LOG OF THE DRIVE — SOUTH SECTION

MILE 65.5, SWIFT RUN GAP. Elevation 2,365 feet. *A.T. crossing. U.S. 33 interchange.* To the west (turn right on U.S. 33), Elkton is seven miles and Harrisonburg twenty-two. Elkton has very limited facilities. Harrisonburg offers a wide choice of food and lodging, a hospital, and access to Interstate 81.

The *Appalachian Trail* crosses the Drive here, and crosses U.S. 33 on the overpass. Distances on the A.T.: North (on the east side, from the north end of the overpass) it's 3.0 miles to the South River Picnic Area. South (on the west side, from the south end of the overpass) it's 1.2 miles to the Drive crossing at Mile 66.7.

History: Swift Run Gap has been an important Blue Ridge crossing for more than 100 years, although the present highway is relatively recent. On the east side it follows the original route closely; on the west it doesn't even touch the old road, except here in the gap. Beside U.S. 33, to the west of the overpass, are a historical sign, a stone pyramid, and a stone monolith. All three refer to the Spotswood expedition (page 30.)

Geology: The Swift Run formation was named and described from an exposure on an old road about a mile to the east. The rocks exposed beside the Drive in the South District of the Park show more variety that those in the other districts. (If you've forgotten the origin of the different formations, you might want to review the explanation that begins on page 74.) All the formations that occur in the Park, except the Erwin, are exposed in roadcuts in the South District. White quartzites of the Erwin formation are visible from several overlooks, and can be reached on foot—for example from the Riprap parking area, page 211.

MILE 66.7, A.T. CROSSING. Elevation about 2,635 feet. There's a 5-car parking area on the west side of the Drive. *Hike to Hightop Summit.* Distances on the A.T.: North (on the west side) it's 1.2 miles to Swift Run Gap, Mile 65.5. South (on the east) it's 3.4 miles to Smith Roach Gap, Mile 68.6.

> HIKE: *Hightop Summit. Round trip* 3.0 miles; total *climb* about 935 feet; *time* required 2:55. Outstanding views. See map, page 187.
> Take the A.T. on the east side of the Drive. It starts out through a much overgrown clearing, then swings left, enters the woods, and begins to climb. (In May look for the red-purple trillium, *Trillium erectum,* starting about a quarter of a mile from the Drive; it's rare elsewhere in the Park.) The trail winds its way up the ridge, then turns right (west) toward the summit. After it swings left around the summit, watch for a side trail on the right that goes ten yards to a viewpoint on a rocky ledge. From there you can see most of the higher peaks in the South Section of the Park. See sketches.

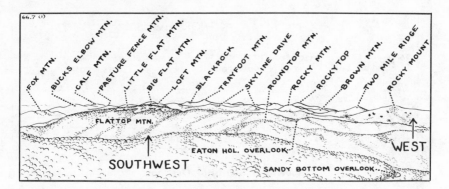

View from Hightop Summit. (No. 1.)

The sharp peak of Trayfoot Mountain (elevation 3,374 feet) is nearly 14 miles away. The cleared summit of Flattop — about four miles away, elevation a little over 3,300 feet — is just outside the Park. To the left of Flattop, on a super-clear day, you can see Bucks Elbow Mountain, near the southern boundary of the Park.

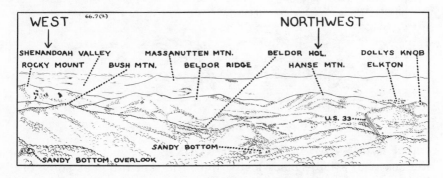

View from Hightop Summit. (No. 2.)

History: On March 18, 1669, the explorer John Lederer first reached the crest of the Blue Ridge. (See page 30.) The ledge you're standing on may be the point from which he first saw the Shenandoah Valley.

If you return to the A.T. and go south about a hundred feet, you come to a side trail on the left that goes 120 yards to the summit of Hightop and the site of a former fire tower. There's nothing left of the tower but its foundation; the whole area is overgrown, and there is no view.

MILE 67.2, SWIFT RUN OVERLOOK. Elevation 2,715 feet. A large overlook with a bulletin board, and with several hemlocks in the island.

The sketch names the principal features of the view. Downhill from the overlook, the Park boundary is only 1/4 mile away. The large hollow below you is private property, although the mountains beyond it are in the Park. Behind you, Hightop Mountain looms over the "north" entrance to the overlook. (The actual direction of the Hightop summit is southeast.) The A.T. is nearly half a mile away, up on Hightop.

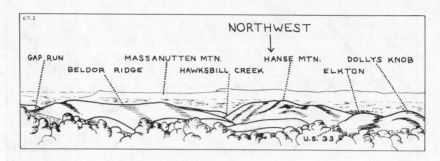

View from Swift Run Overlook.

Geology: The rocks in the island are Pedlar granodiorite, stained by minerals from the lava flow that once covered them. The green color was produced by epidote; the dark brown stains by iron.

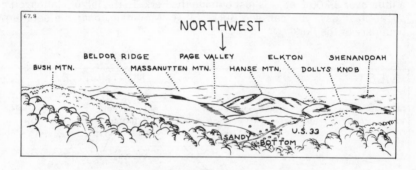

View from Sandy Bottom Overlook.

MILE 67.8, SANDY BOTTOM OVERLOOK. Elevation 2,705 feet. A small overlook with a large black locust tree. The sketch names some of the things you see from here. Sandy Bottom is a small community in the hollow below you. To see it, walk out into the grass beyond the paved walk and look down. If you have binoculars, take them with you. Sandy Bottom is private property, although the mountains beyond it are in the Park.

Hightop is directly east, towering over the north entrance to the overlook. Note the rocky outcrop near the summit. That's the objective of the Hightop hikes from Mile 66.7 and Mile 68.6.

MILE 68.6, SMITH ROACH GAP. Elevation 2,620 feet. Parking for about eight cars. *A.T. crossing. Hike to Hightop Summit.* Distances on the A.T.: South (on the west side of the Drive) it's 1.6 miles to Powell Gap, Mile 69.9 North (on the east side) it's 3.4 miles to the Drive crossing at Mile 66.7.

An old mountaineer road crossed the Blue Ridge here. On the west side of the Drive it has been obliterated. On the East it's still maintained as a fire road, which makes a pleasant, easy, one-mile walk to the Park boundary. (About 3/4 mile from the Drive, where the Hightop A.T. Hut road branches off to the left, keep right.) Outside the Park, it becomes Virginia secondary road No. 626. About 0.3 mile beyond the chain is the site of the old Hightop School.

HIKE: *Hightop Summit. Round trip* 3.7 miles; total *climb* about 950 feet; *time* required 3:25. Outstanding view. A good trail, with an easy slope. See map below; you're near the left-hand edge.

Follow the fire road for about 50 yards, then turn left onto the A.T. Most of the hike is through former pasture, with few mature trees until you get near the summit. Ascend steadily for about a mile; the trail then levels off and crosses the unpaved service road for Hightop A.T. Hut (0.15 mile to the left.) After another 0.1 mile on the A.T., a side trail on the left goes 0.13 mile to the hut, which has a pit toilet and an unprotected spring.

About 0.4 mile beyond the Hightop Hut trail, a side trail on the right

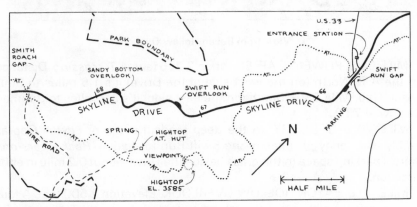

Map of Hightop Area.

goes five yards to an unprotected spring at the foot of a large boulder. Beside the A.T. are shagbark hickories that drop sweet, high-calorie nuts in the fall; if you're lucky, you may find one that the squirrels have overlooked. About 1.8 miles from the start of the hike, the trail levels off and swings around the left side of Hightop summit. A side trail on the right goes 120 yards to the site of a former fire tower. Stay on the A.T. for another 100 feet, and watch for a side trail on the left and goes ten yards to a ledge with a magnificent view. (See sketches, page 185.)

Returning to Smith Roach Gap, stop when you come to the dirt road that crosses the A.T. in an overgrown field. If you turn left and return on the road, it will add less than a quarter of a mile to your hike, with no extra climbing. The road continues through the overgrown field for a short distance; you'll find a variety of wildflowers here in late spring and early summer. After about 0.2 mile, look for an old split-rail fence on the left. Half a mile from the A.T., join another dirt road coming from the left. Keep right, and continue gently downhill another three-quarters of a mile to your starting point.

MILE 69.3, BACON HOLLOW OVERLOOK. Elevation 2,455 feet. A good-sized overlook with a rocky, shady island. The sketch shows most of what you can see from here. Flattop, the mountain with the clearings on top, goes up and to the right, out of the sketch. The ridge at the left of the sketch goes up to Hightop, although you can't see the Hightop summit from here. Behind you, on the other side of the Drive, is Roundtop. Bacon Hollow is directly in front. With binoculars you can see a modern mountain community, with freshly painted houses and late-model cars. The Park boundary is close to the Drive here—not much more than 100 yards below the overlook.

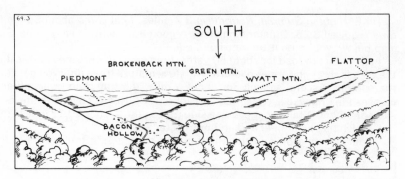

View from Bacon Hollow Overlook.

MILE 69.9, POWELL GAP. Elevation 2,295 feet. *A.T. crossing.* Distances on the A.T.: North (on the west side of the Drive) it's 1.6 miles to Smith Roach Gap, Mile 68.6. South (on the east side) it's 3.2 miles to Simmons Gap, Mile 73.2.

MILE 70.1, GEOLOGY. In the deep roadcut south of Powell Gap are pebbly and sandy phyllites of the Swift Run formation. *Rock lovers only:* there's parking space in the grass beside the Drive, about 0.2 mile in either direction.

MILE 70.6, EATON HOLLOW OVERLOOK. Elevation 2,500 feet. A fairly large overlook, with a shaded island suitable for picnics. There's a view from the north end of the overlook—directly north over Eaton Hollow. Hanse Mountain, four miles straight ahead, has two crests and three talus slopes. To the left of it, and somewhat closer, is Beldor Ridge. To the right of it are three small knobs; the highest, in the middle, is Dollys Knob. A mile and a half diagonally right is the rounded crest of Bush Mountain. Higher up to the right, a mile and a quarter away, is Roundtop — the knob that rises above Bacon Hollow Overlook. To the left of Roundtop is Hightop, three miles away.

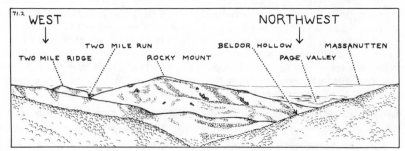

View from Rocky Mount Overlook.

MILE 71.2, ROCKY MOUNT OVERLOOK. Elevation 2,445 feet. In the island are a couple of good-sized basswood trees. Rocky Mount is the peak with numerous talus slopes, directly in front of the overlook (see sketch). The ridge just this side of Rocky Mount ascends to the left and joins the Blue Ridge near Two Mile Run Overlook, Mile 76.2. The Rocky Mount trail goes from Mile 76.1 to the Rocky Mount summit. See page 191.

Geology: The rocks across the Drive from the overlook are dark, much-weathered Catoctin basalt. The talus slopes over on Rocky Mount are white quartzite of the Erwin formation.

MILE 72.2, BELDOR HOLLOW OVERLOOK. Elevation 2,345 feet. This is just a road widening, without an island. Trees divide the view into two parts. From the north end you have a narrow view of Rocky Mount. From the south end (see sketch) you look into the upper end of Beldor Hollow — a very long hollow that runs down below the overlook and far to the right. Beyond the head of the hollow are a number of mountain crests, most of them on the main Blue Ridge. Skyline Drive winds its way among them. If you're going south, this is a preview of your route. If you're going north, you can see where you've been.

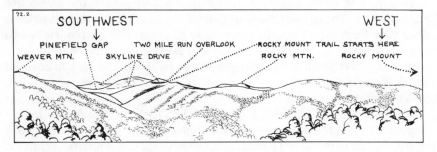

View from Beldor Hollow Overlook.

MILE 73.2, SIMMONS GAP. Elevation 2,255 feet. *A.T. crossing.* Ranger Station. Distances on the A.T.: North (on the east side of the Drive) it's 3.2 miles to Powell Gap, Mile 69.9. South (on the west side) it's 2.2 miles to Pinefield Gap, Mile 75.2.

An old mountaineer road, now a Park fire road, crosses the Blue Ridge here. On the west it goes 1.5 miles to the Park boundary in the head of Beldor Hollow, where it becomes Virginia secondary road No. 628. On the east it goes 0.8 mile to the park boundary in Fork Hollow, where it becomes Virginia secondary road No. 628, as on the other side of the mountain. Along this road, on the east side and within half a mile of Simmons Gap, was a small mountain community that included Simmons Gap Mission and Simmons Gap Post Office.

MILE 74.4, LOFT MOUNTAIN OVERLOOK. Elevation 2,455 feet. The view is bounded on the right by the northeast crest of Loft Mountain, and on the left by Flattop. County Line Mountain is straight ahead (see sketch.) The line crosses it just below the crest. You're in Greene County. The crest of County Line Mountain, and most of what you see beyond it, are in Albemarle County.

Toward the left are houses and farms on the side of Flattop Ridge — very different from the old mountaineer cabins. Most of the homes you see, especially out in the hollow, look fairly prosperous. Many of the people who live in them work elsewhere, and depend on farming for only a part of their income.

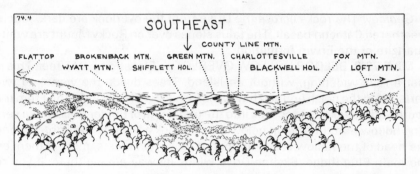

View from Loft Mountain Overlook.

Geology: The rocks exposed in the island and across the Drive are Catoctin basalt. Those near the south end of the island deserve a close look. Colors vary from gray through green-gray to green and purple. Here and there are veins of quartz, and a few small vesicles (gas bubbles in the lava which were later filled with other minerals.) In places the rock is covered with thin sheets of asbestos, which you can recognize by its parallel, fibrous crystals.

MILE 75.2, PINEFIELD GAP. Elevation 2,535 feet. *A.T. crossing.* There's no safe parking at the A.T. crossing, but there's plenty of room in the grass at the entrance to the service road, a hundred yards to the south. Distances on the A.T.: North (on the west side of the Drive) it's 2.1 miles to Simmons Gap, Mile 73.2. South (on the east side) it's 1.6 miles to Ivy Creek Overlook, Mile 77.5.

There is evidence of a mountaineer homesite here in Pinefield Gap. The A.T. south of the crossing follows an old road trace. There are two good springs in the area. There are fruit trees on both sides of the Drive just south of the service road. Oswego tea, *Monarda didyma,* and a cultivated species of *Phlox* are growing nearby.

From the service road entrance, the A.T. is 100 yards north on the Drive and 250 yards down the service road. The Pinefield Gap A.T. Hut is a quarter of a mile from the Drive via service road. That suggests a short semi-circuit hike.

HIKE: *Pinefield A.T. Hut. Semi-circuit* 0.6 mile; total *climb* about 125 feet; *time* required 0.35. Follow the service road, which may be somewhat rough in spots. Twenty-five yards beyond the A.T. is a concrete marker that says "Spring". Go 20 feet left and you'll see the spring. It's unprotected; boil the water before drinking. The hut is 165 yards beyond the A.T., near a small stream. It has a table and fireplace, and there's a pit toilet 50 yards downstream. There's another spring, also unprotected, a short distance upstream.

Return to the A.T. via the service road. Turn right onto the A.T., which continues for about 0.2 mile, through a forest of young maples, to the edge of the Drive. Turn left and return to your starting point.

MILE 75.4, The dirt road on the east side goes 50 yards into the woods, and ends. It's used by the Maintenance Division for earth storage.

MILE 76.0, GEOLOGY. Phyllites and sandstone of the Hampton

formation are exposed in the roadcut here. The closest parking space is at Mile 76.1.

Mile 76.1, ROCKY MOUNT TRAIL. The trail begins at a marker post on the west side of the Drive. There's parking space for one or two cars here, and additional parking at Two Mile Run Overlook, 0.1 mile south.

HIKE: *Rocky Mount Summit. Round trip* 6.9 miles; total *climb* about 2,065 feet; *time* required 6:40. This is a strenuous hike; near the summit, the trail is steep and rough. I have not hiked this trail; the following report is from Ranger-Naturalist Nancy Shives.

The trail descends rather steeply for 0.4 mile, then more gradually. From a low point at about 0.6 mile from the start, the trail skirts the left side of a low knob. Look for a view to the left, toward Two Mile Ridge. (And, in spring, look for the pink flowers of fringed *Polygala* beside the trail.) The trail ascends, passing to the right of a knob and then descending for 0.9 mile to a gap, where the Gap Run trail (named for a different gap, not this one) comes in on the right.

From the gap, the trail climbs nearly a thousand feet in 1.2 miles, with switchbacks, up the south side of Rocky Mount. From the first switchback there's a good view across Two Mile Run to Two Mile Ridge. The high point on the trail is your destination. From there you can climb to a rock with a fine view across Two Mile Ridge to Rocky Mountain and, farther left, to the Blue Ridge and a part of Skyline Drive.

MILE 76.2, TWO MILE RUN OVERLOOK. Elevation 2,770 feet. The sketch shows most of what you can see from here. A graded trail goes to the summit of Rocky Mount from the edge of the Drive a tenth of a mile north of the overlook. (See above.) Diagonally left is Rocky Mountain, with white quartzite cliffs. The sketch shows only the ridge that runs down from it into One Mile Run.

Geology: Looking straight out from the overlook to the far end of Two Mile Ridge, you can see two tiers of cliffs — white quartzite of the Erwin formation. The cliffs rise up from the left, level out, and then curve down to the right — evidence of the deep folding of the earth's crust that occurred when these mountains were formed. The cliffs are somewhat easier to see in winter, when the trees are bare.

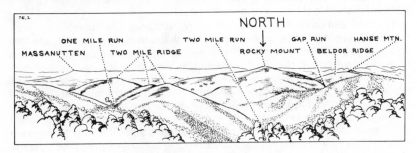

View from **Two Mile Run Overlook.**

MILE 76.9, BROWN MOUNTAIN OVERLOOK. Elevation 2,844. *Hikes.* A long overlook with a large island and a wide view framed by trees. The sketch shows the view from the south end of the overlook — across Big Run to the Rockytop ridge. Rocky Mountain (shown in part at the right-hand

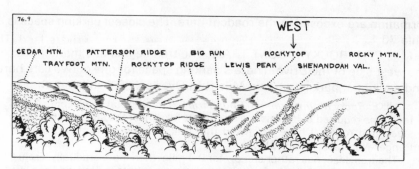

76.9

WEST
↓

CEDAR MTN.   PATTERSON RIDGE   BIG RUN   ROCKYTOP   ROCKY MTN.

TRAYFOOT MTN.   ROCKYTOP RIDGE   LEWIS PEAK   SHENANDOAH VAL.

View from Brown Mountain Overlook.

edge of the sketch) has two humps, and cliffs and talus of white Erwin quartzite. Farther right is the high point on Two Mile Ridge. Still farther right, and higher, is Rocky Mount. You can't see Brown Mountain from the overlook; it's hidden behind the left-hand end of Rocky Mountain.

Geology: The rocks exposed in the roadcut across the Drive are of the Hampton formation: a course-grained quartzite (medium salt-and-pepper gray in a fresh break) and sandstone (finer grained, uniform light gray in a fresh break.)

I will describe two hikes that start here. First, to the top of the talus slope that you can see over there on Rocky Mountain, and return by the same route. Second, a rather strenuous circuit hike to Big Run Portal via the Rocky Mountain/Brown Mountain trail, returning via the Big Run Portal trail.

HIKE: *Rocky Mountain saddle. Round trip* 3.9 miles; total *climb* about 1,140; *time* required 3:40. Good views, and a close look at the white Erwin quartzite. Parts of the trail are moderately steep; parts are rough and rocky. See map, page 202; you're at the upper right.

The trail starts at the opening in the wall. It descends steeply at first, then less so, following the ridge crest to a low point 0.7 mile from the overlook. The blue-blazed Rocky Mountain Run trail comes in on the left here; it's part of the return route for the circuit hike (see below). In the next quarter of a mile dittany, *Cunila origanoides,* grows beside the trail. It's a mint with a wiry stem; a crushed leaf has a pungent minty odor.

The trail climbs to the ridge crest by switchbacks, then levels out. After another 0.3 mile it makes a sharp switchback to the right, around a pine tree and a large rock. Another rock fifteen feet off to the left has a pleasing but narrow view through the trees, back to the main Blue Ridge.

A hundred yards farther on, start to look for turkeybeard, *Xerophyllum asphodeloides,* a member of the lily family. Its basal leaves look like clumps of long, coarse grass. From the middle of the clump rises a flower stalk from two to four feet tall, with long, clasping, thread-like leaves. The unopened flower spike, because of its close-packed buds, resembles a small, green, tapered ear of corn. The flowers begin to bloom, from the bottom of the spike upward, about the end of May, and should be at their best during the first half of June.

Less than a quarter of a mile beyond the first viewpoint, the trail crosses a narrow ridge crest, with a tall rock — white quartzite with black lichens on it — 30 feet to your right. From the top of that rock you have a much better view than from the first one, though it's still partially blocked by trees. From here the trail descends slightly, into the saddle between the two summits of Rocky Mountain. As it levels out and then begins to ascend, watch the ridge crest to your left. When it's about 50 yards away and 15 feet up, and you can see the sky at the base of the trees on the crest, you've reached your destination. Walk up to the ridge crest. You'll come out (I hope) at the top of a talus slope, with a wide view back toward the main Blue Ridge. You can see a section of the Drive, and the overlook where you parked your car, and the ridge you walked on to get here. To the left is Two Mile Run Overlook, with Flattop beyond it. Toward the right is the head of Patterson Ridge, which comes up out of Big Run to join the main Blue Ridge. A little to the right of it, the top of Cedar Mountain appears beyond the Blue Ridge crest.

HIKE: *Big Run Portal. Circuit* 9.9 miles; total *climb* about 2,465 feet; *time* required 9:05. Outstanding views, and the largest stream in the Park. A rather tiring hike, with a lot of climbing. See map, page 202. You're near the upper right. Your route is Rocky Mountain, Brown Mountain, Big Run Portal trail, and the Rocky Mountain Run trail.

As above, to the saddle on Rocky Mountain. Continue to the second crest, where the trail swings gently to the right and begins to descend the long ridge of Brown Mountain. After another half mile you reach a low point, with some big pines on the right. Now watch carefully. The trail begins to ascend, and swings slightly to the left, and aims for the side of a large rock. Here the ridge crest is 30 yards to your left, and 25 feet up. Climb to the crest, to a white quartzite outcropping at the top of a talus slope, and one of the greatest views in the Park. The whole Big Run Valley is spread out below you. The long Rockytop ridge forms the far edge of the Big Run watershed, and Rockytop peak is directly in front of you. To your right is a lower crest on Brown Mountain, and to the left of it the Big Run portal. To your left, the Blue Ridge stands at the head of Big Run, with Cedar Mountain rising above it. Farther right, you can see the peak of Trayfoot Mountain above the Rockytop ridge.

From here the trail continues down the ridge and finally descends by switchbacks, with alternating views of Rockytop and of the cliffs and talus slopes at the lower end of the Rockytop ridge, to the Big Run Portal trail. There you have a good view ahead of the quartzite cliffs and talus slopes that form the west side of Big Run portal. You will probably see a steel bridge to your right. (The bridge is at the edge of a wilderness area, and it may have been removed before you read this.)

Turn left onto the Big Run Portal trail (yellow-blazed, a former fire road). Continue about a mile and a third to a trail junction. Turn left onto the blue blazed Rocky Mountain Run trail and follow it, mostly uphill, for a little more than two miles. Then, as you reach the ridge crest, turn right onto the blue-blazed Rocky Mountain/Brown Mountain trail, and return to your starting point at Brown Mountain Overlook.

CAUTION. Access to Big Run valley from the bottom is precarious because you have to cross private land. The property owners are hostile because of abuses by thoughtless hikers. That's why there's a cable across the road a half mile outside the Park. This cable may have been moved farther out by the time you read this. Hikers may even be forbidden to walk on the private road. For that reason I suggest that you start from the Drive if you want to hike into Big Run. Besides the hike described on page 193 I've recommended three others, on pages 202, 203, and 206.

MILE 77.5, IVY CREEK OVERLOOK. Elevation 2,890 feet. *A.T. access. Hikes.* A pleasant view, framed by trees. Toward the right, outside the sketch, is the northeast summit of Loft Mountain. Farther right, with evergreens on its slope, is the south summit.

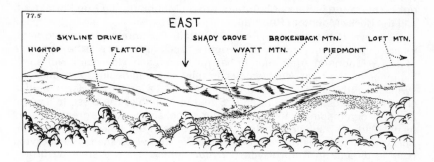

View from Ivy Creek Overlook.

The A.T. passes through the overlook, coming in at one end and going out the other. Distances on the A.T.: North (to the left as you face the view) it's 1.6 miles to Pinefield Gap, Mile 75.3. South (to the right) it's 4.9 miles to the Loft Mountain Campstore. I will describe two hikes that start here.

HIKE: *Ivy Creek. Round trip* 2.8 miles; total *climb* about 695 feet; *time* required 2:30. Woods, stream; a rather easy, pleasant hike.

Take the A.T. at the south end of the overlook. It crosses the Drive twice, reaches the crest of a knob about half a mile from the overlook, then descends for 0.6 mile. There, with the Drive less than 100 yards uphill on the right, the trail swings left, descends, then swings right and crosses Ivy Creek — 1.4 miles from the start. It follows the bank of the stream, climbing easily for nearly 0.3 mile before it swings away to the left. I find this miniature canyon delightful. The A.T. is mostly a ridgetop trail; this is the only place in the Park where it follows a stream.

HIKE: *Loft Mountain Summit. Round trip* 6.4 miles; total *climb* about 1,455 feet; *time* required 5:30. A medium difficult hike with woods, a stream, and a view.

As above to Ivy Creek. Continue another three-quarters of a mile to a trail marker. (From here, the Ivy Creek Trail Maintenance Building is 200 yards to the right. It has pit toilets and an unprotected spring.) Continue uphill on the

A.T. to the partly open grassy saddle between the two crests of Loft Mountain. Where the trail swings sharp right, there's a ledge on the left with a fine view.

At the left of the view is Flattop, with a dirt road and clearings, and with the crest of Hightop showing above it. Farther right, a ridge runs from Flattop down into the Piedmont. The bump on the lower end of the ridge is Wyatt Mountain. County Line Mountain is right out in front of you, three miles away. At the far right is Fox Mountain with three peaks, then a dip, then two peaks more.

Continue on the A.T. to the southwest summit of Loft Mountain. At a concrete marker, the Deadening Trail goes off to the right (see page 197.) Continue on the A.T. for about a tenth of a mile, then take a side trail to the right; it goes 25 yards to a viewpoint. Looking to the left from the viewpoint: at the far end of Pattersons Field is Big Flat Mountain, with the Loft Mountain Campground and two water tanks. To the far right, on the east side of the Blue Ridge, is the Ivy Creek watershed. Everything out in front of you is part of the Big Run watershed. Patterson Ridge almost divides it down the middle. The Big Run portal, at the mouth of the hollow, is four and a half miles to the northwest. Rockytop ridge rises to the left of it and Brown Mountain, with cliffs and talus slopes, to the right. Nearer than Brown Mountain, and farther right, is Rocky Mountain.

MILE 77.6 and 77.7, A.T. CROSSINGS. There is no safe parking at either crossing. Use Ivy Creek Overlook, Mile 77.5.

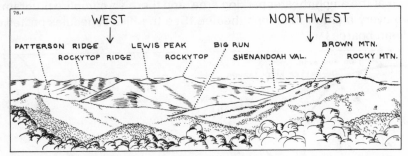

View from Rockytop Overlook.

MILE 78.1, ROCKYTOP OVERLOOK. Elevation 2,860 feet. The view includes a large part of the Big Run watershed. To the left, outside the sketch, the high peak on the horizon is Trayfoot Mountain. If you follow the ridge to the left from Trayfoot you'll see an area of purple-gray talus with larger rocks above it. That, collectively, is Blackrock, which has a spectacular view. You can get there easily by trail. See page 208.

NOTE: According to the Geological Survey, "Rockytop" is the inconspicuous summit to the left of Lewis Peak (see sketch). But in this book, if nowhere else, Rockytop is the higher summit — conspicuously rocky on top — to the right of Lewis Peak.

MILE 78.35, GEOLOGY. There's a parking area on the east side of the Drive, at the foot of a small talus slope of Hampton sandstones, some of them phyllitic (which is to say that in a fresh break you can see glints or luster caused by tiny flakes of mica.) Fifty yards north (uphill) on the Drive is an exposure of Hampton quartzite — medium to dark salt-and-pepper gray in a fresh break; the surface is weathered dark gray, and stained red-brown with iron.

MILE 79.4, DIRT ROAD, east side. This is the service road for Ivy Creek Trail Maintenance Building. It's part of the circuit hike described on page 197.

Geology: You can park in the grass on either side of the Drive near the service road, or in the parking area at the Wayside to the south. From 50 to 150 yards north of the service road are coarse-grained sandstone and quartzite of the Weverton formation. The rocks on the west side have a few thin layers of phyllite, which has a lustrous sheen. Those on the east have nearly white veins of small quartz pebbles.

MILE 79.5, LOFT MOUNTAIN DEVELOPMENT. Beside the Drive on the west side is Loft Mountain Wayside, open from early May to late October. It offers a telephone, food, souvenirs and gifts, gasoline, water, and rest-rooms. From the restaurant you have a view over the gas station to the cliffs on Loft Mountain. Two hikes start at the Wayside and go to the cliffs. (See below.) The rest of the Loft Mountain development is up on Big Flat Mountain, a mile or more from the Drive via the paved road opposite the north end of the Wayside parking area. Facilities — open from early May to late October — include a campground, picnic area, amphitheater, campstore, laundry, showers, and trailer sewage disposal. (See map below.) During the summer season (mid-June to Labor Day), conducted hikes begin at the amphitheater parking area, and there's a campfire program at 8:45 every night in the amphitheater. (See the hike schedules posted on bulletin boards.)

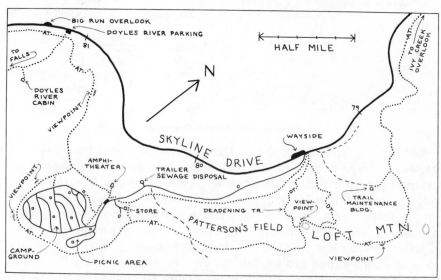

Map of the Loft Mountain area.

Loft Mountain Campground was built in 1964 on Big Flat Mountain. Loft Mountain itself is a mile and a half to the northeast; its name was taken for the campground because it sounds better than Big Flat. Origin of the name Loft is uncertain. Before the Park was created, the tops of Big Flat and Loft Mountains, the saddle between them, and the ridge that goes west to Doyles River Gap were pastures with scattered apple trees. They were part of the extensive holdings of the Pattersons—absentee owners whose lands and cattle were cared for by the Frazier family. Loft Mountain is locally called Frazier Mountain. On some old maps the name is Lost Mountain.

HIKE: *Deadening trail.* (From the Wayside.) *Circuit* 1.4 miles; total *climb* about 455 feet; *time* required 1:35. A *self-guiding* trail with a view. The theme of the walk is succession: the gradual change from pastureland to mature forest. The trail begins at the edge of the Drive, 20 yards north of the road that goes uphill to the campground. (See map, page 196.)

A hundred yards from the Drive, the trail forks. Keep to the right. Near the Loft Mountain summit, the Deadening Trail joins the A.T. Turn left, and look for a side trail on the left. It goes 25 yards to a cliff with a view. To your left, across Pattersons Field, you can see the campground on Big Flat Mountain. To the far right, on the east side of the Blue Ridge, is part of the Ivy Creek watershed. Straight ahead is the Big Run watershed. From the mouth of the hollow the Rocktop ridge rises to the left, and Brown Mountain, with cliffs and talus slopes, rises to the right. Farther right and nearer is Rocky Mountain.

Return to the A.T. and turn left. After 0.1 mile leave the A.T. and take the Deadening Trail to the left. Watch for a miniature natural amphitheater under an overhanging ledge. Except in dry weather water drips from the ledge, and there's a tiny pool of water at its base. To the left of the trail is a chestnut log with a groove around it. This was part of the "deadening," in which trees were girdled to kill them, and thus let light reach the ground so that grass could grow. Farther on there are girdled trees on both sides of the trail. The circuit ends when you get back to the fork in the trail. Continue downhill to the Drive.

HIKE: *Loft Mountain* via *A.T.* (From the Wayside.) *Circuit* 2.7 miles; total *climb* about 570 feet; *time* required 2:25. Good views. From the north end of the Wayside parking area walk 150 yards north on Skyline Drive, then bear right onto a dirt road. (See map, page 196.) At a junction 60 yards from the Drive, turn right and continue 0.3 mile to the Trail Maintenance Building which has a pit toilet and an unprotected spring. Continue about 0.1 mile downhill to the junction with the A.T. Turn right, uphill. The trail climbs Loft Mountain, swings to the right of its northeast summit, then levels off and becomes more open.

Where the trail swings right, watch for a ledge on the left with a view toward the Piedmont. To your left is Flattop, with clearings and a dirt road. County Line Mountain is right out in front of you. To the right is Fox Mountain with three peaks, then a dip, then two peaks more.

Continue on the A.T. across a more or less open saddle to the southwest summit of Loft Mountain. At a concrete trail marker, the Deadening Trail joins from the right. After about a tenth of a mile, watch for a side trail on the right; it goes 25 yards to a cliff with a fine view (see the Deadening Trail hike, above). Return to the A.T., turn right, and continue to the Deadening Trail junction. Turn right. Follow the Deadening Trail downhill to the Drive, where the Wayside is in sight to your left.

HIKE: *Loft Mountain Summit. Round trip* 3.5 miles; total *climb* about 515 feet; *time* required 2:50. Views. The hike starts from the campstore (see map, page 196.) At the bulletin board, as you face the store, turn right and walk to the edge of the lawn, where you have a fine view of the Piedmont. Take the trail that goes 100 yards downhill to the A.T., and turn left onto the A.T. The trail goes at first through former pastures that are still grassy and fairly open. Later you pass through clumps of young black locusts, and then oaks—most of them rather young.

The trail follows the right-hand side of the ridge where, in May, pale blue flowers of *Phacelia* carpet the ground. It passes through a small forest of

Ailanthus (Tree-of-Heaven), then swings left and climbs to the crest, where the Deadening Trail joins from the left. Continue to a side trail on the left, which goes 25 yards to a viewpoint. (See the Deadening Trail hike, page 197.)

You can go back the way you came or, if you wish, return to the junction where the Deadening Trail goes to the right. Turn right. Follow the Deadening Trail for a few yards, then strike out across Pattersons Field toward the campground. If you're quiet you have a good chance of seeing a deer, or maybe a small herd of them. You'll see birds and, in late spring and summer, wildflowers. (CAUTION: Pattersons Field is thick with bushes and brambles and black locust. Crossing it requires a venturesome spirit, and clothes that are either indestructible or expendable.) Follow the field to its low point, bear left to the A.T., and then turn right.

HIKE: *Big Flat Mountain Hike. Circuit* 1.8 miles; total *climb* about 265 feet; *time* required 1:15. This is a rather easy circuit around the campground and picnic area, with an outstanding view. You can start at any of several points. See map, page 196. The following description starts at the amphitheater parking area.

Take the paved walk toward the amphitheater from the north (downhill) end of the parking area. At a junction 30 yards from the start, bear left, walk a quarter of a mile, mostly downhill, to the A.T. Turn sharp left, uphill. The trail climbs steadily for 200 yards to a crest, where a side trail on the left goes 230 yards uphill to the campground at the parking area for A-8 tent sites. To the right of the trail here, and at several points in the next three-tenths of a mile, are rocky ledges with worthwhile views. The sketch shows what you can see from the best of them.

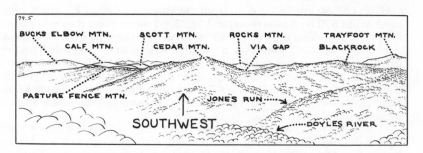

View from A.T. near Loft Mountain Campground.

Out in front and below is the Doyles River watershed. As you follow the course of Doyles River from right to left below you, note that there are two coves going up away to the right. The second and larger one, which comes in at the foot of Cedar Mountain, is Jones Run. There are beautiful waterfalls on both Doyles River and Jones Run, and the Doyles River Trail passes all of them. (See page 200.) With binoculars you can make out the six antenna towers of the FAA radio installation on Bucks Elbow Mountain. Most of Bear Den Mountain is hidden behind Calf Mountain, but with binoculars you can see an antenna tower on top of it. On a very clear day you can see mountains on the Blue Ridge Parkway, far to the south of Calf and Scott Mountains.

As you continue on the A.T. you'll see several trails that go uphill to the left, into the campground. Use any of them if you want to shorten the walk and return to your campsite. The last of these side trails is marked by a concrete post, not quite one mile from the start of the hike. To complete the circuit, stay on the A.T. for another 0.6 mile, to a second marker post. Turn left here. Climb the hill, pass the campstore, and then turn left onto the paved walk beside the campground road. Continue another 0.15 mile to your starting point.

HIKE: *Viewpoint on the A.T. Round trip* 1.5 miles; total *climb* about 260 feet; *time* required 1:15. The view is similar to that from the amphitheater, but it's a pleasant, easy walk. It starts from the amphitheater parking lot (see map, page 196.)

Take the paved walk toward the amphitheater from the north end of the parking area, and after 30 yards, bear left where the trail forks. After a quarter of a mile, the A.T. joins from the left; continue ahead on the A.T., through a former pasture on the ridge crest, with apple trees here and there. From late April until September, you'll find a succession of wildflowers here. Three-tenths of a mile beyond the trail junction, a side trail on the right leads 50 feet to a fairly good viewpoint. Continue on the A.T. for another 200 yards, to a big flat rock on the right. This is your destination.

Looking more or less straight ahead from the rock you'll see a sharp crest on the main Blue Ridge, and under it a stretch of Skyline Drive south of Rockytop Overlook. A little farther left is Rocky Mountain. Still farther left is Brown Mountain, which descends to Big Run portal. Rising on the left of the portal is Rockytop ridge.

MILE 81.1, DOYLES RIVER PARKING. *A.T. access. Hikes. Doyles River Cabin. Doyles River Trail.* There's a small gravelled parking area just off the Drive, and additional parking at Big Run Overlook, a hundred yards to the south. The Doyles River Trail goes downhill from the parking area, and crosses the A.T. after 50 yards. Distances on the A.T.: North (to the left) it's 1.1 miles to the Loft Mountain Amphitheater. (Continue straight ahead when the A.T. turns sharp right.) South (to the right) it's 0.9 mile to Doyles River Overlook, Mile 81.9.

Geology: (Rock lovers only; for others it's too much trouble.) Walk north (i.e. away from the overlook) beside the Drive to Milepost 81. The rock exposed here is of the Weverton formation — with layers of phyllite, sandstone, and quartz gravel. The Weverton formation is younger than the Catoctin lavas, and should therefore lie above them. But in this area the contact has been overturned. The Catoctin formation is exposed beside the Drive a short distance to the north, and it forms the summits of Loft and Big Flat Mountains — high above you to the east. Continue north along the Drive for less than 200 yards, to a culvert and deep hole on the right. Continue another 50 yards to a rock exposure on the right. This is porphyritic Catoctin basalt. "Porphyritic" means that the purplish basalt contains crystals of feldspar; many of them are stained red. They're best seen about six feet above the road surface. Climb a couple of feet up the bank for a close look.

I will describe three hikes that start here at the parking area. First, a relatively easy round trip to the upper falls of Doyles River. Second, a longer one-way hike past two waterfalls on Doyles River and one on Jones Run, to the Jones Run parking area at Mile 84.1. Finally a circuit that follows the Doyles River Trail, as above, and returns to the starting point via A.T.

HIKE: *Upper Doyles River Falls. Round trip* 2.7 miles; total *climb* about 850 feet; *time* required 2:45. A not-too-difficult hike to a small but very pretty waterfall. (See map, page 200.)

Take the Doyles River Trail downhill from the parking area. Cross the A.T. and descend rather steeply for 0.3 mile to an unprotected spring that flows from a pipe in a stone wall on the left. Just beyond the spring, the trail forks. (The left fork climbs rather steeply for 400 feet to the locked *Doyles River Cabin.* To rent the cabin write Potomac Appalachian Trail Club, 1718 N Street, N.W, Washington, D.C. 20036.) Keep right, and continue about 0.6 mile to the Browns Gap fire road. (To the left, the road goes 1.4 miles to the Park boundary, where it becomes Virginia secondary road No. 629. To the right it goes 1.7 miles to Browns Gap, at Mile 83.0 on the Drive.)

Cross the road and continue on the Doyles River Trail, which crosses the Doyles River after 250 yards. Go another 300 yards. Here, as the trail begins to turn right, the top of the falls is about 25 feet to your left; but you can't see the falls from the top. Follow the trail to the right, away from the falls. It swings left in a wide 180-degree curve, to a low point with a marker post. The falls are in sight to your left, in a natural amphitheater, surrounded by giant trees. It's a beautiful thing to see, even (or maybe especially) in winter when it's frozen solid.

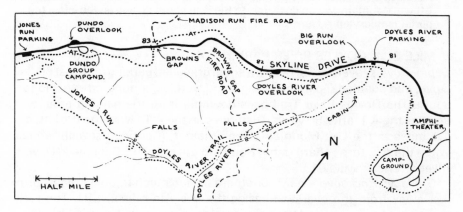

Map of Doyles River area.

HIKE: *Doyles River Trail.* One way 4.8 miles; total *climb* about 1,410 feet; *time* required 4:35. A medium-difficult hike with three waterfalls. Since it's a oneway hike, you'll have to leave a car at the Jones Run parking area, Mile 84.1, or have someone meet you there. See map above.

As above to the upper Doyles River falls. Continue downhill on the Doyles River Trail, through a narrow gorge with the stream downhill on your left, and sometimes pools and cascades worth looking at. The sides of the gorge rise steeply, and you pass some of the biggest trees in the Park. The top of the lower falls is 250 yards from the concrete marker near the upper falls. Again a short side trail on the left goes to the top of the falls, and again there's not much to see there.

Follow the trail to the right, away from the falls. After a hundred yards, look out for a big patch of poison ivy. Fifty yards more and the trail takes a sharp switchback to the left on a slippery slanting rock. Then back through the poison ivy and down to the base of the falls, which is mostly hidden by trees. Fifty yards farther, at a concrete marker, a very rough and rocky side trail on the left goes back to the base of the falls.

About 0.2 mile farther down the gorge you cross a small stream, with a cascade just to the right of the trail. From there it's 0.4 mile to the low point of the hike, where the trail leaves the Doyles River, swings right, and starts uphill beside Jones Run. Where the trail crosses the stream, note the big sycamore just 60 feet to your left. It shows how far down you've come; in Shenandoah, sycamores grow only at lower altitudes.

Continue past cascades that get bigger and more frequent as the trail gets steeper. This is a pleasant walk. In places the whole hillside to your left is terraced with ledges of rock covered with dripping mosses, ferns, and nettles. As you reach the top of a long, gliding cascade, you can see Jones Run Falls up ahead. A nearly vertical cliff blocks the gorge, and the stream plunges over it. The trail swings left to skirt the cliff, makes a sharp switchback, returns to the head of the falls, then turns sharply left, uphill. Less than a quarter of a mile above the falls, the trail swings left and crosses a long shallow ditch that may have been a Civil War trench.

Conjectural history: During the Civil War this area was probably a wide-open pasture. General Jubal A. Early was retreating through Browns Gap, pursued by General Phil Sheridan. If Sheridan had been able to take a few artillery pieces to the head of the falls, he would have made it impossible for the expected reinforcements to reach Early by way of the Browns Gap road. (See map, page 200.) So Early may have had an outpost here.

Half a mile farther up the hollow, the trail joins an old road trace that comes in from the left. The trail crosses Jones Run and later swings left, away from the road trace. It reaches the A.T. about half a mile beyond the stream crossing, and goes on another 25 yards to the parking area.

HIKE: *Doyles River Trail* and A.T. *Circuit* 7.8 miles; total *climb* about 1,825 feet; *time* required 7:00. A rewarding but fairly long and tiring hike with three waterfalls. See map, page 200.

As above, but turn right onto the A.T. just before you reach the Jones Run parking area. Walk three miles north on the A.T., crossing the Drive twice, passing Browns Gap and Doyles River Overlook. Turn left at the marker post when you reach the Doyles River Trail, and go fifty yards uphill to the Doyles River parking area.

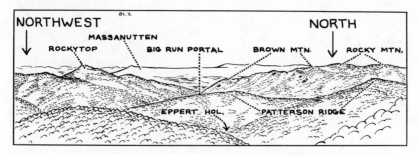

View from Big Run Overlook.

MILE 81.2, BIG RUN OVERLOOK. Elevation 2,860 feet. *Hikes.* This is one of the most beautiful overlooks in the Park, with a deep wide view nicely framed by trees. The sketch shows the right-hand part of the view. To the left, outside the sketch, Rockytop ridge joins the main Blue Ridge. Near the right-hand edge of the sketch is Rocky Mountain, with cliffs and talus slopes of white Erwin quartzite. Farther right, outside the sketch, is Rocky Mount. Still farther right, and closer, you can see Brown Mountain Overlook.

Geology: Across the Drive is a small exposure of Weverton sandstone, with veins of quartz pebbles.

I will describe two hikes that go from the overlook into the head of Big Run — one a round trip and the other a somewhat longer circuit that returns via A.T.

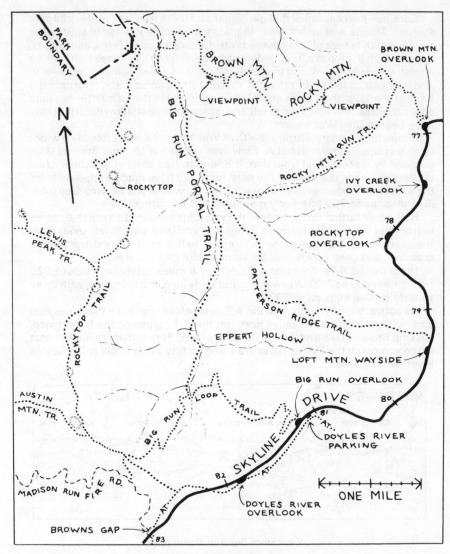

Map of the Big Run area.

HIKE: *Head of Big Run. Round trip* 4.4 miles; total *climb* about 1,250 feet; *time* required 4:00. An interesting walk on a good trail with a few steep parts. See map above.

The trail starts from the overlook and descends by switchbacks. After two-thirds of a mile it switches back sharply to the left and swings around a branch of Eppert Hollow. There are views across the hollow to Patterson Ridge, about a mile away, with parts of Brown Mountain and Rocky Mountain visible beyond it. The trail reaches a ridge crest at 1.2 miles, descends along the crest, then levels off. (In spring, look for dwarf *Iris* here.) After a final switchback to the left the trail descends to the site of Big Run Shelter, which was removed when Big Run was made a Wilderness Area in 1976. Explore at will, then go back the way you came.

HIKE: *Big Run Loop Trail; A.T. Circuit* 5.8 miles; total *climb* about 1,365 feet; *time* required 5:00. See map, page 202.

As above, to the head of Big Run. Take the road trace to the right and then, almost immediately, turn left onto the trail and start climbing. About 1.3 miles from the old road you reach a trail crossing on the ridge crest. (The trail ahead descends 0.3 mile to the Madison Run fire road. The Rockytop trail, to the right, goes to the lower end of Big Run.) Turn left. The trail ascends to the crest of the Blue Ridge, then descends briefly to the A.T. Turn left onto the A.T. and go 1.6 miles (crossing the Drive once and passing through Doyles River Overlook) to the marker at the junction with the Doyles River Trail. Turn left, go 200 feet to the Drive, then turn left again and walk 100 yards to Big Run Overlook.

BIG RUN VALLEY is worth all the time you can give it. I can't tell you what to look for. If you like wildlife or flowers, you'll find them here. Big Run has more water, and probably more fish, than any other stream in the Park. (If you don't care for fishing, try fish watching.) I've seen more small lizards here than anywhere else in Shenandoah. The stream has pools deep enough and wide enough to swim in. In one of those pools, to the left of the road above the first ford, I once saw more than a hundred mallards.

If you have time, check with the rangers about current regulations for backcountry camping. If the regulations permit, consider spending several days exploring the Big Run valley.

MILE 81.9, DOYLES RIVER OVERLOOK. Elevation 2,875 feet. *A.T. access.* The overlook is about 100 yards off the Drive. The entrance road makes a loop around the island, which has shade trees and picnic tables. The A.T. passes through the overlook, coming in one end and going out the other. Distances on the A.T.: North (to the left as you face the view) it's 0.9 mile to the Doyles River parking area, Mile 81.1. South (to the right) it's 1.3 miles to Browns Gap, Mile 83.0.

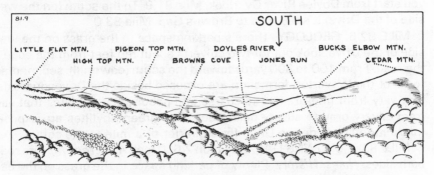

View from Doyles River Overlook.

The overlook has a view of the Doyles River valley. To the left, outside the sketch, is Big Flat Mountain — the site of Loft Mountain Campground. Browns Cove (see sketch), like Browns Gap a mile to the south, was named for the rich and influential Brown family (page 204.) Note that High Top

Mountain is not the same as Hightop, which is farther north and a lot higher.

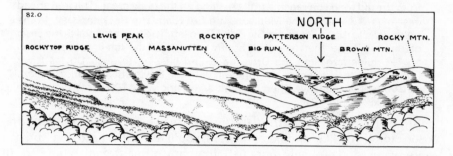

View from Skyline Drive at Mile 82.0.

MILE 82.0, VIEWPOINT AND HISTORY. There's parking space in the grass on the east side of the Drive, about 50 yards south of the milepost. Look out for a culvert near the north end of the grassy strip. From the west side of the Drive you have a clear view into Big Run (see sketch). Just inside the woods on the east side is an artifically levelled area about 25 feet in diameter. That's where General Early posted one of his guns in September, 1864, to command the old road that occupied the present site of Skyline Drive at this point, and thus prevent a cavalry attack from the north against the Confederate troops bivouacked in Browns Gap.

MILE 82.2, A.T. CROSSING. Elevation 2,800 feet. There's very limited parking beside the Drive. If you want to hike north on the A.T. I suggest that you start from Doyles River Overlook, Mile 81.9. To the south (on the west side of the Drive) it's 0.9 mile to Browns Gap, Mile 83.0.

MILE 82.5, GEOLOGY. There's parking space in the grass on the west side of the Drive; look out for two culverts about ten feet from the edge of the road. From 100 to 300 yards toward the south (downhill), sedimentary rocks of the Weverton formation are exposed beside the Drive: quartzites that vary from fine-grained to coarse and pebbly, and phyllites that vary from silvery gray to silvery pale green. The green phyllites are exposed intermittently beside the Drive for a quarter of a mile to the south.

MILE 83.0, BROWNS GAP. Elevation 2,600 feet. *A.T. crossing.* Fire road, both sides. *Hikes. History.* Plenty of parking space in the grass on the east side. The A.T. crosses the Drive just south of the fire road. Distances on the A.T.: North (on the west side of the Drive) it's 1.3 miles to Doyles River Overlook, Mile 81.9 South (on the east side) it's 1.4 miles to the Drive crossing at Mile 84.3.

History: About 1750 Benjamin Brown and his son, also Benjamin Brown, began to buy land in the western part of Albemarle County, including more than 6,000 acres on both sides of what is now Doyles River. They became, of course, one of the most influential families in that part of the county. The older Benjamin Brown had eight sons. I know the names of seven:

Benjamin, Barzillai, Benajah, Bernard, Bernis, Bezaleel, and Brightberry. In 1805-06 Brightberry Brown and William Jarman built a turnpike across the Blue Ridge here. For many years it was one of the principal routes for taking farm produce from the Shenandoah Valley to Richmond.

Browns Gap and the turnpike were used briefly during the Civil War. On May 2, 1862, at the beginning of his Valley Campaign, Stonewall Jackson marched his entire army through Browns Gap. From June 9 to June 12, after the Battle of Port Republic at the end of the Valley Campaign, Jackson's army camped in and near Browns Gap. On September 25, 1864, General Jubal Early and his army, after their defeat at Winchester, fortified themselves here and fought off Sheridan's attacks for two days while awaiting reinforcements.

The turnpike is now a Park fire road. On the west it's Madison Run fire road; it descends five miles to the Park boundary, where it becomes Virginia secondary road No. 663. The lower end of the Madison Run hollow is worth exploring (experienced hikers only.) On the east, the Browns Gap fire road goes a little more than three miles to the Park boundary, where it becomes Virginia secondary road No. 629.

I will describe three hikes that begin at Browns Gap: Upper Doyles River Falls, the Doyles River Trail circuit, and Big Run Portal via Rockytop.

HIKE: *Upper Doyles River Falls. Circuit* 5.3 miles; total *climb* about 1,000 feet; *time* required 4:30. A not-too-difficult hike to a very pretty waterfall. See map, page 200.

Take the fire road on the east side of the Drive. About 0.4 mile from the start, and 25 feet up the bank to the left, is a small white tombstone. (In summer it may be hard to see from the road.) The inscription reads "William H. Howard, F Co., 44 Inf., C.S.A."

About 0.8 mile from Browns Gap the road forks, going uphill to the left and downhill to the right. Keep right. (The other road goes to an abandoned dump.) After another eighth of a mile you may see signs of human settlement, such as the ruins of a barbed wire fence and, half a mile from the fork in the road, the rusty shell of an old car 50 feet in the woods on the right. Three hundred yards farther, up the bank to the left, was a homesite. A part of the chimney is still standing, visible from the road. This part of the hike is a treat for tree lovers. There are several tulip trees and oaks, a hickory, and at least one hemlock, that are nearly four feet in diameter.

Cross the Doyles River and reach the Doyles River Trail 1.7 miles from Browns Gap. Turn right; after 250 yards the trail crosses the stream, goes another 300 yards, and then swings to the right, away from the falls. It makes a wide semicircle to the left, to a low point with a concrete marker. The falls are in view to the left, in a natural amphitheater surrounded by giant trees. They aren't very high, but I find them among the most attractive in the Park.

Return up the Doyles River Trail to the fire road; cross the road and continue uphill another 0.9 mile to the A.T. (Straight ahead at this point, 50 yards up the Doyles River Trail, is Doyles River Parking at Mile 81.9 on the Drive.) Turn left onto the A.T. Walk 0.8 mile to Doyles River Overlook, then another 1.3 miles to Browns Gap.

HIKE: *Doyles River Trail and A.T. Circuit* 6.5 miles; total *climb* about 1,400 feet; *time* required 6:45. A pleasant but moderately difficult hike, with three waterfalls. See map, page 200.

As above to Upper Doyles River Falls; then continue as in the "Doyles River Trail" hike described on page 200. Turn right when you reach the A.T., and walk 1.1 miles, mostly level or downhill, to Browns Gap.

HIKE: *Big Run Portal* via *Rockytop. Circuit* 14.6; total *climb* about 2,900 feet; *time* required 12:20. A long, strenuous, tiring hike. There are a few good views along the trail—most of them where it crosses a talus slope or boulder field—of mountains to the west: Austin Mountain, Lewis Mountain, and Lewis Peak. Wider and more impressive views are available if you climb some of the cliffs and talus slopes that rise up on your right.

Most of the rocks you will see are sandstones of the Hampton formation. But as you begin to skirt the high peak of Rockytop you come to exposures of white Erwin quartzite, which continue almost to the Big Run fire road. In the quartzite are occasional examples of the fossilized burrows of *Skolithos,* an ancient, worm-like organism.

Take the fire road on the west side of the Drive. Turn right onto the A.T., and go 0.6 mile to the blue-blazed Big Run — Rockytop trail. Turn left, and go two-thirds of a mile to a trail junction. The Big Run Loop trail goes downhill to the right. The trail on the left goes to the Madison Run fire road. Go straight ahead, uphill. At a low point 0.4 mile from the junction, the Austin Mountain trail goes off to the left. Then, after about a mile, as you cross a talus slope, there's a crest on your right. According to Geological Survey maps, this is Rockytop. But I will follow the local custom and use the name Rockytop for the very rocky and more conspicuous summit up ahead.

As you skirt the left side of Rockytop there are cliffs and talus slopes above on your right. Continue around the west and north sides of the peak, ascending by switchbacks. Then descend for two miles to the Big Run fire road and turn right.

After half a mile cross a steel bridge (if it's still there) and continue on the former fire road, which is now the Big Run Portal trail. (See note about the BIG RUN VALLEY on page 203.) About four and a half miles from the bridge, you reach a junction with the Big Run Loop trail. Turn right, climb 1.3 miles to the Rockytop trail, and turn left. Continue to the A.T., turn right, and return to Browns Gap.

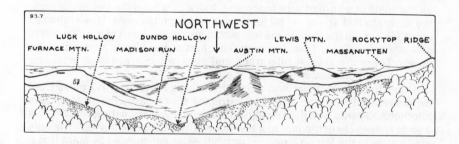

View from Dundo Overlook.

MILE 83.7, DUNDO OVERLOOK. Elevation 2,769 feet. The sketch shows the right-center part of the view. The ridge to the left of Furnace Mountain rises to the summit of Trayfoot Mountain. Most of the bushes in front of the overlook are mountain laurel, which blooms in early June.

Geology: The cliffs and talus slopes on Furnace, Lewis, and Austin Mountains are of white Erwin quartzite. The talus on Trayfoot is Hampton quartzite.

MILE 83.7, DUNDO GROUP CAMP. The entrance is on the east side of the Drive, just south of the overlook. This was originally CCC Camp No. 27. Now it's a campground for organized youth groups — Boy Scouts, for example. The facilities are rather primitive. There are a number of tent sites, each with a table and fireplace. There are pit toilets at each end of the campground, and a water faucet at each campsite. If you'd like to bring *your* youth group here, call Park Headquarters, (703) 999-2243.

MILE 84.1, JONES RUN PARKING. Elevation 2,790 feet. *Hikes.* The A.T. crosses the Doyles River Trail only 30 yards from the parking area. If you want to hike the A.T. I suggest that you start from the Drive crossing at Mile 84.3, to save this parking space for Doyles River Trail hikers.

From here you can take a one-way hike on the Doyles River Trail to Doyles River Parking Mile 81.1, or a circuit that returns from Doyles River Parking via the A.T. Since I've described both those hikes from the other end (pages 200 and 201), I won't repeat them here.

> HIKE: *Jones Run Falls. Round trip* 3.6 miles; total *climb* about 915 feet; *time* required 3:15. A not very difficult hike on a good trail to an attractive waterfall. See map, page 200.
>
> Take the Doyles River Trail at the north end of the parking area. Cross the A.T. and after about half a mile cross Jones Run. The trail follows an old road trace for another third of a mile, then swings left and continues downhill through a very young forest that was pasture when the Park was created. After you cross a shallow ditch that may have been a Civil War trench, and join the stream on your left, continue another 0.2 mile to the head of the falls. The trail swings sharp right, then makes a switchback to the left and returns to the base of the falls. Jones Run drops about 42 feet over a nearly vertical cliff that crosses the gorge and continues for a distance down the left bank of the stream. Where the cliff is watered by spray from the falls, it's covered with a great variety of mosses and flowering plants.

MILE 84.3, A.T. CROSSING. Elevation 2,810 feet. Parking for several cars in the grass on the west side. Distances on the A.T.: North (on the east side of the Drive) it's 1.4 miles to Browns Gap, Mile 83.0. South (on the west side) it's 1.1 miles to Blackrock and 2.3 miles to Blackrock Gap, Mile 87.4.

MILE 84.7, ABANDONED ROAD, east side. This is an exploring possibility for experienced hikers. The entrance is grassy and hard to see; look for the yellow posts and chain. I have not explored this area. Park naturalists Bob Momich and Amanda Moody report as follows:

> The trail passes signs of mountain people and the CCC: wells, rock walls, and piles of decaying chestnut wood. About a mile from the Drive, the trail divides. The right fork is obvious. Take the left fork, which is overgrown and obscure. Where it turns sharp left at some rock walls, keep going straight ahead. Cross a fence, leaving the Park. Enter an open field, with a good view of Cedar Mountain ahead and Via Hollow to the right. Less than 300 yards ahead is the Via family cemetery. The dates on the stones are evidence of high infant mortality among the mountain people. Via is the original (and present) name of the family. Viar and Viare, which appear on some of the stones, are variants.

MILE 84.8, BLACKROCK PARKING, west side. This is the closest approach to *Blackrock* from the Drive. Turn in onto the unpaved road.

A hundred yards from Skyline Drive is parking space for about six cars.

HIKE: *Blackrock Summit. Round trip* 1.0 miles; total *climb* about 175 feet; *time* required 1:10. An easy hike with outstanding views and a little geology. See map below.

Beyond the chain the Trayfoot Mountain trail (a former fire road, which still looks like a road) parallels the Drive for a short distance, then swings up to the ridge top, where it touches the A.T. Step over onto the A.T., and continue in the same direction. Walk a third of a mile on a good trail with a very easy climb, through pleasant woods. Then the trail swings right, onto a talus slope. After another hundred feet you're crossing a talus slope that goes down a tenth of a mile to your right, made of rocks from breadbox size to Buick size. And, beyond the slope, a wide-open breathtaking view across Madison Run and Dundo Hollow. The trail makes a 200-yard loop around three sides of Blackrock summit. In the middle of the loop, the Blackrock Spur trail goes off to the right.

The Blackrock Spur trail descends 0.2 mile to the Trayfoot Mountain trail, which continues another 0.7 mile to Trayfoot Mountain summit, where you'll find the foundation of a former fire tower. (There are no views from the summit.) The Trayfoot Mountain trail continues another 3.9 miles to the Paine Run trail.

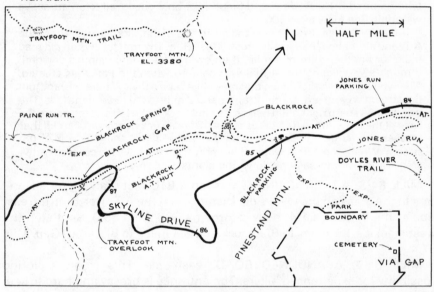

Map of Blackrock area.

There's no trail to the top of Blackrock. The climb is a rock scramble that you can begin at any point on the loop. On the summit, the view is wrapped around you for more than 300 degrees. Looking away from the woods, the high peak in front of you is Trayfoot Mountain, just over half a mile away. (Its elevation is about 3,380 feet; you're at 3,092.) Trayfoot Mountain extends far to the left from its highest point, then descends into Paine Run hollow. The low, free-standing mountain beyond its foot is Horsehead. Buzzard Rock rises to the left of the mouth of the hollow, the far edge of which is formed by Rocks Mountain.

To the right of Trayfoot summit, Furnace Mountain rises at the mouth of Madison Run hollow. (Madison Run was named for a wealthy settler who, about 1750, built an estate called Madison Hall near its mouth. Furnace Mountain gets its name from Mount Vernon Furnace, which was built at its foot in 1848 for the reduction of iron ore.) Farther right are Austin Mountain, Lewis Mountain, and Lewis Peak. The long Rockytop ridge forms the far boundary of the hollow, and joins the main Blue Ridge toward the right, where you see a roadcut beside the Drive. Farther right on a very clear day you can see Hightop, thirteen miles away. Still farther right, and much closer, is Big Flat Mountain — the site of the Loft Mountain Campground.

Legend: In the spring of 1781, during the American Revolution, the British were pressing westward in Virginia. The Virginia Assembly, to avoid capture, fled across the mountain to Staunton. Thomas Jefferson, governor of Virginia, entrusted the State Archives and Great Seal to his friend Bernis Brown. Bernis hid them in a cave here at Blackrock, where they remained throughout the rest of the war.

Geology: Blackrock summit and the talus slopes below it are Hampton quartzite. Maybe you can imagine the great monolith that all this started from. When it was exposed by erosion it had already been cracked and weakened by pressure, and by cycles of heating and cooling. Rain water seeped into the cracks and froze, and melted and seeped and froze again. In a very short time, as geologists measure—probably less than 100,000 years— Blackrock crumbled into the magnificent but messy pile you're standing on.

In a fresh break, the quartzite is medium salt-and-pepper gray. Weathering has stained its surface pale purplish gray-brown, tan, and red-brown. Many of the rocks are covered with close-clinging pale green lichen. (A photographer with a closeup lens, color film, and a taste for abstract art, could spend some time here.) Any blackness that Blackrock may have is due to its burden of rock tripe — a coarse lichen that's dark brown and crispy when it's dry, and gray-green and leathery when it's wet.

Oral history: I have reports from oldtimers who visited the Blackrock Springs Hotel (which was about a mile down the hollow on the Paine Run side) during the early years of this century. The trip up to Blackrock was a favorite excursion for hotel guests. And one of its outstanding attractions — at least the thing the oldtimers remember most vividly — was the chance to scratch ones name or initials on the rocks. Which consisted, I gather, of scratching off the rock tripe.

MILE 86.8, TRAYFOOT MOUNTAIN OVERLOOK. *Drinking fountain* (turned off in winter). Elevation 2,530 feet. The short hollow in front of the overlook drains into the north branch of Moormans River in Via Hollow, at the foot of Pasture Fence Mountain (which has grassy clearings near its top.) To the right of Pasture Fence and more distant, with clearings and radio towers on top, is Bucks Elbow Mountain. From the south end of the overlook on a very clear day you can see far to the right, across the Blue Ridge to the Allegheny Mountains on the far side of the valley.

MILE 87.2, A.T. CROSSING. *Hikes.* Elevation 2,390 feet. There is parking space on the east side, just south of the A.T. (Straight out from the wall, you look across the head of Paine Run: that's Trayfoot Mountain ahead and to the right. To the far left, with three close-together peaks, is Rocks Mountains.) Distances on the A.T.: North (on the west side of the Drive) it's 1.2 miles to Blackrock, and 2.3 miles to the Drive crossing at Mile 84.3. South (on the east side) it's a quarter of a mile to Blackrock Gap, Mile 87.4.

HIKE: *Blackrock A.T. Hut. Round trip* 1.3 miles; total *climb* about 555 feet; *time* required 1:25. See map, page 208. Take the A.T. north from the outside of the curve on the Drive. For most of the hike it follows or closely parallels an old road trace, which is blocked at the edge of the Drive by a yellow pipe. (This is the road on which guests at Blackrock Springs Hotel rode up to Blackrock.)

About half a mile from the start a side trail on the right goes to the hut, which is down in a deep ravine. It has a table, fireplace, spring, and pit toilet.

MILE 87.4, BLACKROCK GAP. Elevation 2,320 feet. Fire road; trail head. *A.T. access.* The A.T. comes to the edge of the Drive on the east side, but does not cross it. Distances on the A.T.: North (to the left) it's a quarter of a mile to the Drive crossing at Mile 87.2. South (to the right) it's 1.8 miles to the Drive crossing at Mile 88.9.

On the west side of the Drive the Paine Run trail goes 3.8 miles to the Park boundary, where it joins Virginia secondary roads Nos. 614 and 661. On the east side the Blackrock Gap fire road goes 1.1 miles to the Park boundary, then continues for 0.4 mile to the north fork of Moormans River in Via Hollow.

Paine Run hollow is big and wild — a great place for exploring and backcountry camping. Although you can reach it from the bottom, you have to cross private land to do so. It might be better to start from Blackrock Gap and walk down the trail.

History: About a mile down the Paine Run trail is Blackrock Springs, which at the turn of the century was a fashionable resort with a hotel, cabins, recreation hall, and bowling alley. The resort reached the height of its popularity in the 1840's and 1850's. It burned down, probably as a result of arson, early in this century. The waters of Blackrock Springs were said to be good for whatever ails you. According to advertisements they contained iron, soda, lime, magnesia, and carbonic acid gas. When Mme. Curie discovered radium, that too was added to the list of ingredients. There were seven springs of different colors and different healing properties, including one for rheumatism, one for arthritis, one for gout, and one for aiding the growth of hair. People still come to Blackrock Gap and carry jugs down the trail to bring back some of the healing water. If you'd like to see where the hotel once stood, or if you're suffering from shortage of hair or other ailment, try this:

HIKE: *Blackrock Springs. Round trip* 2.2 miles; total *climb* about 425 feet; *time* required 2:10. (See map, page 208.) Follow the Paine Run trail downhill on the west side of the Drive, past a switchback to the right, to a sharp switchback to the left. Leave the trail at that point and follow an old road trace straight ahead. In the next few hundred yards you will see level areas where cabins once stood, uphill to the right. Pass a covered spring at the right-hand edge of the road trace. (I don't know which of the seven ailments this one is good for.) The sites of various hotel buildings are straight ahead, as well as ahead and to the left. Explore at will.

MILE 88.6, HORSEHEAD OVERLOOK. Elevation 2,580 feet. The overlook has a clear view over Paine Run hollow (see sketch). Trayfoot Mountain bounds the watershed on the right and Rocks Mountain on the left. From the north end of the overlook, beyond the trees, you can see up into the head of Paine Run. The massive mountain ahead and left is Trayfoot. With your binoculars, follow the ridge to the right from Trayfoot summit, past the low point, until you come to a purplish talus slope. Follow it up to the right, to the jumbled mass of broken rock on the ridge crest. That's

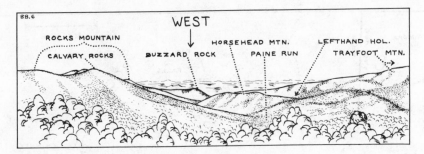

88.6

WEST

ROCKS MOUNTAIN
CALVARY ROCKS
BUZZARD ROCK
HORSEHEAD MTN.
PAINE RUN
LEFTHAND HOL.
TRAYFOOT MTN.

View from Horsehead Overlook.

Blackrock, which gave its name to Blackrock Springs and Blackrock Hotel and Blackrock Gap. The view from there is impressive. For an easy hike to Blackrock, see page 208.

Geology: In the island, and in the roadcut across the Drive, are exposures of interbedded phyllite and sandstone of the Hampton formation. The phyllite is pale gray in a fresh break — thin, flaky, and soft. The sandstone is much harder. The weathered surfaces are stained with iron, from golden brown to nearly black. NOTE: The gray stone in the wall here, and in overlooks to the south, is limestone — brought up from the Valley. It does not occur naturally in the Park.

MILE 88.9, A.T. CROSSING. Elevation 2,620 feet. There's limited parking on the east side. Distances on the A.T.: North (on the east side of the Drive) it's 1.8 miles to Blackrock Gap, Mile 87.4. South (on the west side) it's 1.1 miles to Riprap Parking, Mile 90.0.

MILE 90.0, RIPRAP PARKING. Elevation 2,730 feet. *Riprap Trail. A.T. access.* A paved parking area on the west side of the Drive. A graded trail goes 100 yards uphill to the A.T. Distances on the A.T.: North (to the right) it's 1.1 miles to the Drive crossing at Mile 88.9 South (to the left) it's 2.9 miles to Wildcat Ridge Parking, Mile 88.9.

HIKE: *Chimney Rock. Round trip* 3.4 miles; total *climb* about 830 feet; *time* required 3:10. Good trail, fine views. See map, page 212.

Take the Riprap Trail uphill and turn right when it reaches the A.T. About 0.4 mile from the start, as the A.T. is levelling off, turn left on the Riprap Trail. It goes up and down, mostly down, for another 0.7 mile, to a talus slope that crosses the ridge. The trail swings right, then left; the white rocks on the right here are the first viewpoint shown on the map. That's Paine Run watershed below you, and you can see most of it from here. To your left is a ridge that runs down from Rocks Mountain, and beyond it is Buzzard Rock, just to the left of the mouth of the hollow. In front of you Trayfoot Mountain bounds the far side of the hollow. The free-standing mountain out in the hollow is Horse-head; beyond it, Lefthand Hollow runs up into the side of Trayfoot.

Geology: The rocks at this viewpoint, like Calvary Rocks and Chimney Rock up ahead, are white Erwin quartzite; throughout the area are occasional fossilized burrows of *Skolithos,* an ancient worm-like animal.

After another 0.2 mile, Calvary Rocks rise up ahead of you, to the left of the trail. There was formerly a side trail to the summit, which offered a breathtaking 360 degree view. But the view is now overgrown. This is now a wilderness area; the side trail and the view have both been sacrificed for the sake of wilderness.

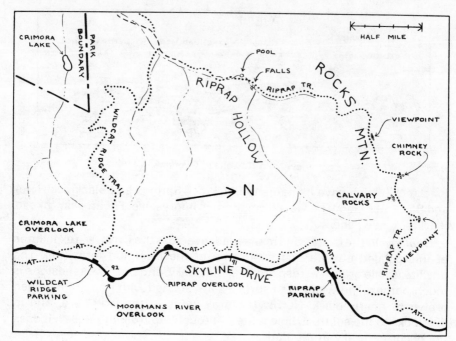

Map of Riprap area.

Continue another 0.2 mile. Where the trail makes a sharp turn to the left, Chimney Rock stands free on your right, across a deep, narrow gorge. (You may see a spike in the rock on each side of the gorge; there was once a bridge here.) From here you can see all of the Paine Run hollow, all the way up to the crest of the Blue Ridge.

HIKE: *Chimney Rock* and *Riprap Hollow* to Park boundary. *One way* 4.9 miles; total *climb* about 620 feet; *time* required 4:15. Views, stream, pool, cascades. At lower elevations parts of the trail are rough, and there are several stream crossings. See map, above.

This *one-way* hike requires that you leave a car in the mouth of Riprap Hollow, or arrange to be picked up there. Parking is limited; I don't recommend this hike for summer weekends. Directions: from Swift Run Gap, Mile 65.5, go west on U.S. 33 to Elton and turn left onto U.S. 340. Go about 23.5 miles to Crimora and turn left onto state road no. 612. (Or, from Rockfish Gap, go west on U.S. 250 to Waynesboro; turn right onto 340; go to Crimora, and turn right onto 612.) Go 1.7 miles on 612, and turn left onto a narrow dirt road. From here it's about a mile to the Park Boundary at the mouth of Riprap Hollow. Because the area is now undergoing rapid subdivision and road-building, I can't predict what you'll find.

The hike starts like the one above. From Chimney Rock continue another 0.4 mile, and watch for another viewpoint on the right. From it you can see most of Paine Run Hollow. Horsehead Mountain is right out in front of you, very close. This is my favorite view into Paine Run because it's completely unobstructed—left, right, across, and down. Sitting on the edge of the cliff with your feet hanging over is like flying without a plane.

Less than 0.2 mile from this point the trail swings left, and begins its descent into Cold Spring Hollow. A mile and a tenth farther on, a stream comes in from the left, and we join Riprap Hollow. Thirty yards downstream is a small but very pretty waterfall. In this area, and for a considerable distance downstream, rhododendrons *(R. catawbiense)* are scattered through the woods. They have big, showy, violet-colored flowers that bloom in May.

The trail fords the stream; a hundred yards beyond, a side trail on the right crosses the stream to the site of Riprap Shelter, beside one of the biggest swimming holes in the Park. (The shelter was considered an "attractive nuisance" because it encouraged illegal camping. It was removed in 1977.) From the shelter site, go downstream about 200 feet to rejoin the trail, which from this point on is a former fire road. Continue for 0.6 mile, crossing the stream twice, to the marker post at the foot of the Wildcat Ridge Trail. Continue another 0.6 Mile on the former fire road, crossing the stream once more, to reach the parking area.

HIKE: *Wildcat Ridge Parking* via *Chimney Rock* and *Riprap Hollow, One way* 7.1 miles; total *climb* about 2,000 feet; *time* required 6:45. Views, stream, cascades, pool. This *one-way* hike requires that you leave a car at Wildcat Ridge Parking, Mile 92.1, or have someone meet you there. Because of the 2,000-foot climb, this hike is moderately difficult. At lower elevations parts of the trail are rough, and there are several stream crossings. See map, page 212.

As above to the marker post at the foot of the Wildcat Ridge Trail. Turn left onto the trail, cross the main stream, and continue beside a tributary. After two-tenths of a mile the trail turns left and crosses the stream. Later, after the trail swings right and crosses the stream for the last time, it climbs a third of a mile to a sharp left turn. Less than half a mile up the ridge the trail makes a sharp switchback to the left. About 60 yards before the switchback, to the right and somewhat back, is an overgrown view of Crimora Lake. You may be able to see it through an opening in the leaves, a few degrees south of directly west. A hundred feet beyond the switchback, look to the left for another chance to see the lake through the leaves. Behind you, down the trail, is a leafy view of Turk Mountain.

The trail continues up Wildcat Ridge for another 1.2 miles to the A.T. Cross the A.T. and continue a little more than 200 yards uphill to the Wildcat Ridge parking area.

HIKE: *Chimney Rock, Riprap Hollow, Wildcat Ridge,* and return via *A.T. Circuit* 9.8 miles; total *climb* about 2,365 feet; *time* required 8:50. A rather long and tiring hike. At lower elevations, parts of the trail are rough; there are several stream crossings. See map, page 212.

As above to the A.T. intersection on Wildcat ridge, Turn left, and walk 2.7 miles on the A.T. to the concrete marker at the Riprap Trail intersection. Turn right and go 90 yards downhill to the Riprap parking area.

MILE 91.4, RIPRAP OVERLOOK. Elevation 2,920 feet. A good-sized overlook with a wide view, and a grassy island with pines and small dogwoods. On a very clear day you can see mountains along the Blue Ridge Parkway, far beyond Scott Mountain (at the left edge of the sketch.) Farther right you can see the Alleghenies on the far side of the Valley. For hikes into Riprap Hollow see above. (The word "riprap" means broken stone, which the hollow has lots of.)

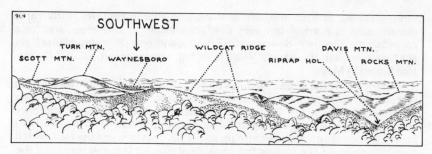

View from Riprap Overlook.

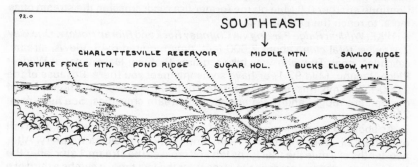

View from Moormans River Overlook.

MILE 92.0, MOORMANS RIVER OVERLOOK. Elevation 2,975 feet. The overlook offers a clear, pleasing 180-degree view. Its most prominent feature is the Charlottesville reservoir (see sketch). Along the foot of Pasture Fence Mountain, the north fork of Moormans River flows from left to right, through Via Hollow and into the reservoir. The buildings and towers on Bucks Elbow Mountain, to the right, are an FAA installation. Between Bucks Elbow and the Blue Ridge, the south fork of Moormans River flows from right to left and into the reservoir. (The reservoir is outside the Park, as are Pasture Fence and Bucks Elbow Mountains.)

History: In the early 1700's, Charles Moorman and his son Thomas bought a great deal of land in this area. In 1741 Thomas Moorman patented 750 acres on the river that thereafter carried his name. It's reported that when Pasture Fence Mountain was first discovered by the settlers it was covered with lush bluegrass. By the time George Washington was a teenager, wealthy landowners from the eastern part of the county had fenced this mountain for grazing.

MILE 92.1, WILDCAT RIDGE PARKING. Elevation 2,980 feet. *Hikes. A.T. access.* The Wildcat Ridge trail crosses the A.T. a little more than 200 yards from the Drive. Distances on the A.T.: North (to the right) it's 2.9 miles to Riprap Parking, Mile 90.0. South (to the left) it's a third of a mile to the Drive crossing at Mile 92.4.

From here you can take a one-way hike through Riprap Hollow to Chimney Rock and Riprap Parking, Mile 90.0. Or you can make that hike a circuit, returning via A.T. Since I've described both those hikes from the other end (page 212), I won't repeat them here.

HIKE: *Riprap Hollow. Round trip* 6.8 miles; total *climb* about 1,670 feet; *time* required 6:15. A moderately difficult hike to a stream, cascades, and pool. At lower elevations parts of the trail are rough, and there are several stream crossings. See map, page 212.

The trail crosses the A.T. about 200 yards from the Drive, and then descends on Wildcat Ridge, swinging back and forth from one side of the ridge to the other. About 1.2 miles from the start it's on the right side of the ridge crest; it then begins a 300-yard crossover to the left side, ending in a sharp switchback to the right. A hundred feet short of the switchback is a view ahead, through the trees, of Turk Mountain. To the right, just a few degrees south of directly west, is Crimora Lake. You may be able to see it through the leaves.

Continue down the ridge another 0.4 mile, to where the trail turns sharp right. The trail descends the ridge, fords the stream, then swings left and passes through a pleasant woods. Soon after you ford the stream again, it joins a larger one that flows down through Riprap Hollow. (From here on, the woods are dotted with rhododendrons, *R. Catawbiense.* They have large, showy, violet-colored flowers that bloom during the last half of May.) The trail fords the stream and continues to the Riprap trail, which is a former fire road. Turn right. Cross the stream twice, and stop at the third crossing. On the far side of the stream the former fire road becomes a narrow trail. Take the side trail that goes to the left, without fording the stream. It goes about 200 feet to the site of Riprap Shelter (which was removed in 1977.) The shelter site faces the stream in a very attractive setting, with a view to the left of one of the Park's biggest swimming holes.

MILE 92.4, A.T. CROSSING. Elevation 3,000 feet. There's space for several cars on the west side. Distances on the A.T.: North (on the west side) it's a third of a mile to the Wildcat Ridge Trail, near the Drive at Mile 92.1. South (on the east side) it's 1.9 miles to the Drive crossing in Turk Gap, Mile 94.1.

MILE 92.6, CRIMORA LAKE OVERLOOK. Elevation 2,985 feet. The overlook has a wide view, from Turk Mountain at the far left to the nearby Wildcat Ridge at the right. Rocks Mountain, with a small white talus slope, is beyond Wildcat Ridge. Crimora Lake is a little to the right of straight out from the overlook; from here, its water looks dark-colored. Farther left is a body of pale greenish water surrounded by piles of bare earth, with a few trees and a little grass. This is a flooded, abandoned, open-pit manganese mine. The piles of raw earth are a result of the mining operation.

History: Mining of the Crimora manganese deposit began in 1867 and continued intermittently under a series of owners — many of whom lost money — until March 1946, when the mill shut down for the last time (up to now.) The Crimora deposit, about 500 feet wide, 200 feet deep, and half a mile long, consists of clay with scattered lumps of manganese ore. It lies under a layer of clay and quartz fragments about 15 feet thick, and it's this material which forms the yellow-orange mounds that you see from the overlook. The Crimora deposit has produced more manganese than any other deposit in the United States.

The first step in processing the ore consists in washing off the clay, which requires tremendous quantities of water. Crimora Lake was formed by damming a stream in Dorsey Hanger Hollow to provide water for processing the ore. Clay-laden water was allowed to settle in sumps at the deep ends of the mine pits, and was then recycled. Even so, a chronic water shortage, as well as competition from imported ores, has kept the mine from being very profitable.

Legend: Samuel W. Donald, the second owner of the mine, named it for the daughter of a friend. She was Crimora Frances Withrow.

Point of view: Take another look at the flooded minepit. I've seen a similar body of pale green water, surrounded by yellow-orange earth and scattered trees, in Yellowstone National Park. It's a major tourist attraction there. Whether the flooded Crimora mine pit is an eyesore or a sight for sore eyes depends on how you look at it.

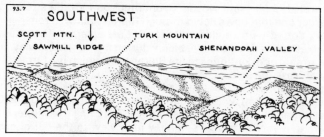

View from Turk Mountain Overlook.

MILE 93.7, TURK MOUNTAIN OVERLOOK. Elevation 2,720 feet. The sketch shows the view toward the left. Turk Mountain is capped by Erwin quartzite; you can see cliffs and talus slopes that slice across it near the top. The high ridge diagonally to your right is Rocks Mountain.

MILE 94.1, TURK GAP. Elevation 2,610 feet. *A.T. crossing.* Distances on the A.T.: North (on the east side of the Drive) it's 1.9 miles to the Drive crossing at Mile 92.4. South (on the west side) it's 1.6 miles to Sawmill Run Overlook, Mile 95.3.

An old road crossed the mountain here; it's now a yellow-blazed horse trail. On the west it's called the Turk Gap trail, which begins at a concrete post about a hundred yards north of the A.T. crossing, and goes 1.6 miles to the Park boundary.

The Turk Mountain trail begins on the A.T. about 0.1 mile from the Drive, on the west side. It's a two-mile round trip, with a good view from the top of a talus slope near the summit.

MILE 94.5, TURK BRANCH TRAIL, east side. There's limited parking in the grass near the trail head. The trail goes down to the south branch of Moormans River, where it joins the fire road that descends from Jarman Gap, Mile 96.8. For experienced hikers.

Geology: From here (Mile 94.5) south to Milepost 95, are intermittent exposures of phyllite of the lower Hampton formation. In a fresh break its color varies from silvery gray to very pale tan — some of it banded, some with veins of pebbly quartzite. The weathered surfaces are mostly stained with iron. (There's more parking space in the grass on the west side at Mile 94.9).

MILE 95.3, SAWMILL RUN OVERLOOK. Elevation 2,200 feet. *A.T. crossing.* From here you look right down the main branch of Sawmill Run. Except for that, the view is similar to what you see from Sawmill Ridge Overlook, Mile 95.9. Looking far to the left you can see a prominent roadcut; above and to the right of it are the two crests of Calf Mountain.

The A.T. crosses the Drive at the north end of the overlook. Distances on the A.T. North (on the west side of the Drive) it's 1.6 miles to Turk Gap, Mile 94.1. South (on the east side) it's 2.0 miles to Jarman Gap, Mile 96.8.

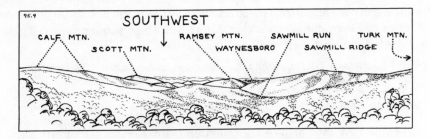

View from Sawmill Ridge Overlook.

MILE 95.9, SAWMILL RIDGE OVERLOOK. Elevation 2,215 feet. There's a good view from the middle of the overlook (see sketch). The Blue Ridge Parkway runs among the distant mountains on the horizon, beyond Scott Mountain. Most of the city of Waynesboro is hidden behind Ramsey Mountain. Sawmill Ridge continues to the right (beyond the edge of the sketch) to join Turk Mountain, which rises higher to the right before descending abruptly into a shallow cut.

Geology: In the roadcut across the Drive are deposits of the Weverton formation: sandstone (fine-grained, medium-gray in a fresh break); quartzite (coarse, nearly white grains in a tan cement); and phyllite (pale lustrous gray in a fresh break, and a thin piece is soft enough to break between your fingers.) Much of the weathered rock surface has been stained brown with iron.

MILE 96.1, FIRE ROAD, west side. This road descends about 1.7 miles to the Park boundary on Sawmill Run at the foot of Ramsey Mountain, where it joins Virginia secondary road No. 611.

MILE 96.8, JARMAN GAP. Elevation 2,175 feet. Fire roads. *A.T. access. Hikes.*

History: Michael Woods settled here in the 1720's, and the area was known as Woods Gap. The buffalo trail that Woods had followed into the mountains was later replaced by the Three Notched Road, which for a time was the principal crossing of the Blue Ridge. About 1800 Thomas Jarman bought a tract of mountain land that included Woods Gap. Since then it has been called Jarman Gap.

This was originally the southern end of Shenandoah National Park, and the road to the south was part of the Blue Ridge Parkway. The Park was later extended to Rockfish Gap, 8.3 miles by road to the south, and the road is now part of Skyline Drive.

On the east side are two unpaved roads. One goes downhill to the left, and follows the south fork of Moormans River to the Charlottesville Reservoir. The road that goes uphill to the right reaches the Park boundary in about 100 yards. It follows the route of the old Three Notched Road into the hollow of Lickinghole Creek.

A.T. access is via either of the fire roads on the east side. To go north, take the left-hand road about 250 yards and turn left onto the A.T. From there it's 1.8 miles to Sawmill Run Overlook, Mile 95.3. To go south on the A.T. see the Beagle Gap hike, below.

> HIKE: *Jarman Gap. Circuit* 0.5 mile; total *climb* about 135 feet; *time* required 0:25. A pleasant, easy hike through the woods.
> Take the left-hand fire road, which curves right and descends rather steeply to a stand of tall tulip poplars. The bank on the right is rich in ferns: Christmas ferns, ebony spleenwort, polypody, and rattlesnake fern. (There's some poison ivy, too.) At the A.T. junction, 250 yards from the start, turn right, uphill, through a grove of big trees — up to three feet in diameter — some of them oaks but mostly tulip poplars. Where the trail turns sharp right, there's a pretty little spring on the left, which may be dry in summer. (Don't drink the water without boiling it.)
> Continue to the Park boundary at the second fire road, a quarter of a mile from the first one. The A.T. continues on the other side of the road. Turn right. A hundred yards down the road the boundary turns left, and you re-enter the Park. It's only a hundred yards more to your starting point.
> HIKE: *Beagle Gap. One way* 2.7 miles; total *climb* about 825 feet; *time* required 2:25. This is a fairly easy hike across the semi-open crest of Calf Mountain, with views from the cleared pasture land. It's a one-way hike, which requires that you leave a car in Beagle Gap, Mile 99.5, or have someone meet you there.
> On the east side of the Drive take the right-hand fire road, which goes uphill 200 yards to the A.T. Turn right onto the A.T. and, after a few tenths of a mile, pass under the power line (see below). About a mile from the start of your hike, pass the Calf Mountain A.T. Hut and spring. Continue to the summit of Calf Mountain (elevation 2,975 feet), 1.7 miles from Jarman Gap. From a point a few feet short of the summit, look back the way you came for a fine view of Bucks Elbow Mountain (with radio towers on top) and, farther left, the Moorman River valley.
> The trail continues along the ridge crest, with white blazes painted on the rocks. It passes to the left of the second summit of Calf Mountain, and descends to the Drive in Beagle Gap.

MILE 97.4, POWER LINE CROSSING. Heavy, multiple wires, on big steel towers. There's parking space in the grass on the west side of the Drive. Under the wires is a bank about ten feet high, which is sometimes clear and sometimes overgrown. When it's clear there's a striking view from the top, down a cleared swath many miles long. A double line of steel towers, strung together by long catenaries of wire, marches down over the ridges and into the hollow of Sawmill Run, out through the mouth of the hollow, past Ramsey Mountain on the left and the foot of Sawmill Ridge on the right, into the Valley. Under some atmospheric conditions the wires make a sizzling sound, like something frying over a low fire, and it seems to come from all around you.

MILE 97.6, GEOLOGY. There's parking in the grass on the west side of the Drive. In the roadcut on the east side is an exposure of sedimentary rocks (laid down in the interval between two ancient lava flows) of the Catoctin formation: coarse sandstone with some small quartz pebbles, and some soft, crumbly phyllite. A good part of the rock surface is covered with poison ivy.

MILE 98.9, CALF MOUNTAIN OVERLOOK. Elevation 2,480 feet. As you approach the overlook the road appears to go right out into the sky. This is a long overlook with a 300-degree wrap-around view. For me, it's one of the superstars. To see all of it you should park you car and walk from one end of

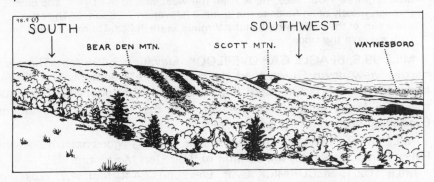

View from Calf Mountain Overlook. (No. 1.)

the overlook to the other. See sketches. From the south end of the overlook you can see a smoky smokestack in Waynesboro. Farther right, on a more distant ridge, Interstate 64 descends into the valley. Calf Mountain rises up behind the overlook.

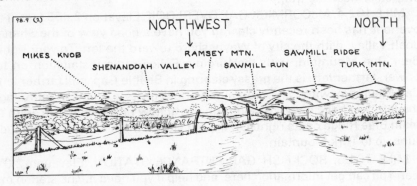

View from Calf Mountain Overlook. (No. 2.)

MILE 99.5, BEAGLE GAP. Elevation 2,530 feet. *A.T. crossing. Hikes.* The Drive passes between Bear Den Mountain on the west side and Calf Mountain on the east. The fence on each side of the Drive is at the Park boundary. The A.T. crosses the Drive here.

Distances on the A.T.: North (on the east side of the Drive) it's 2.7 miles to Jarman Gap, Mile 96.8 South (on the west side) it's 1.8 miles to McCormick Gap, Mile 102.1.

HIKE; *Calf Mountain Summit. Round trip* 2.1 miles; total *climb* about 495 feet; *time* required 1:45. An easy hike through partly open former pasture. Take the A.T. on the east side of the Drive. It ascends along the right flank of the first crest, and continues along the semi-open saddle, where it's marked by white blazes on the rocks. The high point of the trail, on the second crest of Calf Mountain (elevation 2,975 feet) is your destination. From there you have a fine view straight ahead of the summit of Bucks Elbow Mountain, with the radio installations on top. If you follow the trail a few yards more, you can see farther to the left, with a view of the whole length of the Moorman River valley.

HIKE: *Bear Den Mountain. Round trip* 1.2 miles; total *climb* about 355 feet; *time* required 1:05. Take the A.T. on the west side of the Drive, and climb through mostly open fields to the summit (elevation 2,885 feet). The towers are a part of the radio system of the Virginia State Police. There are views on both sides of the ridge.

MILE 99.8, BEAGLE GAP OVERLOOK. Elevation 2,495 feet. There's a narrow view down Greenwood Hollow into the Piedmont. The divided highway you see is Interstate 64, headed for Charlottesville. Note that there's a fence here, about 50 feet from the edge of the pavement. Everything beyond it is private property.

MILE 101.2, PRIVATE ROAD, west side. This road goes half a mile to the Police Radio Station on the summit of Bear Den Mountain.

MILE 102.1, McCORMICK GAP. Elevation 2,440 feet. *A.T. crossing.* There is limited parking on the east side of the Drive. Distances on the A.T.: North (on the west side of the Drive) it's 1.8 miles to Beagle Gap, Mile 99.5. South (on the east side) it's 3.0 miles to Skyline Drive at Mile 105.2 near Rockfish Gap. From McCormick Gap to Rockfish Gap, the A.T. lies on an easement over private land. If you're going south on the A.T., it's best to stay on or near the trail.

MILE 102.4, McCORMICK GAP OVERLOOK. Elevation 2,455 feet. If the overlook has been recently cleared you have a good view of the Shenandoah Valley, with the city of Waynesboro toward the left. To your right is Bear Den Mountain, with the Virginia Police radio installation on top. Lower, farther left, is the grassy clearing in Beagle Gap; still farther left is Calf Mountain, with Calf Mountain Overlook on its left flank. Continuing to the left, you have a view straight up the hollow of Sawmill Run, with the main Blue Ridge on its right. On the left side of the hollow, Sawmill Ridge runs up to Turk Mountain.

MILE 104.6, ROCKFISH GAP ENTRANCE STATION. Elevation 2,070 feet. You can get information here, and help if you need it. The station may be unmanned at night and in the winter.

MILE 105.1, PARK BOUNDARY. South of this point you're on the Blue Ridge Parkway.

MILE 105.2, APPALACHIAN TRAIL. Elevation 1,900 feet. The A.T. goes steeply up the bank on the east side. To the north (on the east side) it's 3.0 miles to McCormick Gap, Mile 102.1. To the south the A.T. follows the road, crossing Interstate 64 and U.S. 250 on the overpasses.

MILE 105.4, ROCKFISH GAP. Elevation 1,900 feet. Interstate 64 and U.S. 250 interchange. The Blue Ridge Parkway continues to the south from here. South of the overpasses and just west of the Parkway are motels, restaurants, and a gas station. Waynesboro, west on U.S. 250 at the foot of the mountain, offers food, lodging, and a hospital.

There is a tourist information center in Rockfish Gap. It's open during the summer travel season, and has information on food, lodging, and tourist attractions in the area. To find it, if you're going south: cross both overpasses and turn right. Look for a large sign beside the road that says "Rockfish Gap Regional Visitor Center." An arrow points to the Center, on the lower level of one of the motel buildings.

History: At first only a buffalo path crossed the mountain here. Later a dirt road was built to carry produce from the Shenandoah Valley to the head of navigation on the Rockfish River. It joined the Three Notched Road (which crossed the mountain in Jarman Gap) near the town of Wayland Crossing. The Blue Ridge Tunnel runs under Rockfish Gap, just outside the Park, and takes the C & O Railroad through the mountain about 500 feet below the surface. The tunnel was engineered by Colonel Claude Crozet, who had crossed the Alps with Napoleon. In 1870 the town of Wayland Crossing was renamed Crozet in his honor. Crozet is visible from the Drive: going north, as you round the curve at Mile 100.4, Crozet is the town at the foot of the mountain, ahead and to the right.

Rockfish Gap was the site of Mountain Top Tavern, one of the most famous taverns in the state. Many important conferences were held here. In 1818 a convention of 28 prominent citizens of Virginia, including Chief Justice Marshall and ex-presidents Madison, Monroe, and Jefferson, met here at Mountain Top Tavern to decide whether the University of Virginia should be in Staunton, Lexington, or Charlottesville.

INDEX

Accidents, cause of   25
Accommodations   15-18
Amphibians   53
Appalachian Trail   57
A.T. = Appalachian Trail

Backcountry camping   18
Backpacking   68
Bacon Hollow
  Overlook   187-188
Baldface Mountain
  Overlook   179
Beagle Gap   219
Beagle Gap Overlook   220
Beahms Gap   116
Bear Den Mountain hike   220
Bearfence Mountain
  hikes   175-177
Bearfence A.T. Hut   177
Bears   44-47
Beldor Hollow Overlook   189
Berry Hollow parking
  areas   141, 147
Bettys Rock hike   151-152
Bicycling   14
Big Devils Stairs hikes   96, 97
Big Flat Mountain hike   198
Big Meadows   164-166
Big Meadows Swamp hike   163
Big Run hikes   202, 203
Big Run Overlook   201
Big Run Portal hikes   193, 206
Birds   51-53
Blackrock Gap   210
Blackrock A.T. Hut   209
Blackrock Springs hike   210
Blackrock Summit hike (central
  section)   166-167
Blackrock Summit hike (south
  section)   208-209
Bluff trail   92, 97
Bolen Cemetery   101
Bootens Gap   173
Brown Mountain
  Overlook   191-192
Browns Gap   204-205
Buck Hollow hike   124

Buck Hollow Overlook   123
Byrds Nest Shelter No. 1   141
Byrds Nest Shelter No. 2   156
Byrds Nest Shelter
  No. 3   129, 132
Byrds Nest Shelter
  No. 4   116, 118
Byrd Visitor Center   164

Cabins   58
Calf Mountain hike   220
Calf Mountain Overlook   219
Campgrounds   16
Camp Hoover
  hikes   170-172, 173
Camping, backcountry   18
Catoctin formation   75
Caverns, Luray   119
Caverns, Skyline   81
CCC = Civilian Conservation Corps
Cedar Run hikes   153, 154
Chimney Rock hikes   211-213
Civilian Conservation Corps   42
Climate   70
Columnar jointing   76
Comfort stations   17
Compton Gap   89
Compton Peak   91
Concessioners   15
Copper mines   143, 161
Corbin Cabin cutoff trail   134
Corbin Cabin hikes   134-136
Cougar   48
Crandall, Aggie   72-74
Crandall, Hugh   77, 78
Crescent Rock Overlook   150
Crescent Rock trail   152
Crimora Lake Overlook   215
Crimora mine   215-216

Dark Hollow Falls hike   163
Davids Spring hikes   162
Deadening trail   197
Dean Cemetery   183
Deer   48
Dickey Ridge Picnic Area   84
Dickey Ridge trail   81
Dickey Ridge Visitor Center   83

ABOUT THE PUBLISHER

The Shenandoah Natural History Association, Inc. of Luray, Virginia 22835 was authorized by an act of Congress to operate within Shenandoah National Park. Its chief purpose is to assist the Park's Interpretive Division in doing a better job of interpreting Shenandoah's natural and cultural history in such a manner as to enhance visitor enjoyment. This is accomplished by making literature, maps, guides and pictorial illustrations of Shenandoah readily available to the traveling public at Park visitor centers or by mail from Luray, Virginia. This book is one of the publications produced by the Association. (Write for a complete list.)